MOTHER-DAUGHTER KNITS

30 Designs to Flatter & Fit

⚜

MOTHER DAUGHTER KNITS

⊰ KNITS ⊱

30 Designs to Flatter & Fit

SALLY MELVILLE & CADDY MELVILLE LEDBETTER

POTTER
CRAFT

NEW YORK

to Andy Sheshko

⚜

Published in the United States by Potter Craft, an imprint of the Crown Publishing Group,
a division of Random House, Inc., New York.
www.pottercraft.com

POTTER CRAFT and colophon is a registered trademark of Random House, Inc.

Library of Congress Cataloging-in-Publication Data is available upon request.

ISBN: 978–0–307–40872–3
Printed in China

Design by Goodesign
Photographs by Rose Callahan

10 9 8 7 6 5 4 3 2 1

First Edition

⚜ ACKNOWLEDGMENTS ⚜

To these folks I am grateful:

Andy...for learning to knit, for giving his knitting over to Caddy, and for being a brilliant husband to my girl. Rosy for knowing that a dual-generation book would be wonderful and for helping us find its focus, the staff at Random House—all a joy to work with—for a job well done, Sandi Minnes for her insight, Michelle Brock for her knitting (and for asking for the hoodie), Lynn Philips for her knitting, Stasia Bania (my rock) for her knitting, Pat Scott for asking for a gray cardigan, Sandra Whittaker for her quick but patient editing, Shannon Moore (my grandson!) for his graphics (despite not knowing what looked like a lamp was actually a sleeve!), the Moores, my loving and extended family for whom I am always grateful, my students and my friends who inspire and lead me, all yarn companies (and their reps) for their help and their stuff, the moose for his goodness and comfort, my son, Jeremy, for being so creative yet so proud of his mom and sister, and—finally—my daughter, Caddy, for her wit, her humor, her intelligence, her work ethic, her company, and her blessed being. ⚜ —SALLY

My warmest thanks to:

The man of my dreams, my husband Andy (I still can't believe my luck), Bridget, and Christina for their encouragement and understanding, Rosy and the staff at Random House for their tireless work and enthusiasm, Sandra for her great editing, the yarn companies for all their wonderful help, the Sheshkos, the Moores, and especially my nephew Shannon for his brilliant work on the schematics (and for reminding me how important it is to take breaks and play video games with him), my unbelievable and unbeatable friends and family for being the kind that everyone wishes for, my brother, Jeremy, whose heart is so big it could carry the world (and I believe it has on a few occasions), and my mom, Sally, whose strength, patience, wisdom, and laughter keep my feet on the ground and the corners of my mouth turned toward the sky. ⚜ —CADDY

❧ CONTENTS ❧

❧

INTRODUCTION

I learned to knit as a child, and my children saw me knitting through their childhoods. Of course, I taught (or tried to teach) them to knit. But I didn't do a wonderful job of it. I think my mistake with Caddy was to say "Do this, and don't worry about mistakes.

BUT DO TRY TO KEEP THE SAME NUMBER OF STITCHES ON YOUR NEEDLE." SHE COULDN'T manage to keep the stitch count the same, and so gave it up—for the next twenty years! (The lesson here should be that we be very careful what we say to our children—and to watch for the reaction to what we have said.) But then, as you will read later, she found me teaching her fiancé to knit and realized that, through years of watching, she knew how to knit. The real surprise was that she loved it!

Fast forward to me with an idea for a book. In speaking with the folks who ultimately became my publisher, I mentioned that my daughter was now teaching, writing, and designing. A two-generation knitting book had been a dream of theirs, and here we were! Well, almost....I was there; my daughter was at home, working full time. Our publisher asked if I thought Caddy would write a book with me? I joyfully and optimistically said I would ask.

That phone call was, indeed, amazing...more than a dream come true because it wasn't a dream that had occurred to me. We got immediately—gratefully, excitedly, and energetically—to work.

Most of the work for the book—the concepts and designs—was done independently. Caddy relied on me less often than I expected. (And isn't that so typical of what a mother might say?) But some of the work we did together. For example, we both adhere to accepted standards for the sizing and writing of patterns. Because I had

more years of experience writing patterns, this felt like the mom's usual job—to tell the daughter what she needs to know in order to follow the rules that need to be followed. But it's also the mom's job to let the daughter live her own life within those rules. So great variety may be found within the design and execution of our work, and who would want it any other way?

But while we recognized our different choices—choices that are reflective of the demographics we represent—we also appreciated our common ground. We wanted garments that flatter and fit. No matter our age, no matter our size, no matter our style, we knitters deserve to make garments that we wear well and proudly. And so we wrote the first chapter of this book and designed projects that are designed to flatter the female form—with all the help we think you need to make this so.

Perhaps the greatest lesson of our experience is to celebrate both our similarities and our differences. And then be patient as life unfolds. ❧ —SALLY

GROWING UP WITH AN AUTHOR FATHER, A DESIGNER MOTHER, AND A CHILD PRODIGY FOR A brother made for quite an inspirational upbringing for me. As a child I tried to knit a few times but gave up, I tried to play the piano but gave up. I tried to be a writer but gave up. In other words, I tried to excel at the things for which my family was exceptional, and of course (in my eyes) couldn't compete. You would think that this would be very discouraging. On the contrary, being surrounded by so much talent and so many ideas gave me the confidence that I would "come into my own eventually." (However, if you had asked me at the time what I thought about all that talent and all those ideas, I would have said something like "Genius is overrated.")

Fast forward to me stealing my husband's knitting (What?) and loving it!

Now it was my turn to blow my family away with my talent and my ideas. And blow them away I did, especially my mom. We began swapping designs and realized that we did as much differently as we did the same. And we worked beautifully and enthusiastically together!

So you can imagine, when I got a phone call from her on the subject of doing a book together, that my reaction was simply and clearly, "Of course! What a brilliant idea!"

We immediately put our little matching heads down and conspired to put a book together. The ingredients were discipline, a lot of giddiness, creativity, and, of course, patience (although my mom brought most of that). Throw that in the oven until golden-brown, and you get a book that celebrates both our similarities and our differences and appeals to all knitters—whatever age or skill level. I must admit that this last sentence thrills me, so I will embellish the point a bit.

Obviously my mom has more experience and so tends to write intermediate to advanced patterns—while I write beginner to intermediate patterns—and that became the focus of the Grape and the Wine chapter. At the same time, we definitely recognize that we have completely different taste, so for the Like Mother Like Daughter or Not chapter we took a similar yarn or concept and went our separate ways. (Highly entertaining by the way; you should try it at home!) But through every decision, we knew that we both want what we wear to look and feel as good as possible, especially when we take the time to knit it ourselves: hence the Knit to Flatter and Fit material. (It is, I'm sure, just as thrilling for any knitter, despite age, to hear not only "Wow, did you knit that?" as "What a great design! It fits you perfectly!")

I can't begin to tell you how excited I am and what it has meant for me to be part of such a book. I hope that you can feel a twinge of that excitement on these pages. But I know that you will—and that you feel that excitement whenever you pick up your needles. 🍇 —CADDY

PS: To further introduce ourselves—our histories, our demographics, and the concepts that the book explores—you will find a dialogue throughout that includes answers to some of the questions we ask each other or that you might ask. We hope you enjoy our musings; but more importantly, we hope they lead to your own dialogue.

CHAPTER ONE

⤜ KNIT TO FLATTER & FIT ⤛

Regardless of size, age, or demographic, a knitter who spends the time and energy to knit something should be happy and proud of the result. It should fit, it should flatter, and there should be no mystery as to how this happened.

SADLY AND TOO OFTEN, A SWEATER IS FINISHED AND THEN PUT ASIDE—LANGUISHING IN A CLOSET, sent to Goodwill, given away. There's something not quite right about it, but it isn't ripped out and altered. To rip out and alter would mean an understanding of what went wrong and how to fix it, and this knowledge is often missing from the picture.

While this sad tale could end here—with the knitter blaming her lack of skill (as we are all wont to do) and fatally discouraged from the craft—it rarely does. Most knitters are ever-optimistic: we rarely break stride before it's off to the yarn shop and into another project! Such optimism and enthusiasm must be rewarded, and the best way I know to do this is to offer the information and skills to make garments that will be proudly worn.

What follows is a discussion of shape and styling (what shapes look good and how to wear them) followed by measurements and fit (the when and how of pattern alterations). The result should make you a confident and proud wearer of the garments you knit.

It is not my intention that you come away from this discussion with a conviction that we all look the same. When we don't wear the unique pieces we knit is when we run that risk. Knitting our own clothing is a statement of our individuality, and this entire book is meant to encourage that. So do not be a slave to these concepts; do not let what I say override your own preferences or good judgment. Do, however, consider what follows as suggestions; find what makes sense for you, and absorb that into your work. Then continue to enjoy expressing your personal style through your hands and into your work. You honor our craft when you do so. ❧

drawing 1
the hourglass

KNIT TO FLATTER

There are many wonderful styling books on the market to help you flatter your figure, build a wardrobe, and dress your best. But what I find missing from them is attention to sweaters. Knits in particular—unless skinny and cashmere—tend to get a bad rap. I believe this need not be so, and

what follows is how I would redress this situation.

THE NATURAL HOUR-GLASS AND HOW TO ACHIEVE IT

The archetype of the female shape is the hourglass—larger bust and hips with an emphasized slimness between. Whether our personal shape is triangle, inverted triangle, oval, slim, or

wide rectangle, and whatever our age, it is some version of the hourglass that we often wish to attain. To interpret the hourglass, we would knit an upper garment that shows a narrowing between the bust and waist then wear it with something that continues the hourglass over the lower half. This is easy enough to do with a form-fitting dress and a perfect figure (drawing 1). But to achieve this with our knits, three things need to be attended to: length and shape, then styling.

The Length and Shape of the Garment

Suppose you want to wear a short, unshaped sweater. Can it suggest the hourglass shape? Absolutely! For most of us, the waist is narrower than the bust and hips, so a short sweater that sits well above the hip will allow the world to see them narrowing toward a waist. The sweater is the upper part of the hourglass, and the exposed near-waist area is the center of the hourglass.

But to where should this short sweater fall? Most of us don't like cropped sweaters, which over-expose our middle, so we'd want a short sweater to give us the hourglass with minimum mid-body exposure.

Two pieces of information are helpful here. First, something that is not cut precisely in half is more visually interesting than something cut right across its middle. And second, I believe that there is a place on our bodies—slightly higher than the midpoint between our feet and the tops of our heads—that puts our upper and lower bodies into an attractive

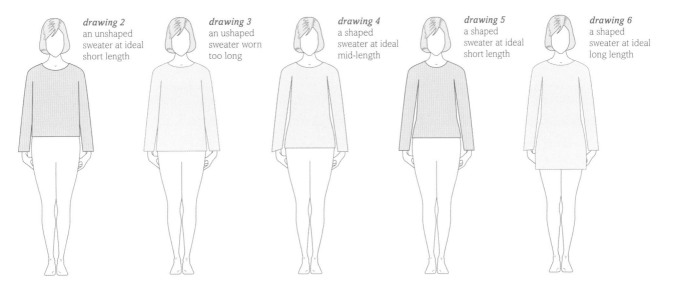

drawing 2
an unshaped sweater at ideal short length

drawing 3
an ushaped sweater worn too long

drawing 4
a shaped sweater at ideal mid-length

drawing 5
a shaped sweater at ideal short length

drawing 6
a shaped sweater at ideal long length

balance. The formula for this appears in the next section.

This I believe to be our "ideal short sweater length" (drawing 2). It gives a slightly long-legged silhouette, and it exposes just the right amount of the mid-section to show the hips narrowing to a waist. On most of us, it will ride near the center of the belly—cutting it in half. Good news, because one of the best ways to make something look smaller is to cut it in half. (If the sweater is shorter than this point, the legs will look longer but we might expose more of our mid-section than we'd like; if the sweater falls below this length—to the mid-point between our head and the floor—our legs will look shorter and, more important, we won't expose enough of the mid-body to show the middle of the hourglass.)

But we don't always want to wear a short sweater. What if we want a longer, mid-length sweater? Can this length still achieve the hourglass shape? Absolutely! But to do so, the sweater itself must be shaped. If the garment has no shaping and ends at the widest part of the hip, it says,

"This is how wide I am at my hips, and I continue at this width up to my bust!" This wide, continuous rectangle is not the shape we wish to offer (drawing 3).

A shaped, mid-length sweater can define an hourglass shape beautifully. All we need is a visible narrowing at the waist to define the center of the hourglass (drawing 4). By the way, waist shaping does not demand that the shaping sit precisely at the actual waist: a slightly high waist is a flattering interpretation of the hourglass. Nor does waist shaping need to sit tight to the actual waist: often the suggestion of a waist is enough. (So, while your waist might be 8" [20cm] narrower than your bust, very successful sweater shapes might show a waist only 4" [10cm] narrower.)

The natural place for this mid-length, shaped sweater to end is the leg break—the top of the hip—which will, by the way, approach the mid-point on the body (halfway between the head and the floor). The formula for this also appears in the next section.

You might ask why the ideal short sweater length was not applied to

this sweater? It could be (drawing 5). It would certainly make the legs look longer. But compare that against the previous diagram to see if the hips—divided in half in the earlier diagram—don't look narrower? (Remember, one of the best ways to narrow something is to divide it in half.) Here you have a choice.

And what of the long sweater that we love? Can it define the hourglass shape? Of course it can, if it has shaping built into it (drawing 6).

There is no ideal length for a long, shaped sweater: its length will be to your personal preference. It might depend upon your height: since longer garments make us look shorter, a tall person might want a longer sweater. Or it might depend upon your shape: some might want the garment to cover more of the thigh. And it might depend upon the style: is it a sweater that you want to be able to wear as a dress?

What We Wear with It

Often we pay attention to the colors we put together but not the shapes or fabrics. And it's sad when a wonderful garment is ruined by styling. For example, a short and unshaped sweater might not look good with slim jeans. If the hips are wide, there's too much emphasis given to the bottom of the hourglass; if the hips are narrow, we may look top heavy. It's important to make the rest of our outfit continue the good work of the sweater's silhouette.

What follows are guidelines for styling the hourglass. Of course, these are not the only possibilities for what to knit and how to wear it (the following section explores others): this is simply a basic introduction to making and wearing sweaters that flatter.

If Your Garment Is Short and Unshaped

Knit it to your ideal short sweater length (page 17) or slightly shorter.

If you choose to make your sweater shorter than this length, you might add something that ends at your ideal short sweater length (putting your body into balance). The added thing could be a belt or a tight top (drawing 7). (Both are good choices and have the potential to camouflage the belly.)

If you like your hips, continue the hourglass with straight pants. But many of us do better to continue the hourglass with an A-line skirt. (I use the term A-line loosely: look for skirts that fit smoothly at the waist and float over the hips.) (drawings 8 and 9)

If Your Garment Is Mid-Length and Shaped

Knit it to your ideal mid-length (page 17). Wear it with an A-line skirt or with straight pants or skirt. (A straight pant or skirt is one that fits the hip and continues straight without tapering on the lower leg. Avoid a tighter leg since it will widen the hip.) (drawings 10 and 11)

If Your Garment is Long and Shaped

Knit it to any length.

Wear it with slim pants or leggings or tights. (The longer the garment, the less of the heavier upper leg is exposed. So wear finer leg coverings for longer garments and heavier leg coverings for shorter garments. All of these choices might be leg coverings you would never wear unless the shapelier parts of your mid-body were covered!) (drawing 12)

Personal Modifications

If you are a standard size (page 158), your bust is 8" larger than your waist, and your hips are 10" larger than your waist. This makes you a natural hourglass who may simply follow the guidelines as written above. But what about those of us with not-so-perfectly proportioned bodies? Welcome to the majority! Few of us own bodies that conform to this idealized silhouette. If you are not the same clothing size top and bottom, you are probably well aware of this and wish to achieve balance. To rectify an imbalance, follow the guidelines above, but wear darker-colored, lighter-weight, less shiny, and lighter-textured pieces on your heavier half. In addition, look for details that draw attention to the half of the body that is slimmer: a large collar, a wide neckline, a puffed sleeve, or a shoulder wrap will draw the eye up and widen the upper half; pockets, stitching, or bold patterns will draw the eye down and widen the lower half.

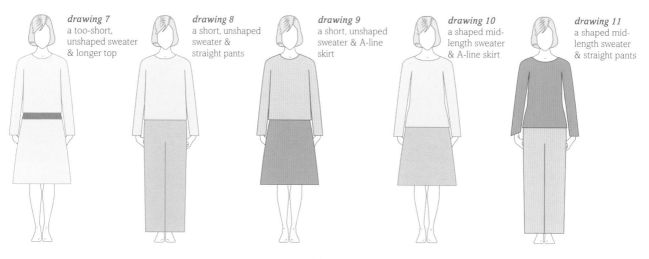

drawing 7
a too-short, unshaped sweater & longer top

drawing 8
a short, unshaped sweater & straight pants

drawing 9
a short, unshaped sweater & A-line skirt

drawing 10
a shaped mid-length sweater & A-line skirt

drawing 11
a shaped mid-length sweater & straight pants

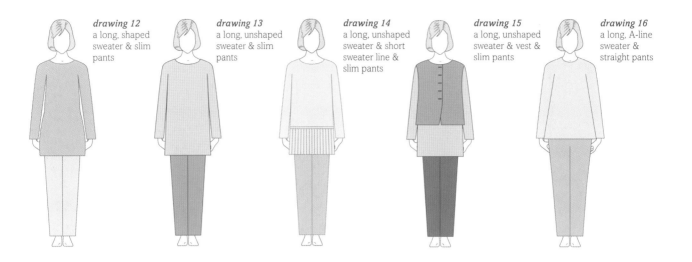

drawing 12
a long, shaped sweater & slim pants

drawing 13
a long, unshaped sweater & slim pants

drawing 14
a long, unshaped sweater & short sweater line & slim pants

drawing 15
a long, unshaped sweater & vest & slim pants

drawing 16
a long, A-line sweater & straight pants

OTHER DESIRABLE SHAPES AND HOW TO ACHIEVE THEM

So first we learn how to achieve the illusion of a natural hourglass shape. But what about other shapes? Wouldn't life be dull—and style severely limited—if what we wear could only be drawn to this one, tightly prescribed silhouette? And truly, there are days when we don't feel like an hourglass and don't want to make any attempt to look like one. We just want to put on a big, long sweater and head off to the cottage or the grocery store or out to walk the dog. Can we still look good? Of course we can! In fact, these sweaters can take us into high fashion! All we need do is re-examine our assumptions about length, shape, and styling.

The Length and Shape of the Garment

For big, long sweaters with no waist shaping we forgo the hourglass shape. But what's the next best thing to the hourglass—a style that's occasionally been the epitome of female beauty? The slim rectangle! Since the eye extends what it sees (and

won't imagine what it cannot see), we want a long sweater to fall to a slim part of us. The eye will then extend our slim rectangle upward—no hips, no butt, no belly. Where this length would be is somewhere below the widest point of the hips. The next section explains how to take this measurement.

In addition, this sweater needs to have enough ease built into it that there is no suggestion of the body parts we wish to cover. We could produce a big, long, and unshaped sweater that is generous from top to bottom—hips + 6" (15.5cm) or more (drawing 13). And while we love that these sweaters hang loose and free, they do run the risk of looking like a sack. One way to improve them is to put some sort of demarcation (a change of color, yarn, or texture) at the ideal short sweater length (drawing 14). Alternatively, try topping it with a vest that falls to your ideal short sweater length or shorter (drawing 15). These modifications will make you look taller.

Another way to draw a fabulous silhouette (my personal favorite) is to make big sweaters generous at the

hip only—big, long, and A-line (diagram 16). Because its extra-generous hem makes the hip look slim in comparison, and because it then describes an upwardly narrowing silhouette, this shape needn't cover as much of the leg: it may be worn shorter—to just above crotch length. And this is good, because anything that exposes the full length of the leg makes us look taller.

What We Wear with It

We want to wear a long sweater with something slim enough to show the narrowness of the leg—the template for that slim rectangle.

If Your Sweater Is Long and Unshaped

Knit it to fall to a slim part of the leg.

Wear it with slim pants, leggings, or tights. (The same suggestions hold true here as for styling a long, shaped sweater in the preceding section.) (drawings 14 and 15)

If Your Sweater is Long and A-line

Knit it to the leg break or longer.

Wear it with slim or straight pants or a slim or straight skirt. (drawing 16)

drawing 17
5 Places to Personalize a Pattern

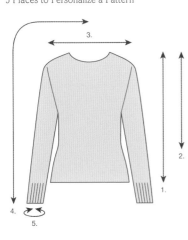

KNIT TO FIT

From the preceding discussion, you would draw the conclusion that there are ideal garment lengths for you. You might then wonder how any designer can know yours? How can this person know your height, your shape, and your preferences? It's not possible! (This explains why my answer to a question once asked— "What is the most common mistake knitters make?"—was that they follow the pattern!) There are directions in every pattern that you should never follow blindly.

In this book, we've alerted you to the directions you should personalize: you are told in the Pattern Notes what to watch for, and you are told within the pattern where to shorten or lengthen. Many knitting patterns do not offer these directions, but you should be able to apply what follows to all other patterns.

There are five places where individual fit should override a pattern. (drawing 17)

1. The finished garment length

2. The waist length (if the garment has waist shaping)

3. The shoulder width (if the garment has shoulder seams)

4. The sleeve length

5. The number of stitches in a fitted cuff

To make garments that fit, measure your bust and then follow the sizing chart of standard body measurements (page 158) to determine which size to knit. Most of us know to do that. But beyond that, there are other personal measurements you'll need. You'll then want to change your patterns to follow these measurements. Directions for all these measurements and changes follow. (Do be aware that if you change any of the pattern's directions, this will change the yardage used. And, it really is a good rule to never be a slave to the pattern's yardage. Better to always have a little extra on hand.)

Measuring for Your Ideal Short Sweater Length

*   Take your height in inches.
*   Divide this by 2.
*   Subtract 2½" and call this your "balance point."
*   Hold something rigid on your head, and have someone measure from the top of your head to the top of your shoulder on your collarbone. (If you are alone, back into a wall and hold a rigid ruler at your head and then on your collarbone; mark the wall with a pencil, and measure between these two points. Make sure the ruler is parallel to the floor.)
*   Subtract the head + neck mea-surement from your balance point. (drawing 18)

Using the Sizing Chart on page 158, make the following adjustments. (These adjustments are to override extra girth.)

*   If you knit size XS, do nothing.
*   If you knit size S, add ½" (13mm)
*   If you knit size M, add 1" (2.5cm).
*   If you knit size L, add 1½" (3.8cm).
*   If you knit size 1X, add 2" (5cm).
*   If you knit size 2X, add 2" (5cm).
*   For larger sizes, continue to add ½" (13mm) per size.

This is your ideal short, unshaped sweater length (drawing 18).

Measuring for Your Ideal Mid-length Sweater

*   Stand straight, and hold a tape measure at the top of one shoulder on the collarbone. Let the tape measure ride over the bust and down the leg.
*   Hold the tape measure to the leg break—the top of your leg that is evident when you bend it.

This is your ideal mid-length sweater (drawing 19).

Measuring for Your Ideal Big and Long Sweater

*   Wear the lower body covering you would wear with your big and long sweater.
*   Looking in a mirror, note the place where you'd like to define your slim rectangle. For a long straight sweater, it will be below your leg break and just before your legs widen to hip. For a long,

A-line sweater, it might be at your leg break and just above your crotch, or it could be longer.

- Look at yourself from the back, and adjust.
- Stand straight, and hold a tape measure at the top of your shoulder on the collarbone. Let the tape measure ride over the bust and down to this point on the leg.

This is your ideal long, unshaped sweater length (drawing 20).

Measuring for Your Waist Length

- Find the most prominent bone at the base of the back of your neck.
- Have someone measure you from this point down your back and to your waist.

This is your back waist length (drawing 21). In sweaters with waist shaping, you might want this to occur at the natural waist. But you might want it to occur 1–2" (2.5–5cm) above the natural waist—to give the illusion of a long leg.

To Change a Pattern's Finished Length

- For every garment, find the finished length of the garment (in the measurements or schematics).
- If this is different from your measurement, add or subtract this difference (the number of inches or centimeters) where the pattern says, "shorten or lengthen here."

Because some patterns do not tell you to shorten or lengthen, here are some guidelines for when to do this.

- In garments with no armhole shaping, change finished length before the neck.

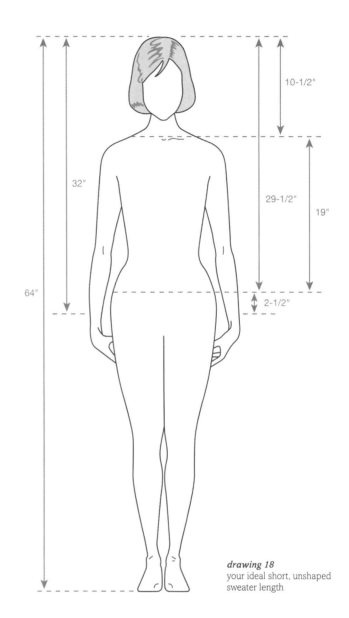

drawing 18
your ideal short, unshaped sweater length

- In garments with armhole shaping, change finished length before the armhole. (The armhole depth is particular to the size of the sleeve and should not be changed.)
- In garments with waist shaping, change finished length before the waist and waist length between the waist and armhole.

As an example, here's a situation you might encounter—a mid-length garment with waist shaping where the pattern's waist length is 1" (2.5cm) too short for you, but the finished length is perfect. (What follows illus-trates why you need to work this out before much knitting is done and why you might want to photocopy and mark up your schematic.)

- The pattern's waist length is 16" (40.5cm), but yours is 17" (43cm).
- The pattern's finished length is 22" (56cm), as is yours.
- The pattern will tell you to shorten or lengthen for waist length before the armhole: you'll add 1" (2.5cm) more rows.
- But, you've now added 1" (2.5cm) to the finished length. Therefore, where the pattern tells you to

shorten or lengthen before waist shaping, you will work 1" (2.5cm) fewer rows.

Measuring for Your Shoulder Width

The shoulder width is the seam-to-seam measurement across a garment with shoulder definition. This, then, applies to the set-in sleeve but not to the drop shoulder or raglan. It also applies to a sleeveless garment and to a garment with shoulder straps (although we never make straps to our actual shoulder width or they'd fall off).

Patterns are sometimes written with ever-larger shoulder widths per size. But just because you are a size small does not mean you have narrower-than-average shoulders, and just because you are a size extra-large does not mean you have wider-than-average shoulders. On the other hand, patterns can be written with the same shoulder widths for all sizes, but this may not be your measurement, either. What you want is a shoulder width that fits your body.

- Find the points on the top of your shoulders, toward the edge, that are sensitive when you press on them.

or

- Find and wear a set-in sleeve garment whose shoulder seams fit you.
- Have someone measure you across the back between these points (or seams).

This is your body's shoulder width (drawing 22). And this might be the width to which you shape your shoulders—but not always. If the garment is sleeveless, you might make the shoulders 1" (2.5cm) wider, to give yourself the illusion of a wider shoulder. If the garment has sleeves, you might make the shoulders 1" (2.5cm) narrower, because the sleeves may pull the garment off the shoulders. (This latter is more likely to occur if the yarn is heavy and/or the sleeve is not a tight fit at the armhole.)

To Change the Pattern's Shoulder Width

- Find the finished shoulder width (in the measurements or schematics).
- If it is different from your measurements, then you will change the "Shape Armhole" directions.
- Multiply the stitches per inch (or centimeter) by your shoulder width. Make this a whole number and then odd or even, as suits the pattern. Add 2 stitches (if needed, for seams).
- Bind off as directed at the underarm.
- When decreasing to shoulder width, work more or fewer decreases in order to attain the stitches of your shoulder width. (For smaller sizes, you might actually have to increase to your shoulder width. Do this gradually as you approach the shoulder.)
- You will have different numbers of stitches for all of the pattern's subsequent directions. Do not change the neck numbers: absorb your changes into the shoulder instructions. (It's not that difficult, I promise. For example, if you have 4 fewer stitches for the shoulder width, then bind off 2 fewer than directed for each

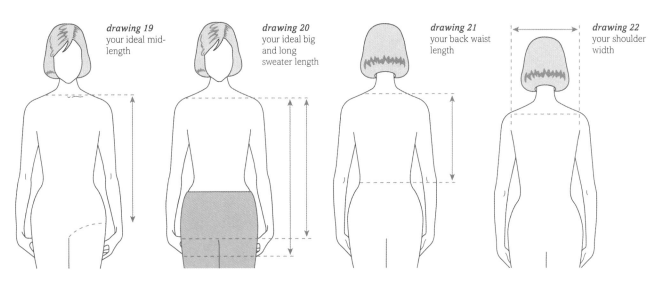

drawing 19 your ideal mid-length

drawing 20 your ideal big and long sweater length

drawing 21 your back waist length

drawing 22 your shoulder width

shoulder. Do make all shoulders match!)

Measuring for Your Sleeve Length

Sleeve length is something many knitters struggle with. It's confusing, but here's how to make sense of it.

- Stand with your arm bent 90 degrees at the elbow.
- Have someone measure you from the center and base of your neck, across your shoulders, and around your arm to your wrist break.

This is your sleeve length (drawing 23).

You might note that it is not actually the length of your sleeve, because half the width of the garment—from center neck to top of sleeve—is included. But in the tailoring world, this measurement is called sleeve length. (The reason for this terminology is so this measurement can cover all manner of styles and armhole shapings.)

The patterns in this book give you finished sleeve lengths. But many do not. Go to the schematics, and do the following.

- Find the garment's width from top of sleeve to top of sleeve: in a set-in sleeve this will be shoulder width; in a drop shoulder, it will be front/back width. Divide by 2.
- Find the total length of the sleeve—including the sleeve cap if there is one.

The sum of these two numbers is the pattern's sleeve length. Compare this against your sleeve length.

You may knit most long-sleeved garments to your sleeve length. Or you might knit them 1" shorter, because heavy sleeves can pull a sweater off the shoulders to make a longer sleeve. Alternatively, for a garment with a tight-fitting cuff that blouses out to a loose sleeve, you may need to add 1" (2.5cm) to your sleeve length to accommodate the extra length that blousing demands. For shorter sleeves, measure yourself to see where you'd like this sleeve to fall on your arm. And it's always helpful to double-check these measurements against a similar garment.

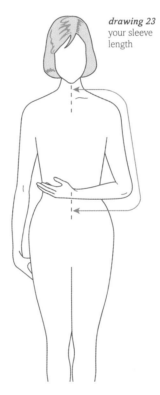

drawing 23
your sleeve length

To Change a Pattern's Sleeve Length

- Find the difference (the number of inches or centimeters) between your sleeve length and the pattern's.
- Work more or fewer rows where the pattern says, "shorten or lengthen here." In styles with armhole shaping, this will happen before the armhole. (The armhole depth is specific to the size of your sleeve and should not be changed.)

Determining the Number of Stitches for Your Cuff

The number of stitches that is appropriate for a fitted cuff is dependent upon the size of your bones and hands. What you want is a cuff that fits your wrist but is not so tight that your hand can't pass through.

- Do not knit the sleeves first.
- Find a part of your garment knit in the same stitch pattern as your cuff. (The bottom band is the logical place. But you may use any cast-on edge knit with the same yarn and needles as the cuff.)
- Wrap this piece around your hand, and count the minimum number of stitches that will allow your hand to pass through.

This is the correct number of stitches for your cuff.

To Change the Number of Stitches in the Cuff

- Cast on the number of stitches for the cuff as determined above.
- Work the cuff to the desired length.
- When starting the sleeve itself, decrease or increase to match the number of stitches directed.

IN CONCLUSION

The preceding discussion should alert you to the following....

- You should never follow a pattern without personalizing it to your measurements. (I know I've said that before, but it bears repeating.)
- You should never judge a garment's length by how it falls on the model. (For example, I make my garments for a 5'4"–5'6" woman—a woman of average height—but the model might be somewhat taller, so the garment could look short on her.)
- Whether you are short- or long-waisted will not affect your ideal sweater lengths. (In fact, this body anomaly is corrected if you knit to your ideal length.)
- Because you may have shortened or lengthened, you should not expect to see a total number of stitches after picking up for the front band of a cardigan. (I'll give you a proportion and—if necessary—a multiple, but never a total.)
- If you change a pattern, you may need different yardage.

What follows are just a few other things to consider....

KNIT TO FLATTER

Sometimes we follow all the rules for length, size, and styling, but the garment still does not flatter. It's the right color and style, but there's something still not quite right.

Have you ever thought about which fabrics look good on you—and which do not—in terms of the following: shiny or matte? stiff or drapey? small, dense patterning or larger, less-dense patterning? (The first two would translate to yarn aesthetics and fiber content, and the third would translate to the color work of the garment.)

Prevailing wisdom says that shiny fabric, stiff fabric, or small patterning make you look bigger. But I know from experience that other issues override this assumption. (I am small and small-boned, and I look wrong—truly terrible, in fact—in shiny or stiff fabrics and in small and busy patterning.) Which is right for you? You need to address these issues in order to avoid buying yarn that's wrong for you and that will sabotage the garment from its inception.

You might also consider what styles look good on you: raglan, drop shoulder, set-in sleeve? boat neck, V-neck, round neck?

Here's what I know about these different styles.

- The raglan may emphasize the shoulders and bust (making narrow shoulders look narrower and a bigger bust look bigger).
- The drop shoulder is not comfortable unless shaped generously. (Some knitters—especially those with a larger bust—might not like the excessive fabric at the underarm.)
- The set-in sleeve is considered "universally attractive" (as long as it fits the shoulders, page 19).
- The boat neck will shorten the neck and make it look slim (because the opening is so much wider than the neck itself).
- The V-neck will lengthen the neck and make it look slim. It will also expose the good skin we older girls have on our upper chest (mainly because the chin has shaded it from the sun all these years, plus gravity has had a go with our fleshier, lower regions, so this skin has been stretched—something akin to a face lift!).
- The V-neck is also good for a larger bust because it cuts the bust in half, and a good way to make something look smaller is to cut it in half.
- The round-neck is considered "universally attractive" (as long as it doesn't sit too tight to the base of the neck, which would make the neck look wider). And we older girls might love a deep round neck (for the same reasons we like the V-neck).

CHAPTER TWO

❧ THE GRAPE AND THE WINE: ❧
Thoughts to an Adult Daughter

We are warned when we are expecting a child. The older folk say, "Your life will change." And we, the pregnant couple, say, "Oh yes, we know; we are prepared." The older folk just shake their heads.

Once that baby comes, we realize what we did not know: that nothing could have prepared us. The moment we look at this baby, it feels as if our hearts are breaking, splitting in two, growing to twice their size. But as our hearts grow big, our fears grow bigger, too. Everything scary is anything that could harm this child. Yet life is not all scary, because we learn to laugh as we never have. And we also learn to cry as we never have: sometimes from fear, but often from something offered, from pride, or from joy.

With a change as profound as the life of a new baby, every emotion is thrown into turmoil. And, at the same time, everything we thought we knew is brought to judgment. What do I know for sure that is right for this child? What do I not know that could put this child in harm's way? It's a frightening thing—the responsibility of a new life.

So today my child is grown, and I wonder what I have learned since those early moments of turmoil and uncertainty. Whether we speak of knitting or of life, what do I know for sure that I would wish for her? Success and accomplishment: peace and prosperity; comfort and contentment: happiness beyond measure. Certainly. But would

I wish her never to be scared? No, that would mean she'd never hold my grandchild. Would I wish her never to cry? That would be as terrible as wishing her never to laugh. Never to know pain? Pain teaches us what we need to know, and suffering brings compassion. Never to struggle? That would mean she'd never learn, plus most of us old folk say that it's when we were struggling that we were happiest. And never to fail? Chekov said, "One would have to be God to see success and failure and know one from the other."

Albert Einstein said that the most significant decision we make is whether we live in a friendly or a hostile universe. To me, living in a friendly universe means that we can have faith that life's journey, wherever it takes us, will grant us peace and lead us home.

I love my daughter beyond measure, and I always will. Through whatever she endures or celebrates, I love her and I always will. And what I wish for her is this. May she know life in all its fullness. May she live in a friendly universe. May she learn through life's uncertainties. May she find the peace that leads her home. ❧ —SALLY

❖ NO-MESS HEADBAND ❖

Designed by Caddy

I WEAR HEADBANDS A LOT, AND APPARENTLY I'M NOT ALONE. BUT MOST WOMEN HAVE THE SAME COMPLAINTS I DO: THEY SLIDE OFF YOUR HEAD AND MAKE YOUR HAIR AT THE BACK OF YOUR HEAD BUNCH UP (ESPECIALLY IF YOU HAVE SHORT HAIR!). SO I SET OUT TO DESIGN A HEADBAND THAT LOOKS REALLY CUTE, STAYS PUT, AND IS NARROW ENOUGH AT THE BACK TO NOT MESS WITH THE TRESSES. AND IF I MAY SAY SO..."MISSION ACCOMPLISHED!"

SKILL LEVEL
Beginner

SIZE
- One size
- Finished width (at widest point) 2½" (6.5cm)
- Finished length (minus elastic) 13½" (33cm)

MATERIALS
- 28 yd (25m)/1 ball Estelle Young Touch Cotton DK (100% cotton, each approximately 1¾ oz [50g] and 114 yd [105m]), in color 23 maroon, ❸ light/double knitting
- One pair size 6 (4mm) needles, or size needed to obtain gauge
- 6" (15cm) of black elastic, ¼" (3mm) wide
- Tapestry needle

GAUGE
16 stitches and 30 rows/15 garter ridges = approximately 2½" (6.5cm) in garter stitch

HEADBAND
Cast on 4 stitches.
Knit 8 rows.
Increase row K1, kf&b, knit to last 2 stitches, kf&b, k1.
Work 7 rows even.
Repeat the last 8 rows 5 times more—16 stitches. End after working 8 rows even.
Decrease row K1, skp, knit to last 3 stitches, k2tog, k1.
Work 7 rows even.
Repeat the last 8 rows 5 times more—4 stitches. End after working 8 rows even.
Bind off.

FINISHING
Thread the elastic onto a tapestry needle. Bring the needle through one end of the headband.
Tie the elastic to itself twice (to make a double knot around the end of the headband). Repeat for the other end, leaving approximately 2" (5cm) of elastic between each end. Trim the elastic.

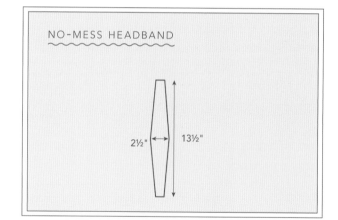

NO-MESS HEADBAND

2½"   13½"

⋇ BUTTONED MUFFLER ⋇

Designed by Sally

INSPIRED BY CADDY'S TABBED CUFFS (PAGE 28), I THOUGHT ABOUT HOW THE TABS COULD BE USED IN OTHER WAYS AND FOR DIFFERENT TYPES OF GARMENTS. AND SINCE THE CUFFS ARE A BEGINNER PATTERN, I SUPPOSE IT WAS OBVIOUS THAT MY FIRST INSTINCT WOULD BE TO DESIGN A SCARF—THE QUINTESSENTIAL BEGINNER GARMENT. SO HERE IT IS, A TABBED ALTERNATIVE TO THE SCARF. I LOVE ITS POLISHED LOOK AND THE WAY IT FITS AROUND THE COLLAR OF A COAT OR JACKET.

SKILL LEVEL
Beginner

SIZE
- One size
- Finished height 8" (20cm)
- Finished length 28" (71cm)
- Circumference (buttoned) 20" (50.5cm)

MATERIALS
- 105 yd (95m) / 2 skeins Malabrigo Aquarella (100% wool, each approximately 3½ oz [100g] and 65 yd [58m]), in color 02 Soriano, 6 super bulky
- One pair size 11 (8mm) needles, or size needed to obtain gauge
- Tapestry needle
- 3 Buttons, 1" (2.5cm) wide

GAUGE
9 stitches and 16 rows / 8 garter ridges = 4" (10cm) in garter stitch

MUFFLER
Long-tail cast on 64 stitches.
*Knit 7 rows.
Next row (RS) Bind off 4 stitches, knit to end.
(On right-side rows, the tail is to the left.)
Decrease row (WS) Knit to last 3 stitches, k2tog, k1.
Knit 1 row.
Repeat decrease row once—58 stitches.
Next row (RS) E-wrap cast on 4 stitches then knit to end—62 stitches.
Repeat from * once—60 stitches.
Knit 7 rows.
Bind off.

FINISHING
Sew 3 buttons to match placement as shown on the schematic.
(The first button is 1½" [3.8cm] up and in from the lower corner.)
Force buttons through fabric to create buttonholes.
(These will enlarge and become permanent.)

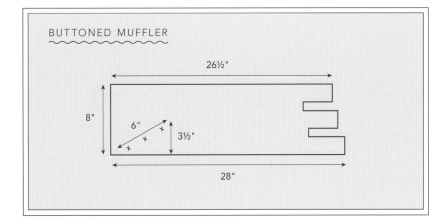

BUTTONED MUFFLER

26½"

8"

6"

3½"

28"

❧ TABBED CUFFS ❧

Designed by Caddy

THESE CUFFS ARE PERFECT FOR PEOPLE WHOSE HANDS ARE ALWAYS COLD BUT WHO NEED THEIR FINGERS FREE—FOR TYPING, FOR PLAYING MUSICAL INSTRUMENTS, FOR KNITTING. THEY ARE ALSO A FUNKY AND FASHIONABLE ALTERNATIVE TO THOSE DARN MITTENS WITH THE FINGER FLAP.

SKILL LEVEL
Beginner

SIZE
- One size
- Finished circumference 6–8" (15–20cm)
- Finished length 8" (20cm)

MATERIALS
- 170–200 yd (155–180m) / 2 balls Estelle Young Touch Cotton DK (100% cotton, each approximately 1¾ oz [50g] and 114 yd [105m]), in color 23 maroon, (3) light/double knitting
- One pair size 7 (4.5mm) needles, or size needed to obtain gauge
- Stitch holder
- Tapestry needle
- Pins
- 6 Buttons, 1" (2.5cm) wide

or
- 12 Buttons, ½" (13mm) wide

GAUGE
20 stitches and 40 rows / 20 garter ridges = 4" (10cm) in garter stitch

PATTERN NOTES
- These cuffs are knit lengthwise.
- The buttons are used to attach the tabs to the main pieces but are purely decorative (There are no buttonholes!), so be sure to sew your buttons through both layers.

MAIN PIECE
Cast on 40 stitches.
Knit until piece measures 1" (2.5cm) short of fitting around your wrist.
(Place the piece on a table, lay your arm on top, and use your other hand to wrap, stretching slightly: tighter is better than looser.)
Next row K10. Place remaining 30 stitches on a holder. Turn.

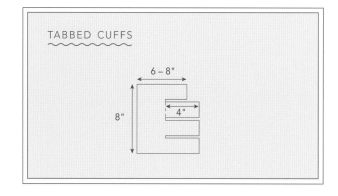

PALM PIECE

Knit these 10 stitches to 2" (5cm). Bind off so the tail will be at the top. Leave a long tail for seaming.

TAB 2

Return to remaining stitches, join yarn, and knit the next 10 stitches to 4" (10cm).
Bind off, leaving a tail to sew button(s).

TABS 3 AND 4

Work as for Tab 2.

FINISHING

(Be sure to sew each cuff so one fits the right hand and the other fits the left! Make one, see which hand it fits, then reverse the sewing for the other hand.)
Sew the Palm Piece to the Main Piece, sewing 10 bind-off stitches of the Palm Piece to the first 10 cast-on stitches of Main Piece. (Take the bind-off and cast-on edges to the wrong side.) Do not cut the remaining yarn: you will use this for the final step.

Put the cuff on, and wrap Tab 2 around your wrist to fit snugly. Pin in place. Repeat for Tabs 3 and 4.
With tab tails, sew Tabs to Main Piece with one large button (or two small buttons).
With remaining tail, sew the cast-on edge of the Main Piece to the wrong side of Tabs.

WHY DO YOU KNIT?

SALLY: I knit because I must. Rare is a day that passes without knitting, and those are not days I enjoy. While my hands need knitting, I think my brain needs it more—the soothing and peaceful place to which it retreats.

I also knit because I've always been fidgety—needing to do two things at once. How does anyone watch a hockey game without knitting?

Lastly, I knit because I love to make my own clothes. From the first time I got to say, "I made it myself!" I was hooked.

CADDY: I knit because my hands tell me to.

Knitting is my meditation; I'm sure that my heart rate is lower when I'm knitting—unless I'm ripping something out! But that is strangely pleasing, too.

I knit because I believe one of the greatest gifts you can give yourself is the outlet to create.

⁓ TABBED SPATS / LEGWARMERS ⁓

Designed by Sally

I LOVE BOOTS—SHORT OR TALL. BUT I CANNOT ALWAYS FIND THE PERFECT BOOT FOR EVERY OUTFIT. SOMETIMES IT'S THE WRONG HEIGHT, WRONG COLOR, WRONG MATERIAL, WRONG HEEL. SO HOW FUN TO TAKE CADDY'S CONCEPT OF TABS AND APPLY IT TO THE LEG—TO MAKE A PAIR OF PERFECT KNITTED BOOTS (WHICH ARE APPARENTLY OH-SO FASHIONABLE) BUT STILL WEAR THEM OVER OUR MOST COMFORTABLE SHOES!

SKILL LEVEL
Easy

SIZES
- One size, two heights
- Spats (Legwarmers)
- Circumference at base 11 (11½)" (28 [29]cm)
- Circumference at top 9 (12)" (23 [30.5]cm)
- Height 8 (16½)" (20 [42]cm)

MATERIALS
Spats
- 160 yards (144m) / 1 ball Lana Grossa Luxor (31% merino wool, 49% microfiber, each approximately 1¾ oz [50g] and 165 yd [150m]), in color 009 brown, 🧶4️⃣ medium/worsted weight

Legwarmers
- 300 (270m) yards / 2 balls Berroco Peruvia (100% wool, each approximately 3½ oz [100g] and 174 yd [160m]), in color 7114 brown, 🧶4️⃣ medium/worsted weight

Both
- One pair size 9 (5.5mm) needles, or size needed to obtain gauge
- Tapestry needle
- 8 (20) Buttons, ½–¾" (13–20mm) wide

GAUGE
17 stitches and 28 rows / 14 garter ridges = 4" (10cm) in garter stitch

PATTERN NOTES
- For the long version, you will know the top from the bottom because the circumference is larger at the top. But you can, of course, wear them upside down!
- The spats are rolled over at the top; the legwarmers are not.
- All pieces are knit lengthwise.
- The first number is for the spats. The second number (in parentheses) is for the legwarmers. When only one number is given, it applies to both.

RIGHT LEG
Leaving a long tail for seaming, long-tail cast on 35 (70) stitches.
Work in garter stitch to 4" (10cm). End after working a right-side row.
(On right-side rows, the tail is to the left.)

Ankle Short-row Shaping, Both Versions
Next (short) row (WS) K32. Turn.
Next 5 RS rows Wyif slip 1 purlwise, knit to end.

Next 5 WS (short) rows Knit 3 fewer stitches than previous wrong-side row. Turn.
(The final short row will have 17 stitches.)
Next (RS) row Wyif slip 1 purlwise, k16.
Next (WS) row K35 (70).

Upper Leg Short-row Shaping, Tall Version only
Next (short) row (RS) K32. Turn.
Next 7 WS rows Wyif slip 1 purlwise, knit to end.
Next 7 RS (short) rows Knit 4 fewer stitches than previous wrong-side row. Turn.
(The final short row will have 4 stitches.)
Next (WS) row Wyif slip 1 purlwise, k3.
Next (RS) row K70.

Both Versions
Continue in garter stitch to 9½" (24cm), measuring along top (center) not including the short rows.
End after working a wrong-side row.
(On wrong-side rows, the tail is to the right.)

Tabs (from top to bottom)
Short version only, next row (RS) Bind off first 14 stitches, then continue as follows over remaining 21 stitches.
*All Versions, next row (RS) K7. Turn.
Knit these 7 stitches for 7 more rows, then bind off. Cut yarn, leaving 10" (25.5cm) tail.
Return to remaining stitches, right side facing.
Repeat from * 2 (9) times more—3 (10) tabs.

FINISHING
With cast-on tail, sew cast-on edge to wrong side behind tabs and—for top of short version only—behind 14 bind-off stitches.
With tails, sew down tabs by sewing a button through both layers.

Top Tab, Short Version only
Fold upper edge over to depth of 7 stitches.
Pick up and knit 7 stitches along the bumps that line up with the base of the other tabs.
Knit 7 more rows.
Bind off.
With tail, sew down tabs by sewing a button through both layers.

LEFT LEG
Work as Right Leg to 4" (10cm). End after working a wrong-side row.
(On wrong-side rows, the tail is to the right.)

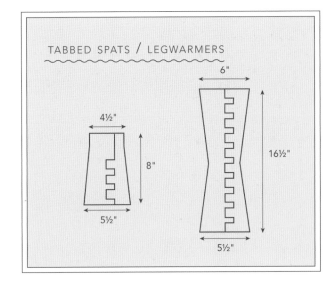

TABBED SPATS / LEGWARMERS

Ankle Short-row Shaping, Both Versions
Next (short) row (RS) K32. Turn.
Next 5 WS rows Wyif slip 1 purlwise, knit to end.
Next 5 RS (short) rows Knit 3 fewer stitches than previous wrong-side row. Turn.
(The final short row will have 17 stitches.)
Next (WS) row Wyif slip 1 purlwise, k16.
Next (RS) row K35 (70).

Upper Leg Short-row Shaping, Tall Version only
Next (short) row (WS) K32. Turn.
Next 7 RS rows Wyif slip 1 purlwise, knit to end.
Next 7 WS (short) rows Knit 4 fewer stitches than previous wrong-side row. Turn.
(The final short row will have 4 stitches.)
Next (RS) row Wyif slip 1 purlwise, k3.
Next (WS) row K70.

Both Versions
Continue in garter stitch to 9½" (24cm), measuring along top (center) not including the short rows.
End after working a wrong-side row.
(On wrong-side rows, the tail is to the right.)

Tabs (from bottom to top)
*All versions, next row (RS) K7. Turn.
Knit these 7 stitches for 7 more rows, then bind off. Cut yarn, leaving 10" (25cm) tail.
Return to remaining stitches, right side facing.
Repeat from * 2 (9) times more—3 (10) tabs.
Short version only, next row Bind off final 14 stitches.

FINISHING
Work as for Right Leg.

❧ THE SLOUCH ❧

Designed by Caddy

TRY WEARING THIS SLOUCH WITH THE RIBBON OFF TO ONE SIDE, OR TO FRONT-AND-CENTER TO ACCEN-
TUATE THE BUST, OR DOWN THE BACK FOR A DRAMATIC LOOK. TO CINCH THE RIBBON, SIMPLY PULL FROM
THE BOTTOM AND TIE A KNOT TO SECURE.

SKILL LEVEL
Beginner

SIZES
- XS (S, M, L, 1X)
- Finished bust 30 (34, 38, 42, 46)" (76 [86, 96.5, 106.5, 117] cm)
- Finished length 10 (11, 12, 13, 14)" (25.5 [28, 30.5, 33, 35,5]cm)

MATERIALS
- 220 (245, 270, 300, 320) yd (200 [220, 245, 270, 290]m) / 3 (4, 4, 4, 5) balls Classic Elite Duchess (40% merino, 28% viscose, 10% cashmere, 7% angora, 15% nylon, each approximately 1¾ oz [50g] and 75 yd [68m]), in color 1016 Natural, (5) bulky
- One size 11 (8mm) circular needle, 20–24" (50–60cm) long, or size needed to obtain gauge
- Stitch marker
- 2 yd (1.8m) ribbon, 1½–2" (4–6cm) wide
- Tapestry needle

GAUGE
12 stitches and 16 rows = 4" in stockinette stitch

PATTERN NOTES
- This garment is knit in the round.

SLOUCH
Cast on 90 (102, 114, 126, 138) stitches. Place stitch marker onto the right needle, and begin to work in the round.
(As you join the round, make sure your cast-on row is not twisted.)
Work 1x1 rib (*k1, p1; repeat from *) for 3 rounds. End at marker.
Next round Knit.
Knit in rounds until piece measures 9 (10, 11, 12, 13)" (23 [25.5, 28, 30.5, 33]cm). End at marker.
Next round Work 1x1 rib.
Work 1x1 rib for 2 more rounds. End at marker. Bind off in rib.

FINISHING
Block lightly.
Cut the ribbon into two pieces of equal length. Thread both pieces of ribbon through a tapestry needle. (The ribbon is doubled through what follows.)
Starting anywhere in the cast-on edge, bring the needle

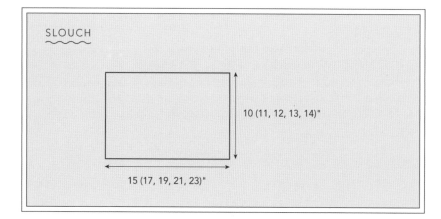

SLOUCH

10 (11, 12, 13, 14)"

15 (17, 19, 21, 23)"

from the back to the front through a stitch above the cast-on stitch.

*Take the ribbon up 2 rows then through to the back. Take the ribbon under 2 rows then through to the front. Repeat from * to the top of the slouch.

(Be sure to maintain a straight line by threading through the same stitch column all the way to the top.)

At the top of the slouch, bring 8" (20.5cm) of ribbon through to the right side.

Tie a double bow at the top. Trim to suit.

Pull the ribbon from the bottom to cinch as desired.

Trim the ribbon at the bottom to suit.

WHAT DO I DO THAT'S DIFFERENT FROM WHAT MY DAUGHTER/ MOM DOES?

SALLY: Sad but true, my daughter is more energetic and more adventurous than me. And she is also boundlessly optimistic. (She has yet to knit her share of bad sweaters—inevitable steps in our learning curve.) And while she's doing and trying and making new stuff, I tend to rely upon the tried and true. (I also think it's something that comes with age—an appreciation of styles that are classic and timeless.)

CADDY: I remember telling my mom that I was going to knit shelves. She smiled and nodded, biting her tongue. Needless to say, the shelves didn't quite work out.

❧ TWO-WAY SHRUG ❧

Designed by Caddy

HAVING AN ALTERNATIVE TO A SWEATER OR CARDIGAN, WHEN YOU NEED SOME WARMTH BUT DON'T WANT TO HIDE THE OUTFIT UNDERNEATH, IS A MUST. THIS PATTERN WAS DEVELOPED TO BE SUCH AN ALTERNATIVE. IT CAN BE WORN OPEN—OR BUTTONED—AND IT'S EASY TO KNIT SINCE IT'S ALL ONE PIECE!

SKILL LEVEL
Easy

SIZES
- XS-S (M-L, 1X)
- Finished bust (closed) 34 (39, 44)" (86 [98.5, 112]cm)
- Finished length (at back, including collar) 17½ (20½, 25½)" (44.5 [52, 64.5]cm)

MATERIALS
- 30 (35, 40) yd (27 [32, 36]m) / 1 ball Lana Grossa Luxor (51% merino wool, 49% microfiber, each approximately 1¾ oz [50g] and 165 yd [150m]), in color 005 charcoal (CC), (**4**) medium/worsted weight
- 370 (430, 485) yd (335 [390, 435]m) / 3 [3, 3] balls Lana Grossa Luxor, in color 006 silver (MC), (**4**) medium/ worsted weight
- One pair size 10 (6mm) needles, or size needed to obtain gauge
- Tapestry needle
- 1 Button, ½" (13mm) wide
- 1 Button, ¾" (20mm) wide

GAUGE
16 stitches and 24 rows = 4" in stockinette stitch

PATTERN NOTES
- This shrug is knit from the bottom up.
- Work all increases as lifted increases.
- To help get your bearings, remember that the top of your shrug does not have a border.
- Because of the loosely-knit nature of the shrug, there is no need for buttonholes: the buttons are easily forced through the fabric.

SHRUG
With CC, cast on 126 (144, 162) stitches.
Work 1x1 rib for 3 rows.
With MC, knit 1 row, then purl 1 row.
Decrease row (RS) K1, skp, knit to last 3 stitches, k2tog, k1.
Work 3 (5, 7) rows even.
Repeat the last 4 (6, 8) rows 15 (13, 13) times more—94 (116, 134) stitches. End after working 3 (5, 7) rows even.

Shape Collar

Increase row (RS) K1, increase 1 in next stitch, knit to last 2 stitches, increase 1 in next stitch, k1.

Work 5 rows even.

Repeat the last 6 rows 5 times more—106 (128, 146) stitches. End after working 5 rows even.

Bind off.

FINISHING

Side Edgings

With right side facing and CC, pick up and knit 1 stitch for every row along entire side edge.

Work 1x1 rib for 2 rows, then bind off in rib.

Repeat for the second edge.

Assembly

Referring to the schematic, fold the shrug over to match points A to the points B below, then sew the edges together toward points C and D for 1½" (4cm).

With right side facing, sew the large button onto the top left corner of the ribbed edge (as shown by the large circle on the schematic).

Sew the smaller button onto the top right corner, ¾" (2cm) from the ribbed edge (as shown by the small circle on the schematic).

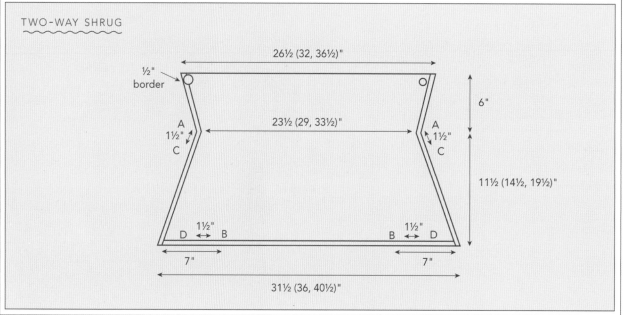

TWO-WAY SHRUG

½" border

26½ (32, 36½)"

23½ (29, 33½)"

6"

A
1½"
C

A
1½"
C

11½ (14½, 19½)"

1½"
D   B

1½"
B   D

7"

7"

31½ (36, 40½)"

⤛ CAMELOT COAT ⤜

Designed by Sally

I CALL THIS THE CAMELOT COAT BECAUSE IT SEEMS LIKE SOMETHING JACKIE MIGHT HAVE WORN DURING THOSE MAGICAL YEARS OF THE KENNEDY WHITE HOUSE. THE WORLD SEEMED SO INNOCENT THEN, AND HER STYLE—ICONIC, CLEAN, SIMPLE—EXPRESSED IT PERFECTLY. AND SO, WE HAVE THE SIMPLE LINES OF THIS COAT, WORKED IN SWEET, FRESH COLORS. I LOVE TO WEAR IT, IN NOSTALGIC REMEMBRANCE OF A TIME GONE BY.

SKILL LEVEL
Intermediate

SIZES
- S (M, L, 1X, 2X)
- Finished bust 38 (42, 46, 50, 54)" (96.5 [106.5, 117, 127, 137]cm)
- Finished hem 56 (62, 68, 74, 80)" (142 [157.5, 172.5, 188, 203]cm)
- Finished length (without fulling) 38 (38½, 39, 39½, 40)" (96.5 [97.5, 99, 100, 101.5]cm)
- Finished shoulder width 15" (38cm)
- Finished waist length 16½ (17, 17½, 18, 18½)" (42 (43, 44, 47, 48]cm)
- Finished sleeve length 26½ (27, 27½, 28, 28½)" 67 [68.5, 69.5, 71, 72]cm)

MATERIALS
- 1400 (1550, 1720, 1890, 2065) yd (1260 [1400, 1550, 1700, 1860]m) / 3 (4, 4, 4, 5) balls Cascade Eco+ (100% wool, each approximately 8¾ oz [250g] and 478yd [437m]), in color 6922 coral or 6902 periwinkle, (5) bulky
- One pair size 8 (5mm) needles, or size needed to obtain gauge
- One pair size 6 (4mm) needles
- Stitch holder
- Tapestry needle
- 6 Buttons, 1" (2.5cm) wide

GAUGE
16 stitches and 22 rows = 4" (10cm) in stockinette stitch, over larger needles and after blocking

PATTERN NOTES
- If you choose to change lengths, adjust finished length before the waistband and waist length between the waistband and the armhole (page 17).
- The back skirt is knit in two pieces that are seamed in the center. This gives stability to the "seat."
- The e-wrap cast-on is used because the lower edgings are picked up and knit down later.
- To work rib as established means to knit the k's and purl the p's.
- The coral version was fulled after knitting. (See finishing directions.) This did not change the width but did shorten the garment by 1–2" (2.5–5cm). It also made the fabric firmer.

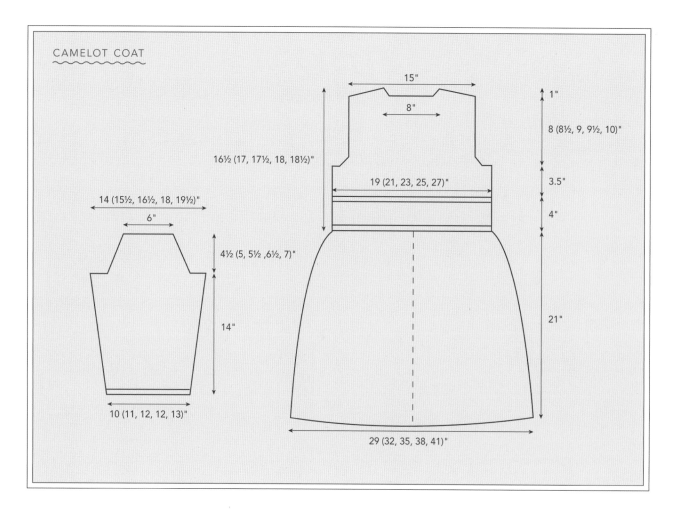

CAMELOT COAT

BACK

Skirt Pieces (Make 2)

With larger needles, e-wrap cast on 59 (65, 71, 77, 83) stitches.

Work stockinette until the piece measures 21" (53cm). End after working a wrong-side row. (Shorten or lengthen for finished length here, page 18.)

For the first piece, cut the yarn, leaving a long tail for seaming. Place stitches on a holder.

For the second piece, do not cut the yarn. Leave stitches on needle.

Waistband

Continuing over the piece just knit, work as follows:

Decrease row With smaller needles, *k1, k2tog; repeat from * to last 2 stitches, skp; introduce piece on holder, k2tog, *k2tog, k1; repeat from * to end—78 (86, 94, 102, 110) stitches.

Knit 1 (WS) row, purl 1 row, then knit 2 rows.

Increase row (WS) *P2, k2; repeat from *, AT THE SAME TIME increase 12 stitches across row [by making k2 with kf&b or p2 with pb&f] in each 5th (7th, 7th, 7th, 9th) stitch,

end with p2—90 (98, 106, 114, 122) stitches.

(For some sizes, you will run out of increases before the end of the row.)

Following RS rows *K2, p2; repeat from * to last 2 stitches, k2.

Following WS rows *P2, k2; repeat from * to last 2 stitches, p2.

(At any time during the waistband, use the tail from the first piece to sew the center Back seam.)

Work 2x2 rib until rib measures 3" (7.5cm). End after working a wrong-side row.

Decrease row (RS) *K5 (6, 6, 7, 8), k2tog; repeat from * to last 6 (2, 10, 6, 2) stitches, knit to end—78 (86, 94, 102, 110) stitches.

Knit 1 (WS) row, purl 1 row, then knit 1 row.

Upper Body

Change to larger needles, and work stockinette until piece measures 28½" (72cm). End after working a wrong-side row.

(Shorten or lengthen for waist length here, page 18.)

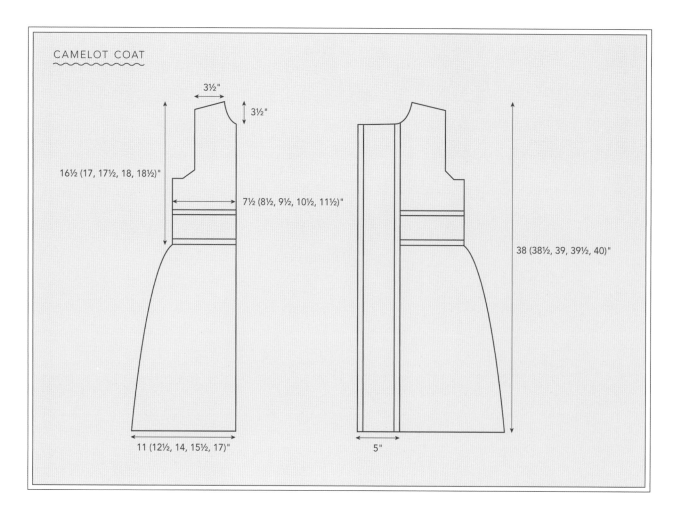

CAMELOT COAT

3½"

3½"

16½ (17, 17½, 18, 18½)"

7½ (8½, 9½, 10½, 11½)"

38 (38½, 39, 39½, 40)"

11 (12½, 14, 15½, 17)"

5"

SHAPE ARMHOLE
Bind off 5 (6, 7, 8, 9) stitches at the beginning of the next 2 rows—68 (74, 80, 86, 92) stitches.
Decrease row (RS) K1, skp, knit to last 3 stitches, k2tog, k1.
Purl 1 (WS) row.
Repeat the last 2 rows 3 (6, 9, 12, 15) times more—60 stitches.
(Adjust shoulder width here, page 19.)
Work even until armhole measures 8 (8½, 9, 9½, 10)" (20.5 [21.5, 23, 24, 25.5]cm). End after working a wrong-side row.

SHAPE RIGHT SHOULDER AND BACK NECK
Bind off 5 stitches at the beginning of the next right-side row. Work to 11 stitches on right needle. Place remaining 44 stitches on holder. Turn.
Bind off 1 stitch at the next 2 neck edges.
Bind off 5 stitches at the next armhole edge then 4 stitches at the final armhole edge.

SHAPE LEFT SHOULDER AND BACK NECK.
Return to remaining 44 stitches, right side facing.
Bind off center 28 stitches, k16.
Bind off 5 stitches at the next 2 armhole edges and 1 stitch at the next 2 neck edges.
Bind off final 4 stitches at armhole edge.

RIGHT FRONT
Skirt
With larger needles, e-wrap cast on 45 (51, 57, 63, 69) stitches.
Work stockinette until piece measures same length as Back skirt. End after working a wrong-side row.

Waistband
Decrease row With smaller needles, *k1, k2tog; repeat from * to last 3 stitches, k1, skp—30 (34, 38, 42, 46) stitches.
Knit 1 (WS) row, purl 1 row, then knit 2 rows.
Increase row (WS) *P2, k2; repeat from *, AT THE SAME TIME increase 5 stitches across row [by making k2 with kf&b or p2 with pb&f] in every 5th (5th, 7th, 7th, 9th)

stitch, end with p3—35 (39, 43, 47, 51) stitches.
(For some sizes, you will run out of increases before the end of the row.)
Following RS rows K3, *p2, k2; repeat from * to end.
Following WS rows *P2, k2; repeat from * to last 3 stitches, p3.
Work 2x2 rib as established until rib measures same length as Back. End after working a wrong-side row.
Decrease row (RS) *K4 (5, 6, 7, 8), k2tog; repeat from * to last 5 (4, 3, 2, 1) stitches, knit to end—30 (34, 38, 42, 46) stitches.
Knit 1 (WS) row, purl 1 row, then knit 1 row.

Upper Body
Change to larger needles, and work stockinette until piece measures same length as Back to armhole. End after working a right-side row.

SHAPE ARMHOLE
Bind off 5 (6, 7, 8, 9) stitches at the beginning of the next wrong-side row—25 (28, 31, 34, 37) stitches.
Decrease row (RS) Knit to last 3 stitches, k2tog, k1.
Purl 1 (WS) row.
Repeat the last 2 rows 3 (6, 9, 12, 15) times more—21 stitches.
(Adjust shoulder width as for Back.)
Work even until armhole measures 5½ (6, 6½, 7, 7½)" (14 [15, 16.5, 17.5, 19]cm). End after working a wrong-side row.

SHAPE NECK AND SHOULDER
Bind off 2 stitches at the next 2 neck edges, then 1 stitch at the next 3 neck edges.
AT THE SAME TIME, when armhole measures same length as Back, bind off 5 stitches at the first 2 armhole edges then 4 stitches at the final armhole edge.

LEFT FRONT
Work as Right Front to increase row in waistband.
Increase row (WS) P3, *p2, k2; repeat from *, AT THE SAME TIME increase 5 stitches across row [by making k2 with kf&b or p2 with pb&f] in every 5th (5th, 7th, 7th, 9th) stitch, end with p2—35 (39, 43, 47, 51) stitches.
(For some sizes, you will run out of increases before the end of the row.)
Following RS rows *K2, p2; repeat from * to last 3 stitches, k3.
Following WS rows P3, *k2, p2; repeat from * to end.
Work 2x2 rib as established until rib measures same length as Back. End after working a wrong-side row.
Continue as Right Front from decrease row of waist-band to end of upper body. End after working a wrong-side row.

SHAPE ARMHOLE
Bind off 5 (6, 7, 8, 9) stitches at the beginning of the next right-side row—25 (28, 31, 34, 37) stitches.
Work 1 wrong-side row.
Decrease row (RS) K1, skp, knit to end.
Purl 1 row.
Repeat the last 2 rows 3 (6, 9, 12, 15) times more—21 stitches.
(Adjust shoulder width as for Back.)
Work even until armhole measures same length as Right Front. End after working a right-side row.
Work as Right Front, Shape Neck and Shoulder.

SLEEVES
Edging
With smaller needles, long-tail cast on 40 (44, 48, 48, 52) stitches.
Purl 1 row, knit 1 row, then purl 2 rows.

Body
Beginning with a right-side knit row, work stockinette for 6 rows.
(Work lifted increases through Sleeve shaping.)
Increase row (RS) K1, increase 1 in next stitch, knit to last 2 stitches, increase 1 in next stitch, k1.
Work 5 (5, 5, 3, 3) rows even.
Repeat the last 6 (6, 6, 4, 4) rows 7 (8, 8, 11, 12) times more—56 (62, 66, 72, 78) stitches.
Work even until piece measures 14" (35.5cm). End after working a wrong-side row.
(Shorten or lengthen for Sleeve length here, page 20.)

SHAPE SLEEVE CAP
Bind off 5 (6, 7, 8, 9) stitches at the beginning of the next 2 rows—46 (50, 52, 56, 60) stitches.
Decrease row (RS) K1, skp, knit to last 3 stitches, k2tog, k1.
Purl 1 (WS) row.
Repeat the last 2 rows 10 (12, 13, 15, 17) times more—24 stitches.
Bind off 2 stitches at the beginning of the next 2 rows.
Bind off 4 stitches at the beginning of the next 2 rows.
Bind off final 12 stitches.

FINISHING
Sew shoulder seams.

COLLAR
With larger needles and right side facing, begin at Right Front neck to pick up and knit as follows:
1 stitch for every bind-off stitch and 1 stitch for every

2-row step between bind-off stitches around Front and Back neck shaping,

1 stitch at each end of Back neck bind-off (if needed, to close holes),

2 stitches for every 3 rows along rows worked even. —71 stitches.

(If needed, increase or decrease on the next row to attain this number.)

Beginning with a purl row, work 3 rows in stockinette.

Next (decrease) row (RS) K8, *k2tog, k7; repeat from * to end—64 stitches.

Work 3 rows in stockinette.

Next (decrease) row (RS) K7, *k2tog, k6; repeat from * to last 9 stitches, k2tog, k7—57 stitches.

Work 3 rows in stockinette.

Next (decrease) row (RS) K6, *k2tog, k5; repeat from * to last 9 stitches, k2tog, k7—50 stitches.

Work 3 rows in stockinette.

Place stitches onto holder. Cut yarn.

Left Front Button Band

With smaller needles, right side facing, and beginning at holder, pick up and knit as follows along Left Front edge:

5 stitches for every 7 rows along stockinette, and 2 stitches for every 3 rows along the waistband.

(To pick up and knit 5 stitches for 7 rows, pick up and knit 3 stitches for 4 rows then 2 stitches for 3 rows.)

Count stitches on needle. While working the next row, increase or decrease to make a multiple of 7 stitches + 4.

Knit 1 (WS) row, purl 1 row, then knit 2 rows.

Increase row (WS) P3, *k2, p2, kf&b, p2; repeat from * to last stitch, p1.

Work 2x2 rib as follows and for 22 rows.

RS rows K3, *p2, k2; repeat from * to last stitch, k1.

WS rows P3, *k2, p2; repeat from * to last stitch, p1.

Row 23 (RS), make buttonhole K3, p2, k1, skp, yo, p1, continue rib as established.

(There is a buttonhole in the button band so the inside collar may be buttoned.)

Row 24 (WS) Work rib.

Row 25 (RS) Work rib, but at buttonhole purl through the yo (below the next stitch on the left needle) then drop the next stitch from the left needle—a larger buttonhole is made.

Work 3 more rows rib.

Decrease row (RS) K3, *k2tog, k6; repeat from * to last 7 stitches, k7.

Knit 1 (WS) row, purl 1 row, then knit 1 row. Bind off purlwise, leaving long tail.

With long tail, sew bind-off edge of edging to selvedge. Mark spaces on button band for 5 evenly-spaced buttons, all in p2's.

(Place the first opposite the buttonhole already formed, place the 5th near the bottom of the waistband, space the remaining 3 evenly.)

Right Front Buttonhole Band

Work as Left Front Button Band to end of Row 22.

Make buttonholes to match placement of buttons as follows.

Row 23 (RS), make buttonholes *Work rib to k2 before each buttonhole, k1, skp, yo, p1, repeat from * until 5 buttonholes are made, then rib to end.

Row 24 (WS) Work rib.

Row 25 (RS) Work rib, but at each buttonhole purl through the yo (below the next stitch on the left needle) then drop the next stitch from the left needle—larger buttonholes are made.

Work 3 more rows rib.

Decrease row (RS) K3, *k2tog, k6; repeat from * to last 7 stitches, k7.

Knit 1 (WS) row, purl 1 row, then knit 1 row. Bind off purlwise, leaving long tail.

With long tail, sew bind-off edge of the edging to selvedge.

Collar Edging

With smaller needles and right side facing, pick up and knit along edge of Front bands and around the Collar as follows: 5 stitches for every 7 rows along edge of Front bands, and 1 stitch for every stitch on hold—100–106 stitches.
Knit 1 (WS) row, purl 1 row, then knit 1 row. Bind off purlwise leaving long tail.
With long tail, sew bind-off edge to selvedge.

Front Lower Edgings

With smaller needles and right-sides facing, pick up and knit along Front hems as follows: 1 stitch for every cast-on stitch, and 5 stitches for every 7 rows along the edge of the Front bands—72 (78, 84, 90, 96) stitches.
Knit 1 (WS) row, purl 1 row, then knit 1 row. Bind off purlwise.

Back Lower Edging

With smaller needles and right side facing, pick up and knit 1 stitch for every cast-on stitch (except for stitches taken into seam allowances at center back) along lower Back hem—116 (128, 140, 152, 164) stitches.

Knit 1 (WS) row, purl 1 row, then knit 1 row. Bind off purlwise.

Sew buttons onto Left Front band to correspond to buttonholes on Right Front band.
Sew inside button to wrong-side of Right Front band.
Sew Sleeves into armholes.
Sew side and Sleeve seams.
Block well.
(This garment must be blocked, and washing in a wool-wash solution then drying flat is the best method.)

Fulling (*optional*)

After washing in a wool-wash solution and while still damp, place the garment in a dryer, with towels, and on air fluff setting until fulled to desired texture.
(This may take only a few minutes, so do not leave the garment unattended. You are not trying to dry it; all you want to achieve is a fuller, fatter fabric. When fulled appropriately, the garment may become 1–2" [2.5–5cm] shorter.) Dry flat.

WHAT IS YOUR KNITTING DEMOGRAPHIC?

SALLY: I'm one of the old girls (whose age need not be quantified) who feared that knitting would die with us. But then knitting became the new yoga, the new black, the new pantyhose, the new lip gloss! As a result, knitting's resurgence in popularity attracted knitters of all ages. The fact that my daughter became part of this group is one of the great joys of my life.

CADDY: I'm a new knitter. (I only started at twenty-four!) And I'm part of the group I like to call "absolutely, fabulously, mad about knitting!"…also known as AFMAK.

I'd also like to say that I'm glad we have knitting as an alternative to pantyhose. Thanks, Mom.

⊰ KNIT-ACROSS SWEATER ⊱

Designed by Caddy

WEAR THIS SWEATER PULLED DOWN LONG, BLOUSED UP SHORT, OR TUCKED INTO A PAIR OF HIGH-WAISTED
PANTS. YOU'LL LOOK FABULOUS, AND YOU'LL BE SHOCKED BY HOW COMFORTABLE YOU ARE. ENOUGH SAID.

SKILL LEVEL
Easy

SIZES
- XS (S, M, L, 1X)
- Finished hem 22 (24, 27, 30, 32)" (56 [61, 68.5, 76, 81.5] cm)
- Finished bust 35 (39, 43, 47, 51)" (89 [99, 109, 119.5, 129.5] cm)
- Finished length (flat) 22 (23, 24, 25, 26" (56 [58.5, 61, 63.5, 66]cm)
- Finished sleeve length 24¼ (24¾, 25¼, 25¾, 26¼)" (62 [63, 64, 65.5, 67] cm)

MATERIALS
- 825 (920, 1010, 1100, 1195) yd (750 [830, 915, 995, 1080]m) / 9 (10, 11, 12, 13) balls Tahki Yarns New Tweed (60% merino wool, 26% viscose, 14% silk, each approximately 1¾ oz [50g] and 92 yd [85m]), in color 051 yellow-green, medium/worsted weight
- One size 8 (5mm) circular needle, 16–20" (40–50cm) long, or size needed to obtain gauge
- 2 Stitch holders
- Tapestry needle

GAUGE
18 stitches and 20 rows = 4" in 1x1 rib
20 stitches and 24 rows = 4" in 4x1 rib

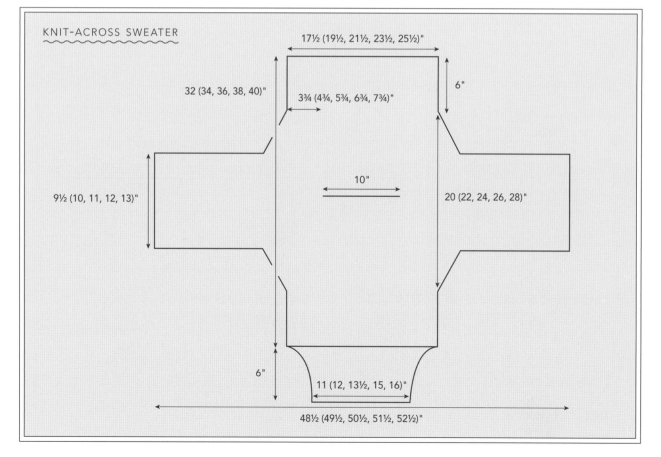

KNIT-ACROSS SWEATER

17½ (19½, 21½, 23½, 25½)"

32 (34, 36, 38, 40)"

3¾ (4¾, 5¾, 6¾, 7¾)"

6"

9½ (10, 11, 12, 13)"

10"

20 (22, 24, 26, 28)"

6"

11 (12, 13½, 15, 16)"

48½ (49½, 50½, 51½, 52½)"

PATTERN NOTES

- The long waist ribbing gives this garment shaping. It could be knit to your ideal mid-length, but it could be bloused and worn shorter.
- Work all increases as lifted increase (and knitwise into knit stitches).
- As a new rib pattern is established, continue in rib as newly established until directed otherwise.
- The garment is knit from side to side and in one piece, and then the long waistband is picked up and knit down.

UPPER BODY

Sleeve

Cast on 43 (47, 51, 55, 59) stitches.

WS rows P2, *k1, p1; repeat from * to last 3 stitches, k1, p2.

RS rows K2, *p1, k1; repeat from * to last 3 stitches, p1, k2.

Work 1x1 rib until Sleeve measures 12½ (12, 11½, 11, 10½)" (32 [30.5, 29.5, 28, 26.5] cm). End after working a wrong-side row.

(Shorten or lengthen for Sleeve length here, page 20.)

SHAPE UNDERARM

First increase row (RS) K2, p1, *increase 1 in next stitch, p1; repeat from * to last 2 stitches, k2—62 (68, 74, 80, 86) stitches.

WS rows P2, *k1, p2; repeat from * to end.

Work 2x1 rib for 5 rows.

Second increase row (RS) *K1, increase 1 in next stitch, p1; repeat from * to last 2 stitches, increase 1 in next stitch, k1—83 (91, 99, 107, 115) stitches.

WS rows *P3, k1; repeat from * to last 3 stitches, p3.

Work 3x1 rib for 5 rows.

Third increase row (RS) *K2, increase 1 in next stitch, p1; repeat from * to last 3 stitches, k1, increase 1 in next stitch, k1—104 (114, 124, 134, 144) stitches.

WS rows P4, *k1, p4; repeat from * to end.

Work 4x1 rib for 5 rows.

Body

Cast on 30 stitches at the beginning of the next 2 rows— 164 (174, 184, 194, 204) stitches.

(Shorten or lengthen for finished length here, page 18, by casting on fewer or more stitches. Be sure to make the number of stitches cast on a multiple of 5.)

Work 4x1 rib for 3¾ (4¾, 5¾, 6¾, 7¾)" (9.5 [12, 14.5, 17, 20] cm). End after working a wrong-side row.

Neck

Next row (RS) Work 4x1 rib across 82 (87, 92, 97, 102) stitches, place these stitches on a holder, work 4x1 rib to end.

Work even over remaining 82 (87, 92, 97, 102) stitches in 4x1 rib as established (with k2 at the beginning of RS rows and p2 at the end of WS rows) until neck opening measures 10" (25.5cm). End after working a wrong-side row. Place these stitches on a holder. Cut yarn.

Return to stitches on first holder. Beginning with a wrong-side row, work 4x1 rib as established (with p2 at the beginning of wrong-side rows and k2 at the end of right-side rows) until neck opening measures 10" (25cm). End after working a wrong-side row.

BODY

Next row (RS) Work 4x1 rib across all 164 (174, 184, 194, 204) stitches.

Work even for 3¾ (4¾, 5¾, 6¾, 7¾)" (9.5 [12, 14.5, 17, 20] cm). End after working a wrong-side row.

Bind off 30 stitches at the beginning of the next 2 rows— 104 (114, 124, 134, 144) stitches.

(If you shortened or lengthened, bind off the same number of stitches you cast on.)

Work 4x1 rib for 5 rows.

SHAPE UNDERARM

First decrease row (RS) *K1, k2tog, k1, p1; repeat from * to last 4 stitches, k1, k2tog, k1—83 (91, 99, 107, 115) stitches.

Work 3x1 rib for 5 rows.

Second decrease row (RS) *K1, k2tog, p1; repeat from * to last 3 stitches, k2tog, k1—62 (68, 74, 80, 86) stitches.

Work 2x1 rib for 5 rows.

Third decrease row (RS) K2, p1, *k2tog, p1; repeat from * to last 2 stitches, k2—43 (47, 51, 55, 59) stitches.

Sleeve

WS rows P2, *k1, p1; repeat from * to last 3 stitches, k1, p2.

RS rows K2, *p1, k1; repeat from * to last 3 stitches, p1, k2.

Work 1x1 rib until second Sleeve measures the same as the first.

Bind off in rib.

FINISHING

Sew side and Sleeve seams.

Waistband

With right side facing, pick up and knit 1 stitch for every 2 rows around entire bottom edge of sweater—98 (110, 122, 134, 146) stitches.

(If needed, increase or decrease on the next row to attain this number.)

Work 1x1 rib in the round until piece measures 6" (15cm) when stretched to fit the waist.

Bind off loosely.

❧ LONG-AND-SHORT-OF-IT PULLOVER ❧

Designed by Sally

I AM TOLD THAT BIG SWEATERS OVER SKINNY PANTS ARE COMING BACK. HONESTLY, IT COULDN'T COME TOO QUICKLY FOR ME. I LOVED THEM THEN (HOW LONG AGO WAS THAT?), AND I WILL LOVE THEM THIS TIME AROUND, TOO. BUT THIS SWEATER HAS FEATURES I KNEW NOTHING OF BACK THEN. FOR EXAMPLE, I NOW KNOW THAT THIS LONG SHAWL COLLAR IS FLATTERING BECAUSE A SLIM CENTER PANEL MAKES THE WHOLE FRONT LOOK SLIM. HOWEVER, THE MOST IMPORTANT FEATURE IS HOW THIS SWEATER CAN BE PERSONALIZED: KNIT TO YOUR IDEAL LONG SWEATER LENGTH WITH THE BOUNDARY BETWEEN THE UPPER AND LOWER SECTIONS AT YOUR IDEAL SHORT SWEATER LENGTH.

SKILL LEVEL
Intermediate

SIZES
- S (M, L–1X, 2X)
- Finished bust 43 (48½, 54½, 60)" (109 [123, 138.5, 152]cm)
- Finished length 25 (26, 27, 28)" (63.5 (66, 68.5, 71)cm)
- Finished length above rib 19½ (20, 20½, 21)" 49.5 [50.5, 52, 53]cm)
- Finished sleeve length 28 (29, 30½, 32)" 71 [73.5, 77.5, 81]cm)

MATERIALS
- 1165 (1350, 1600, 1835) yd (1050 [1215, 1440, 1655]m) / 12 (14, 17, 19) balls Autunno Dive (100% merino wool, each approximately 1¾ oz [50g] and 98 yd [90m]), in color yellow/green-brown-turquoise 32965, (**5**) bulky
- One pair size 10 (6mm) needles, or size needed to obtain gauge
- 2 Stitch holders
- Tapestry needle

GAUGE
14 stitches and 20 rows = 4" (10cm) in box lace

PATTERN NOTES

- This garment is long and unshaped. It could fall to your ideal long-sweater length. But it also has a demarcation (the reverse stockinette boundary) that could fall to your ideal short-sweater length (page 17).
- When joining a new ball of variegated yarn, try to match the color sequence.
- If you think the lace pattern is too challenging, knit the upper sections and sleeves in stockinette.
- To work even means to continue in the stitch pattern as established.
- Work all increases as lifted increase.

STITCH PATTERNS

2x2 Rib (over a multiple of 2 stitches + 2)
RS rows *K2, p2; repeat from * to last 2 stitches, k2.
WS rows *P2, k2; repeat from * to last 2 stitches, p2.
Box Lace (over a multiple of 10 stitches + 7)
Rows 1, 3, 5, 7 K1, *k6, yo, k2tog, yo, k2tog; repeat from * to last 6 stitches, k6.
Row 2 and all WS rows Purl.
Rows 9, 11, 13, 15 K1, *skp, yo, skp, yo, k6; repeat from * to last 6 stitches, skp, yo, skp, yo, k2.
(See chart, page 52)

BACK
Ribbing
Cast on 86 (94, 106, 114) stitches.

Work 2x2 rib to 5½ (6, 6½, 7)" (14 [15, 16.5, 18]cm). End after working a wrong-wide row.
(Shorten or lengthen here for difference between finished length and ideal short sweater length, page 18.)

Reverse Stockinette Boundary
Next row (RS) *K7 (11, 9, 14), k2tog; repeat from * to last 5 (3, 7, 2) stitches, knit to end—77 (87, 97, 107) stitches.
Knit 1 row, purl 1 row, then purl 1 row.

Lace Section
Beginning with Row 1, work box lace until lace section measures approximately 18 (18½, 19, 19½)" (45.5 [47, 48, 49.5]cm). End after working Row 2 or 10.
(Working to these particular rows will make the stitch pattern end nicely. But your ideal length should override this.)
(Shorten or lengthen for ideal short sweater length here, page 18.)

SHAPE RIGHT BACK NECK
Continuing box lace, work to 24 (29, 34, 39) stitches on right needle. Place remaining 53 (58, 63, 68) stitches on holder. Turn.
*Bind off 1 stitch at the next 2 neck edges—22 (27, 32, 37) stitches.
Work even to the end of the next wrong-side row.
Bind off loosely.

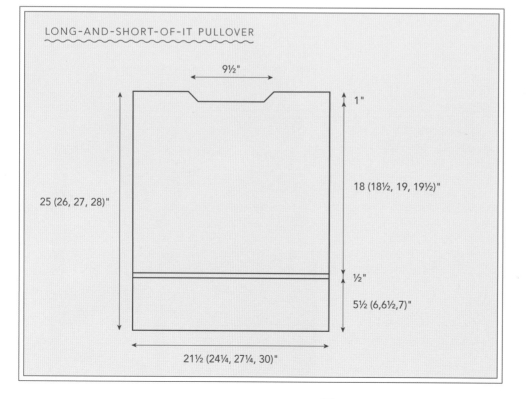

LONG-AND-SHORT-OF-IT PULLOVER

9½"

1"

18 (18½, 19, 19½)"

25 (26, 27, 28)"

½"

5½ (6,6½,7)"

21½ (24¼, 27¼, 30)"

Continue box lace until lace section measures 10"
(25cm). End after working a wrong-side row.
(Shorten or lengthen as for Back.)
Decrease row (RS) Work to last 3 stitches, k2tog, k1.
(Through what follows, do not work box lace once
decreases interfere.)
Work 7 rows even.
Repeat the last 8 rows 5 times more—22 (27, 32, 37)
stitches.
Work even to same length as Back to shoulder. End after
working a wrong-side row.
Bind off loosely.

Right Front, Lace Section

Bind off center 21 stitches, then continue over remaining
28 (33, 38, 43) stitches with Row 1 of box lace as follows:
K8 (3, 8, 3), *yo, k2tog, yo, k2tog, k6; repeat from * to
end.
Continue box lace as established until lace section
measures same length as Left Front. End after working a
wrong-side row.
Decrease row (RS) K1, skp, work to end.
(Through what follows, do not work box lace once
decreases interfere.)
Work 7 rows even.
Repeat the last 8 rows 5 times more—22 (27, 32, 37)
stitches.
Work even to same length as Left Front to shoulder. End
after working a wrong-side row.
Bind off loosely.

SLEEVES
Ribbing
Cast on 34 (34, 42, 42) stitches.
Work 2x2 rib to 3" (7.5cm). End after working a wrong-
wide row.

Reverse Stockinette Boundary
Next row (RS) *K9 (9, 7, 7), increase 1 in next stitch;
repeat from * to last 4 (4, 2, 2) stitches, k4 (4, 2, 2)—37 (37,
47, 47) stitches.
Knit 1 row, purl 1 row, then purl 1 row.

Lace Section
Beginning with Row 1, work box lace to end of Row 4.
Increase row (RS) K1, increase 1 in next stitch, work box
lace to last 2 stitches, increase 1 in next stitch, k1.
Work 3 rows even.
Repeat the last 4 rows 12 (14, 12, 14) times more—63 (67,
73, 77) stitches.

SHAPE LEFT BACK NECK
Return to remaining 53 (58, 63, 68) stitches, right side
facing.
Place first 29 stitches on holder, work a right-side row
over 24 (29, 34, 39) stitches.
Work 1 wrong-side row.
Work as Shape Right Back Neck from * to end.

FRONT
Work as Back through Ribbing and Reverse Stockinette
Boundary.

Left Front, Lace Section
Beginning with Row 1, work box lace over first 28 (33, 38,
43) stitches. Put remaining 49 (54, 59, 64) stitches on
holder. Turn.

(Work another repeat of box lace once you have enough stitches.)

Work even until Sleeve measures approximately 17" (43cm). End after working Row 8 or 16.

(Shorten or lengthen for Sleeve length here, page 20.)

Bind off loosely.

FINISHING

Sew shoulder seams.

Collar

With right side facing, begin at lower edge of Right Front opening to pick up and knit around neck edge as follows:

6 stitches for every 7 rows along vertical edges,

1 stitch for every bind-off stitch and 1 stitch for every 2-row step between bind-off stitches at back neck shaping,

1 stitch for every stitch on holder.

Count stitches on needle. While working the next row, increase or decrease to make a multiple of 4 stitches + 2. Beginning with a wrong-side row, work 2x2 Rib until collar measures 7" (17.5cm). End after working a wrong-side row.

Next (short) row (RS) Rib to 4 stitches on left needle. Turn.

Next (short) row (WS) Wyif slip 1 purlwise, p1, rib to 4 stitches on left needle. Turn.

Next (short) row (RS) Wyib slip 1 purlwise, k1, rib to 8 stitches on left needle. Turn.

Next (short) row (WS) Wyif slip 1 purlwise, p1, rib to 8 stitches on left needle. Turn.

Repeat last 2 rows, leaving 4 more stitches behind each time until 60 stitches have been left behind at the end of a wrong-side row.

Work 1 right-side row over all stitches (to bottom of Collar).

Next row (WS) Bind off in rib.

Sew lower edge of Right Front Collar to 21 bind-off stitches at reverse stockinette boundary (taking ½ stitch of Collar into seam allowance).

Sew lower edge of Left Front Collar behind lower edge of Right Front Collar.

Sew Sleeves to Front and Back (matching center of Sleeves to shoulder seams, and seaming 2 stitches for every 3 rows).

Sew side and Sleeve seams.

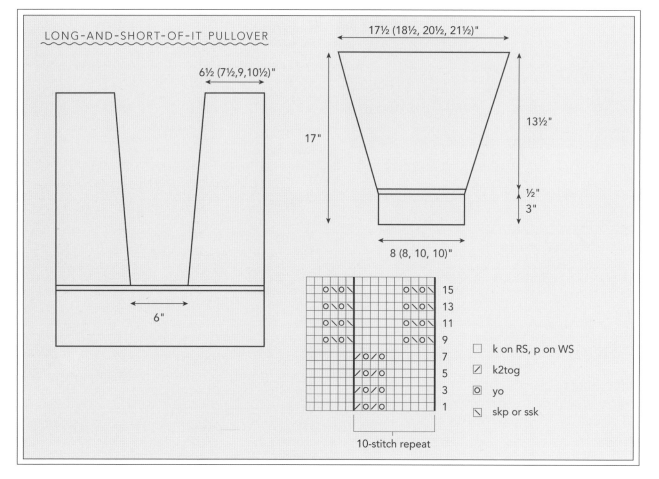

LONG-AND-SHORT-OF-IT PULLOVER

6½ (7½, 9, 10½)"

17½ (18½, 20½, 21½)"

17"

13½"

½"
3"

8 (8, 10, 10)"

6"

15
13
11
9
7
5
3
1

□ k on RS, p on WS

☑ k2tog

◎ yo

◹ skp or ssk

10-stitch repeat

❧ SCARF-CLOSING CARDIGAN ❧

Designed by Sally

THIS IS A SIMPLE, TEXTURED JACKET WITH AN UNUSUAL FRONT CLOSURE: ITS REVERSE STOCKINETTE
FRONT EDGINGS EACH HAVE FIVE ALTERNATING SPACES THROUGH WHICH A COORDINATING SCARF IS
THREADED. THIS METHOD OF CLOSURE LENDS VERSATILITY TO THE GARMENT, BECAUSE THE SCARF CAN
BE CHANGED WITH THE OCCASION OR THE SEASON.

SKILL LEVEL
Intermediate

SIZES
- S (M, L, 1X, 2X)
- Finished bust 36 (40, 44, 48, 52)" (91.5 [101.5, 112, 122, 132]cm)
- Finished length 19 (19½, 20, 20½, 21)" (48 [49.5, 51, 52, 53.5]cm)
- Finished shoulder width 15" (38cm)
- Finished sleeve length 29 (29½, 30, 30½, 31)" (73.5 [74.5, 76, 77.5, 78.5]cm)

MATERIALS
- 990 (1100, 1200, 1320, 1430) yd (890 [990, 1100, 1210, 1320]m) / 11, (12, 13, 15, 16) balls Nashua Julia (50% mohair, 25% kid mohair, 25% alpaca, each approximately 1¾ oz [50g] and 93 yd [85m]) in color 6086 Velvet moss, [4] medium/worsted weight
- One pair size 6 (4mm) needles, or size needed to obtain gauge
- One pair size 4 (3.5mm) needles
- Stitch holder
- Tapestry needle
- 20 Markers (may be pins or scraps of yarn)
- One rectangular scarf, 60–70" [150–175cm]) long

GAUGE
20 stitches and 30 rows = 4" (10cm) in stitch pattern, over larger needles and after blocking

PATTERN NOTES
- This garment is short and unshaped. It could fall to your ideal short sweater length (page 17).

- The long, rectangular scarf should be narrow enough to fit through the spaces and not add bulk to your bust.
- The chart represents stitch pattern between the *'s. There is a stockinette selvedge at the edge of each garment piece (for seaming).
- Maintain stitch pattern through all shaping.

MOCK CABLE STITCH PATTERN
(OVER A MULTIPLE OF 10 STITCHES)
Row 1 *P4, k1, p1, k4; repeat from *.
Row 2 *P3, k2, p2, k3; repeat from *.
Row 3 *P2, k2, p1, k1, p2, k2; repeat from *.
Row 4 *P1, k2, p2, k2, p2, k1; repeat from *.
Row 5 *K2, p3, k3, p2; repeat from *.
Row 6 *K1, p4, k4, p1; repeat from *.
(See chart, page 57)

BACK
Edging
With larger needles and MC, long-tail cast on 92 (102, 112, 122, 132) stitches.
Purl 2 rows.

Body
Begin stitch pattern with Row 1 and as follows.
RS rows K1, work 10-stitch repeat to last stitch, k1.
WS rows P1, work 10-stitch repeat to last stitch, p1.
Work until piece measures 10½" (26.5cm). End after working a wrong-side row.
(Shorten or lengthen for finished length here, page 18.)

SHAPE ARMHOLE
Bind off 4 (5, 7, 9, 11) stitches at the beginning of the next 2 rows—84 (92, 98, 104, 110) stitches.
Decrease row (RS) K1, k2tog or p2tog (as stitch pattern demands), work to last 3 stitches, k2tog or p2tog, k1.
Work 1 wrong-side row.
Repeat the last 2 rows 3 (7, 10, 13, 16) times more—76 stitches.
(Adjust shoulder width here, page 19.)
Work even until armhole measures 7½ (8, 8½, 9, 9½)" (19 [20.5, 21.5, 23, 24]cm). End after working a wrongside row.

SHAPE RIGHT SHOULDER AND BACK NECK
Bind off 5 stitches at the beginning of the next right-side row. Work to 19 stitches on right needle. Put remaining 52 stitches on holder. Turn.
*Bind off 1 stitch at the next 2 neck edges and 6 stitches at the next 2 armhole edges.
Bind off final 5 stitches at armhole edge.

SHAPE LEFT SHOULDER AND BACK NECK.
Return to remaining 52 stitches, right side facing.
Put center 28 stitches on holder (for center Back neck), work 1 right-side row over 24 stitches.
Bind off 5 stitches at the next armhole edge.
Work as Shape Right Shoulder and Back Neck from * to end.

RIGHT FRONT
Edging
With larger needles and MC, long-tail cast on 47 (52, 57, 62, 67) stitches.
Purl 2 rows.

Body
Begin stitch pattern with Row 1 and as follows.
S (L, 2X) SIZES ONLY
RS rows K1, work from A to repeat line, work 10-stitch repeat to last stitch, k1.
WS rows P1, work 10-stitch repeat to last 6 stitches, work to A, p1.
M (1X) SIZES ONLY
RS rows K1, work 10-stitch repeat to last stitch, k1.
WS rows P1, work 10-stitch repeat to last stitch, p1.
ALL SIZES
Work even to same length as Back to armhole. End after working a right-side row.

SHAPE ARMHOLE
Bind off 4 (5, 7, 9, 11) stitches at the beginning of the next wrong-side row—43 (47, 50, 53, 56) stitches.
Decrease row (RS) Work to last 3 stitches, k2tog or p2tog, k1.
Work 1 wrong-side row.
Repeat the last 2 rows 4 (8, 11, 14, 17) times more—38 stitches.
(Adjust shoulder width as for Back.)
Work even until armhole measures 5½ (6, 6½, 7, 7½)" (14 [15, 16.5, 18, 19]cm). End after working a wrongside row.

SHAPE NECK
Bind off 8 stitches at the next neck edge, 3 stitches at the next neck edge, 2 stitches at the next neck edge, then 1 stitch at the next 3 neck edges—22 stitches.
Work even until armhole measures same length as Back.

SHAPE SHOULDER
Bind off 5 stitches at the next armhole edge, 6 stitches at the next 2 armhole edges, then 5 stitches at the final armhole edge.

LEFT FRONT
Edging
With larger needles and MC, long-tail cast on 47 (52, 57, 62, 67) stitches.
Purl 2 rows.

Body
Begin stitch pattern with Row 1 and as follows.
S (L, 2X) SIZES ONLY

RS rows K1, work 10-stitch repeat to last 6 stitches, work to B, k1.

WS rows P1, work from B to repeat line, work 10-stitch repeat to last stitch, p1.

M (1X) SIZES ONLY

RS rows K1, work 10-stitch repeat to last stitch, k1.

WS rows P1, work 10-stitch repeat to last stitch, p1.

ALL SIZES

Work even to same length as Back to armhole. End after working a wrong-side row.

SHAPE ARMHOLE

Bind off 4 (5, 7, 9, 11) stitches at the beginning of the next right-side row—43 (47, 50, 53, 56) stitches.

Work 1 row even.

Decrease row (RS) K1, k2tog or p2tog, work to end.

Work 1 wrong-side row.

Repeat the last 2 rows 4 (8, 11, 14, 17) times more—38 stitches.

(Adjust shoulder width as for Back.)

Work even until armhole measures 5½ (6, 6½, 7, 7½)" (14 [15, 16.5, 18, 19]cm). End after working a right-side row.

SHAPE NECK AND SHOULDER

Work as Right Front.

SLEEVES

Edging

With larger needles and MC, long-tail cast on 42 (42, 42, 52, 52) stitches.

Purl 2 rows.

Body

Begin pattern stitch with Row 1 and as follows.

RS rows K1, work 10-stitch repeat to last stitch, k1.

WS rows P1, work 10-stitch repeat to last stitch, p1.

Work to 6 rows.

Increase row (RS) K1, M1, work to last stitch, M1, k1.

Work 7 (7, 5, 5, 5) rows even.

Repeat the last 8 (8, 6, 6, 6) rows 11 (14, 17, 16, 20) times more—66 (72, 78, 86, 94) stitches.

Work even until piece measures 17" (43cm). End after working a wrong-side row.

(Shorten or lengthen for Sleeve length here, page 20.)

SHAPE SLEEVE CAP

Bind off 4 (5, 7, 9, 11) stitches at the beginning of the next 2 rows—58 (62, 64, 68, 72) stitches.

Decrease row (RS) K1, k2tog or p2tog, work to last 3 stitches, k2tog or p2tog, k1.

Work 1 wrong-side row.

Repeat the last 2 rows 13 (15, 16, 18, 20) times more—30 stitches.

Bind off 2 stitches at the beginning of the next 2 rows.

Bind off 4 stitches at the beginning of the next 2 rows.

Bind off remaining 18 stitches.

FINISHING

Sew shoulder seams.

Neck edging

With smaller needles, MC, and right side facing, begin at Right Front neck to pick up and knit as follows:

1 stitch for every bind-off stitch and 1 stitch for every 2-row step between bind-off stitches around Front and Back neck shaping,

1 stitch for every stitch on holder,

2 stitches for every 3 rows along rows worked even.

—approximately 100 stitches.

Knit 1 row, then purl 1 row.

Next row *K5, k2tog; repeat from * to end—approximately 85 stitches.

Bind off tightly and purlwise.

Front Edgings

Along Right Front, mark 10 spots, evenly spaced.

(Begin 1" [2.5cm] from top, and end 1" [2.5cm] from bottom. Use stitch pattern to help you keep even distance between spaces.)

Place identical markings onto Left Front.

On each side, number marks from 1–10, starting at top.

On Right Front, remove marks 1, 3, 5, 7, 9.

On Left Front, remove marks 2, 4, 6, 8, 10.

Right Front Edging

With smaller needles, MC, and right side facing, begin at the lower Right Front edge to pick up and knit 2 stitches for every 3 rows along the Front edge.

AT THE SAME TIME, make 5 spaces through which to tie the scarf as follows:

work to first marker;

*pick up and knit 4 stitches past this marker, place a marker in the spot of this 4th stitch;

remove the last 7 stitches from the right needle;

turn, cable cast on 6 stitches;

turn, beginning at the spot you just marked, continue picking up and knitting (2 stitches for every 3 rows) to the next marker;

repeat from * until 5 spaces are made;

after 5 spaces are made, continue picking up and knitting (2 stitches for every 3 rows) to end.

Knit 1 row, purl 1 row, knit 1 row, then bind off purlwise.

Sew bind-off row to selvedge except at spaces; at spaces, sew bind-off edge to cast-on edge.

Left Front Edging
Work as Right Front Edging, beginning at upper Left Front edge.

Sew Sleeves into armholes.
Sew side and Sleeve seams.

Back shaping (*optional*)
At center back, 4" (10cm) up from lower edge, mark spots 3" (7.5cm) to right and 3" (7.5cm) to left of center. Attach doubled yarn to one spot. With a running stitch, thread doubled yarn through the garment (to pleat it) across to the other spot. (Keep most of the yarn to the wrong side with only small appearances to the right side.)

Gather as desired.
Secure the yarn at this one end, then, on the wrong side, thread the yarn through the gather a second time.

Scarf
Begin with one end of the scarf at the Front hem. Leaving as little as possible of this end of the scarf at the hem, thread the remainder up and through all alternating spaces.
At the top, wrap the rest of the scarf around your neck, wrapping twice, if possible. Pull what remains through to suit.
Optional If you need to, pin the bottom corner of the scarf to the wrong side of the Front, to secure it and tuck it from sight.

MOCK CABLE CHART

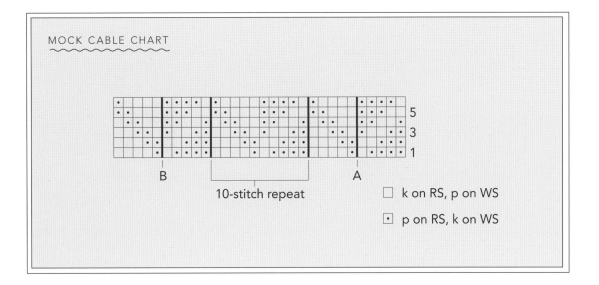

5

3

1

B

10-stitch repeat

A

☐ k on RS, p on WS

⊡ p on RS, k on WS

SCARF-CLOSING CARDIGAN

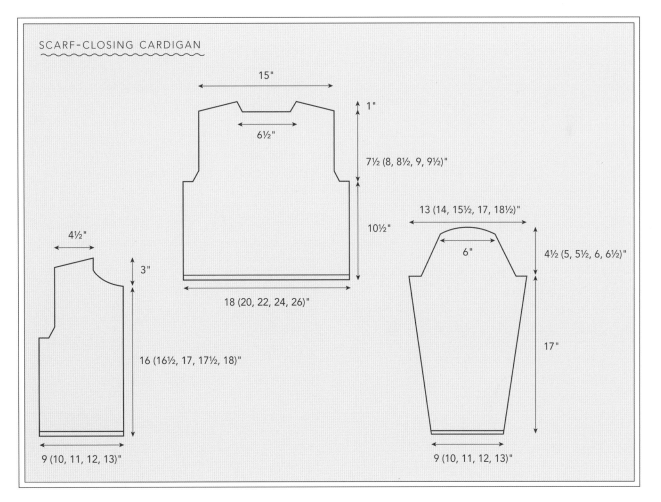

15"

1"

6½"

7½ (8, 8½, 9, 9½)"

13 (14, 15½, 17, 18½)"

10½"

6"

4½ (5, 5½, 6, 6½)"

4½"

3"

18 (20, 22, 24, 26)"

16 (16½, 17, 17½, 18)"

17"

9 (10, 11, 12, 13)"

9 (10, 11, 12, 13)"

❊ CLASSIC SHIRT ❊

Designed by Sally

WHEN STUDENTS ASK ME HOW TO BECOME MORE CREATIVE, MORE ACCOMPLISHED, OR MORE SUCCESS-FUL KNITTERS, I TELL THEM TO GO TO THEIR CLOSET, FIND THEIR FAVORITE ITEM, THEN FIND A WAY TO KNIT IT. SO I THOUGHT I OUGHT TO DO THIS AND WITH THE GARMENT WE ALL OWN—THE CLASSIC BUTTON-FRONT SHIRT.

SKILL LEVEL
Intermediate

SIZES
- S (M, L, 1X, 2X)
- Finished hem (and bust) 36 (40, 44, 48, 52)" (91 [101, 111.5, 122, 132]cm)
- Finished waist 30 (34, 38, 42, 46)" (76 [86, 96.5, 106.5, 117]cm)
- Finished length 22½ (23, 23½, 24, 24½)" (57 [58, 59.5, 61, 62]cm)
- Finished waist length 16½ (17, 17½, 18, 18½)" 41.5 [43, 44, 45.5, 47]cm)
- Finished shoulder width 14" (35.5cm)
- Finished sleeve length (with cuff extended) 31" (31½, 32, 32½, 33") (78.5 [80, 81, 82.5, 83.5]cm)

MATERIALS
- 865 (960, 1060, 1150, 1250) yd (780 [865, 955, 1035, 1125]m) / 4 (5, 5, 5, 6) balls Needful Mohair Royal (80% kid mohair, 20% nylon, each approximately ⅞ oz [25g] and 235 yd [215m]), in color 1650 off-white, **(2)** fine/sport

or

- 1080 (1200, 1320, 1440, 1560) yd (970 [1080, 1200, 1320, 1440]m) / 4 (5, 5, 6, 6) skeins Louet Euroflax Sport Weight (100% linen, each approximately 3½ oz [100g] and 270 yd [246m]), in color 01 Champagne **(2)** fine/sport
- One pair size 6 (4mm) needles, or size needed to obtain gauge
- 2 Stitch markers
- Stitch holder
- One pair size 4 (3.5mm) needles
- 10 Buttons, ⅜" (9mm) wide
- *Optional* 2 more Buttons (for turned-back cuffs)

GAUGE
20 stitches and 28–30 rows = 4" (10cm) in stockinette stitch, over larger needles and after steam-pressing

PATTERN NOTES
- This garment is hourglass-shaped, so it could fall between your ideal short length and mid-length. (The linen version is shown to the length written above, and the mohair version is 2" [5cm] longer.) You may adjust the waist length between the waist and the armhole, and adjust the finished length before the waist (page 17).
- The linen version measured 28 rows = 4" (10cm), while the mohair measured 30 rows = 4" (10cm). The pattern is written to accommodate either row gauge.
- I cannot explain, nor can the yarn companies, why the heavier linen—knit to a looser row gauge—took more yarn. But it definitely did!
- Work all pieces in stockinette unless otherwise indicated.
- Work all increases as lifted increase.
- The sleeves are long enough for the cuffs to be turned back. If you do not wish them to be worn this way, make the sleeves 1½" (4cm) shorter.

BACK
With larger needles, long-tail cast on 92 (102, 112, 122, 132) stitches.
Beginning with a wrong-side row, work until piece measures 2" (5cm). End after working a right-side row.
Next row (WS) P30 (35, 40, 45, 50), pm, p32, pm, p30 (35, 40, 45, 50).
Decrease row (RS) K1, skp, knit to 2 stitches before marker, skp, k32 (to marker), k2tog, knit to last 3 stitches, k2tog, k1.
Work 9 rows even.

(Shorten or lengthen for finished length by changing the number of rows worked even between decreases, page 18.)

Repeat decrease row.

Repeat the last 10 rows twice more—32 stitches between markers, 22 (27, 32, 37, 42) stitches at sides.

Work 2" (5cm) even.

Increase row (RS) K1, increase 1 in next stitch, knit to stitch before marker, increase 1 in next stitch, knit to marker, increase 1 in next stitch, knit to last 2 stitches, increase 1 in next stitch, k1.

Work 9 rows even.

(Shorten or lengthen for waist length here, page 18, by changing the number of rows worked even between increases.)

Repeat increase row.

Repeat the last 10 rows twice more—92 (102, 112, 122, 132) stitches.

Work even until piece measures 14" (35.5cm). End after working a wrong-side row. Remove markers.

SHAPE ARMHOLE

Bind off 4 (5, 7, 9, 11) stitches at the beginning of the next 2 rows—84 (92, 98, 104, 110) stitches.

Decrease row (RS) K1, skp, knit to last 3 stitches, k2tog, k1.

Purl 1 row.

Repeat the last 2 rows 6 (10, 13, 16, 19) times more—70 stitches.

(Adjust shoulder width here, page 19.)

Work even until armhole measures 7½ (8, 8½, 9, 9½)" (19 [20.5, 21.5, 23, 24]cm). End after working a wrong-side row.

SHAPE SHOULDERS

Bind off 5 stitches at the beginning of the next 2 rows.

SHAPE RIGHT SHOULDER AND BACK NECK

Bind off 5 stitches at the beginning of the next row, knit to 12 stitches on right needle. Put remaining 43 stitches on holder. Turn.

*Bind off 1 stitch at the next 2 neck edges and 5 stitches at the next 2 armhole edges.

SHAPE LEFT SHOULDER AND BACK NECK

Return to remaining 43 stitches, right side facing. Place first 26 stitches on holder.

Knit 1 right-side row over 17 stitches.

At the next armhole edge, bind off 5 stitches.

Work as Shape Right Shoulder and Back Neck from * to end.

RIGHT FRONT

With larger needles, long-tail cast on 45 (50, 55, 60, 65) stitches.

Beginning with a wrong-side row, work even until piece measures 2" (5cm). End after working a right-side row.

Next row (WS) P30 (35, 40, 45, 50), pm, p15.

Decrease row (RS) Knit to marker, k2tog, knit to last 3 stitches, k2tog, k1.

Work 9 rows even.

(Shorten or lengthen as for Back.)

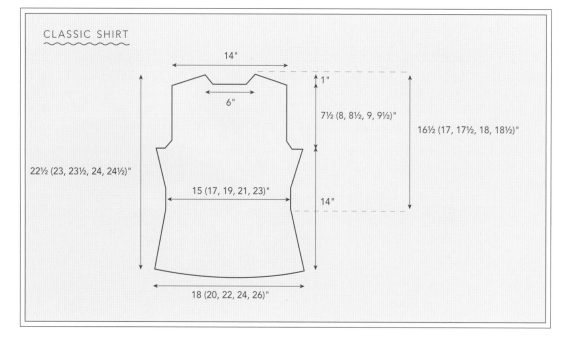

CLASSIC SHIRT

14"

6"

1"

7½ (8, 8½, 9, 9½)"

16½ (17, 17½, 18, 18½)"

22½ (23, 23½, 24, 24½)"

15 (17, 19, 21, 23)"

14"

18 (20, 22, 24, 26)"

Repeat decrease row.

Repeat the last 10 rows twice more—37 (42, 47, 52, 57) stitches

Work 2" (5cm) even.

Increase row (RS) Knit to marker, increase 1 in next stitch, knit to last 2 stitches, increase 1 in next stitch, k1.

Work 9 rows even.

(Shorten or lengthen as for Back.)

Repeat increase row.

Repeat the last 10 rows twice more—45 (50, 55, 60, 65) stitches.

Work to same length as Back to armhole. End after working a right-side row. Remove marker.

SHAPE ARMHOLE

Bind off 4 (5, 7, 9, 11) stitches at the beginning of the next wrong-side row—41 (45, 48, 51, 54) stitches.

Decrease row (RS) Knit to last 3 stitches, k2tog, k1.

Purl 1 row.

Repeat the last 2 rows 7 (11, 14, 17, 20) times more—33 stitches.

(Adjust armhole width as for Back.)

Work even until armhole measures 5½ (6, 6½, 7, 7½)" (14 [15, 16.5, 18, 19]cm). End after working a wrong-side row.

SHAPE NECK

Bind off 4 stitches at the next neck edge, 3 stitches at the next neck edge, 2 stitches at the next neck edge, then 1 stitch at the next 4 neck edges—20 stitches.

Work even until armholes measures same length as Back. End after working a right-side row.

SHAPE SHOULDER

Bind off 5 stitches at the next 4 armhole edges.

LEFT FRONT

Work as Right Front until piece measures 2" (5cm). End after working a right-side row.

Next row (WS) P15, pm p30 (35, 40, 45, 50).

Decrease row (RS) K1, skp, knit to 2 stitches before marker, skp, knit to end.

Work 9 rows even.

(Shorten or lengthen as for Back.)

Repeat decrease row.

Repeat the last 10 rows twice more—37 (42, 47, 52, 57) stitches

Work 2" (5cm) even.

Increase row (RS) K1, increase 1 in next stitch, knit to stitch before marker, increase 1 in next stitch, knit to end.

Work 9 rows even.

(Shorten or lengthen as for Back.)

Repeat increase row.

Repeat the last 10 rows twice more—45 (50, 55, 60, 65) stitches.

Work even to same length as Back to armhole. End after working a wrong-side row. Remove marker.

SHAPE ARMHOLE

Bind off 4 (5, 7, 9, 11) stitches at the beginning of the next row—41 (45, 48, 51, 54) stitches.

Purl 1 row.

Decrease row (RS) K1, skp, knit to end.

Purl 1 row.

Repeat the last 2 rows 7 (11, 14, 17, 20) times more—33 stitches.

(Adjust shoulder width as for Back.)

Work even until piece measures 5½ (6, 6½, 7, 7½)" (14 [15, 16.5, 18, 19]cm) above armhole. End after working a right-side row.

SHAPE NECK AND SHOULDER

Work as Right Front, Shape Neck and Shape Shoulder.

SLEEVES

With larger needles, long-tail cast on 38 (42, 46, 50, 54) stitches.

Beginning with a wrong-side row, work 7 rows.

Increase row (RS) K1, increase 1 in next stitch, knit to last 2 stitches, increase 1 in next stitch, k1.

Work 5 (5, 5, 3, 3) rows even.

Repeat the last 6 (6, 6, 4, 4) rows 15 (16, 18, 20, 22) times more—70 (76, 84, 92, 100) stitches.

Work even until piece measures 16" (40.5cm), End after working a wrong-side row.

(Shorten or lengthen for Sleeve length here, page 20.)

Shape Sleeve Cap

Bind off 4 (5, 7, 9, 11) stitches at the beginning of the next 2 rows—62 (66, 70, 74, 78) stitches.

Decrease row (RS) K1, skp, knit to last 3 stitches, k2tog, k1.

Purl 1 row.

Repeat the last 2 rows 15 (17, 19, 21, 23) times more—30 stitches.

Bind off 2 stitches at the beginning of the next 2 rows.

Bind off 4 stitches at the beginning of the next 2 rows.

Bind off final 18 stitches.

FINISHING

Steam-press all pieces.

Left Front Button Band

With larger needles and right side facing, pick up and knit 3 stitches for every 5 rows.

(To work 3 stitches for 5 rows, pick up and knit 1 stitch in 2 rows then pick up and knit 2 stitches in 3 rows.)

Beginning with a purl (WS) row, work Rows 2–7 in stockinette.

Row 8 (turn row, WS) Knit.

Rows 9–14 Beginning with a knit row, continue in stockinette.

Bind off loosely, leaving long tail.

With long tail, sew bind-off row to selvedge.

Sew lower edge of band closed.

Steam-press band.

Mark spaces for 7 evenly spaced buttons, with the first 1" (2.5cm) from the top and the last 4" (10cm) from the bottom.

Right Front Buttonhole Band

Work as Left Front Button Band to end of Row 3.

Make buttonholes to match placement of buttons as follows.

Row 4 (WS), make buttonholes While purling the row, [yo, p2tog] at all marked spaces—7 buttonholes made.

Row 5–7 Continue in stockinette.

Row 8 (turn row, WS) Knit.

Rows 9–11 Continue in stockinette.

Row 12 (WS), make buttonholes In same manner and in same place, work as Row 4 to make buttonholes on wrong side of band.

Rows 13–14 Continue in stockinette.

Bind off loosely, leaving a long tail.

With long tail, sew bind-off row to selvedge, and sew buttonholes together.

Sew lower edge of band closed.

Steam-press band.

Neck Band

Sew shoulder seams.

With smaller needles and right side facing, begin at upper edge of Right Front band to pick up and knit as follows:

2 stitches for every 3 rows through both layers at top edge of Front bands,

1 stitch for every bind-off stitch and 1 stitch for every 2-row step between bind-off stitches around Front and Back neck shaping,

1 stitch for every stitch on holder,

3 stitches for every 4 rows along rows worked even.
—96 stitches.

(Count stitches. If needed, adjust decreases on next row.)

Row 2 (WS) [P8, p2tog] 3 times, [p4, p2tog] 6 times, [p8, p2tog] twice, purl to end—85 stitches.

Rows 3–4 Continue in stockinette.

Row 5 (RS), make buttonhole K3, yo, k2tog, knit to end.

Row 6 Purl.

Rows 7–9 Knit.

Row 10 Purl.

Row 11 (RS), make buttonhole In same manner and in same place, work as Row 5 to make buttonhole on wrong side of band.

Rows 12–13 Continue in stockinette.

Row 14 (WS) [P8, increase in next stitch] 3 times, [p4, increase in next stitch] 6 times, [p8, increase in next stitch] twice, purl to end—96 stitches.

With larger needle, bind off loosely, leaving a long tail.

With long tail, sew bind-off row to selvedge, and sew buttonhole together.

Sew open edges of band closed.

Steam-press band.

Sew buttons onto Left Front band to correspond to buttonholes on Right Front band.

Collar

With smaller needles and right side facing, begin in 4th stitch from edge of Right Front neck band. Pick up and knit 9 stitches for every 10 purl bumps along edge of neck band. End in 4th stitch from edge of Left Front neck band—73 stitches.

Next row (WS) Cast on 1 stitch at beginning of row, purl across. Turn, cast on 1 stitch—75 stitches.

Increase row (RS) K2, increase 1 in next stitch, knit to last 3 stitches, increase 1 in next stitch, k2.

Work 3 rows even.

Repeat the last 4 rows 4 times more—85 stitches.

(Lengthen collar by making more rows, increasing as above each alternate right-side row.)

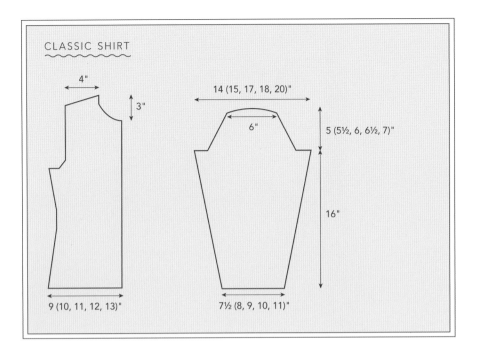

CLASSIC SHIRT

4"

3"

14 (15, 17, 18, 20)"

6"

5 (5½, 6, 6½, 7)"

16"

9 (10, 11, 12, 13)"

7½ (8, 9, 10, 11)"

Purl 1 row, then knit 1 row.

Change to larger needles.

Next (turn) row (WS) Knit.

Next 2 rows Beginning with a knit row, continue in stockinette.

Decrease row (RS) K2, skp, knit to last 4 stitches, k2tog, k2. Work 3 rows even.

Repeat the last 4 rows 4 times more—75 stitches.

Purl 1 row.

Final row (RS) Bind off 1 stitch at beginning of row, knit to end. Turn, p1, slip 1, bind off 1 stitch, slip 1 from right needle onto left. Cut yarn to 1 yd (.9m).

Graft live stitches to inside edge of neck band (remembering that there are 9 collar stitches for every 10 stitches of neck band).

Pull grafting tight enough to seam but not so tight as to bind.

Taking 1 stitch from each edge into seam allowance, sew open front edges of Collar closed.

Steam-press Collar.

Sew Sleeves into armholes.

Sew side and Sleeve seams.

Cuffs

With larger needles, long-tail cast on 42 (46, 50, 54, 58) stitches.

Work even until piece measures 3" (7.5cm). End after working a right-side row.

Next (turn) row (WS) Knit.

Continue until piece measures 3" (7.5cm) past turn row. End after working a wrong-side row.

Final row (RS) Bind off 1 stitch at beginning of row, knit to end. Turn, p1, slip 1, bind off 1 stitch, slip 1 from right needle onto left. Cut yarn to 1 yard (.9m).

With right sides facing, graft live stitches to cast-on edge of Sleeve as follows.

ATTACH RIGHT CUFF

Hold cuff above Sleeve, matching first stitch of cuff to 8th stitch to left of Sleeve seam.

*Beginning at this point, and grafting from right to left, graft stitches of cuff to cast-on row of Sleeve.

After grafting to circumference of Sleeve, 4 stitches remain on needle; sew these stitches to cast-on row under grafted edge of cuff.

ATTACH LEFT CUFF

Hold cuff below Sleeve, matching first stitch of cuff to 8th stitch to left of Sleeve seam.

Work as Attach Right Cuff from * to end.

BOTH CUFFS

Fold cuffs over, and steam-press.

Sew cast-on edges of cuffs to seam allowances.

Taking 1 stitch from each edge into seam allowance, sew open edges of cuffs closed.

Sew one button through all layers of each cuff.

Optional If wearing cuffs turned back, sew a button to the wrong side of each cuff.

⤜ SWING TOP ⤛

Designed by Sally

I HAD TROUBLE NAMING THIS PIECE. "SUMMER TOP," BECAUSE IT CAN BE WORN IN THE SUMMER? THAT DIDN'T ADDRESS ITS ALL-SEASONS, DRESS-UP POTENTIAL. "HIPPIE TOP," BECAUSE IT REMINDED ME OF SOMETHING I'D HAVE WORN IN THE '70S? THAT BELIED THAT FACT THAT IT WAS ACTUALLY MODELED AFTER SOMETHING I BOUGHT IN 2005. MY EDITOR SUGGESTED "SWING TOP," AND I THINK THAT'S PRETTY DESCRIPTIVE. WHATEVER ITS NAME, IT'S A FUN PIECE TO KNIT AND A VERSATILE PIECE TO WEAR.

SKILL LEVEL
Intermediate

SIZES
- S (M, L, 1X, 2X)
- Finished bust 29 (32, 37, 41, 45)" (74 [81, 94, 104, 114]cm)
- Finished hem 62 (70, 76, 82, 88)" (157.5 [178, 193, 208, 223.5]cm)
- Finished length (not including strap) 20 (21½, 23, 24½, 26)" (50.5 [54.5, 58, 62, 66]cm)
- Finished shoulder width 9" (23cm)

MATERIALS
- 480 (535, 590, 640, 695) yd (432 [480, 530, 575, 625]m) / 7 (7, 8, 9, 10) skeins Berocco Bonsai (97% bamboo, 3% nylon, each approximately 1¾ oz [50g] and 77 yd [71m]), in color 4143 Kin gold (MC), **④** medium/worsted weight
- 140 (150, 165, 180, 195) yards (125 [135, 150, 160, 175]m) / 2 (2, 2, 2, 2) balls of Berocco Suede (100% nylon, each approximately 1¾ oz [50g] and 120 yd [111m]), in color 3746 Palomino (CC), **④** medium/worsted weight
- One pair size 10 (6mm) needles, or size needed to obtain gauge
- One pair size 6 (4mm) needles, or size needed to obtain gauge
- Stitch holder
- Tapestry needle
- One size G–6 (4mm) crochet hook
- *Optional* 18 Beads with large holes

GAUGE
14 stitches and 24 rows = 4" (10cm) in stockinette stitch, over MC and larger needles

22 stitches and 28 rows = 4" (10cm) in floret stitch pattern, over MC and CC and smaller needles

PATTERN NOTES
- This garment is a long A-line, so the length may fall to your long sweater length (page 17) or shorter. The straps will add 5" (12.5cm) to the finished length, and the lower piece measures 1" (2.5cm) longer than gauge indicates because it is knit on a slight diagonal.
- The lower piece may stretch up to 2" (5cm) with wearing.
- The bust area of the garment will stretch 4–6" (10–15cm) to fit the sizes given.
- The top may be worn with the V to the front or the back.
- The lower pieces are worked side to side, and the reverse stockinette side becomes the right side.
- When one set of numbers appears, it applies to all sizes.
- The beads are decorative and negate the need to sew in the tails at the bottom. Do not sew in any tails at the hem if you wish to use beads, and cut all tails to 6" (15cm).

BACK
Lower Pieces (Make 2)
With MC and larger needles, long-tail cast on 49 (52, 55, 58, 61) stitches.
(Shorten or lengthen for finished length here, page 18, by casting on fewer or more stitches. Make the difference a multiple of 3. Additional stitches will increase not only the length but also the hem circumference; fewer stitches will decrease not only the length but also the hem circumference.)
Rows 1–3 Knit.

*Continue in MC.

Row 4 Wyib slip 1 purlwise, k48 (51, 54, 57, 60).

Row 5 Purl.

Repeat the last 2 rows 7 (8, 9, 10, 11) times more—16 (18, 20, 22, 24) rows in stockinette. End after working a purl row. Cut MC, leaving 6" (15cm) tail.

(If tails slip, knot them together.)

Use CC for the next 6 rows.

Next 2 rows Knit.

First Short row K46 (49, 52, 55, 58). Turn (leaving 3 stitches behind).

Next Row Wyif slip 1 purlwise, k45 (48, 51, 54, 57).

Second Short row K43 (46, 49, 52, 55). Turn.

Next Row Wyif slip 1 purlwise, k42 (45, 48, 51, 54). Cut CC. Use MC to end.

Third Short row Wyib slip 1 purlwise, k39 (42, 45, 48, 51). Turn.

Next Row Wyif slip 1 purlwise, p39 (42, 45, 48, 51).

Repeat the last 2 rows, leaving 3 more stitches behind each time, 12 (13, 14, 15 16) times more. (The final 2 short rows will have only 4 stitches.) End after a purl row.

Next 6 rows Knit all stitches.

Repeat from * 3 times more.

End the piece after knitting 4 rows over all stitches (rather than 6).

Bind off loosely.

Top

Turn the Lower Piece so the reverse stockinette side is facing.

With smaller needles and MC, pick up and knit along the upper edge as follows: 1 stitch between all garter ridges, and 1 stitch in every row of stockinette—81 (89, 101, 113, 125) stitches.

(Increase or decrease over the next row to attain this number.)

Next row (WS) In MC, knit.

Continuing over smaller needles, work floret stitch as follows.

Row 1 (RS) In CC, knit.

Row 2 (WS) In CC, p1, *[p3tog, do not remove these stitches from the left needle, yo, p3tog through the same stitches again, then remove], p1; repeat from * to end.

Row 3 (RS) In MC, knit.

Row 4 (WS) In MC, [p2tog, do not remove these stitches from the left needle, purl into the first stitch only, then remove], p1, *[p3tog, do not remove these stitches from the left needle, yo, p3tog through the same stitches again, then remove], p1; repeat from * to last 2 stitches, [p2tog, do not remove these stitches from the left needle, purl into the first stitch only, then remove].

Repeat these 4 rows until the top measures approximately 3" (7.5cm). End after working Row 2.

SHAPE ARMHOLE

Continuing floret stitch, bind off at armhole edges as follows.

(To carry yarns through bind off, bind off 1 stitch in MC, then 1 stitch in CC, etc.)

Bind off 8 (10, 12, 14, 16) stitches at the beginning of the next 2 rows.

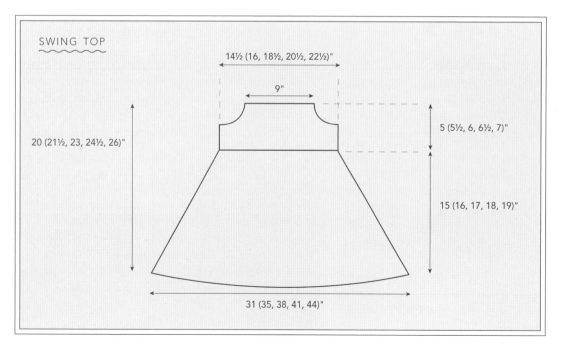

SWING TOP

14½ (16, 18½, 20½, 22½)"

9"

20 (21½, 23, 24½, 26)"

5 (5½, 6, 6½, 7)"

15 (16, 17, 18, 19)"

31 (35, 38, 41, 44)"

Bind off 4 stitches at the beginning of the next 2 (2, 4, 4, 4) rows.

Bind off 2 stitches at the beginning of the next 2 (4, 4, 8, 12) rows.

Bind off 1 stitch at the beginning of the next 6 rows—47 stitches.

If you ended with MC rows, work 2 rows even in CC.

Next row (RS) In MC, knit.

Next row (WS) In MC, bind off knitwise.

FRONT

Work as Back to Shape Armhole.

SHAPE LEFT FRONT ARMHOLE AND V-NECK

Continue floret stitch through all shaping.

(To carry yarns through bind off, bind off 1 stitch in MC, then 1 stitch in CC, etc.)

L (1X, 2X) SIZES ONLY

Bind off 12 (14, 16) stitches at the beginning of the next 2 rows—77 (85, 93) stitches.

Bind off 0 (4, 4) stitches at the beginning of the next 0 (4, 4) rows—77 (69, 77) stitches.

Bind off 0 (0, 2) stitches at the beginning of the next 0 (0, 4) rows—77 (69, 69) stitches.

ALL SIZES

*Bind off 0 (10, 4, 2, 2) stitches at the next armhole edge.

Work to 40 (34, 34, 32, 32) stitches on right needle. Turn.

Place remaining 41 (45, 39, 35, 35) stitches on holder.

Bind off 3 stitches at the next 7 neck edges.

AT THE SAME TIME, bind off 8 (4, 4, 2, 2) stitches at the next armhole edge, 4 (2, 2, 2, 2) stitches at the next armhole edge, 2 stitches at the next armhole edge, then 1 stitch at the next 3 armhole edges.

Bind off final 2 stitches.

SHAPE RIGHT FRONT ARMHOLE AND V-NECK

Return to remaining 41 (45, 39, 35, 35) stitches, right side facing.

Place first stitch on holder.

Begin with the next row in the sequence, work floret stitch for 1 right-side row over 40 (44, 38, 34, 34) stitches.

Beginning with a wrong-side row, work as Shape Left Front Armhole and V-neck from * to end, ignoring directions to place stitches on holder.

FINISHING

Sew side seams.

Right Armhole Edging

With smaller needles, right side facing, and MC, work as follows.

Beginning at the top of the Right Front (and ending at the top of the Right Back), pick up and knit 1 stitch for every bind-off stitch—approximately 34 (42, 54, 66, 78) stitches.

Next row Bind off knitwise.

Left Armhole Edging

Beginning at the top of the Left Back (and ending at the top of the Left Front), work as Right Armhole Edging.

V-neck Edging

With smaller needles, right side facing, and MC, work as follows.

Beginning at the top of the Left Front (and ending at the top of the Right Front), pick up and knit 1 stitch for every bind-off stitch, and 1 stitch on holder (at center front)—43–45 stitches.

Next row Bind off knitwise.

Steam-press all pieces, pressing armhole seam allowances to wrong side.

Sew in all tails except at hem (if using beads), and use tails to sew down seam allowances if needed.

Straps (Make 4)

With crochet hook and MC, chain 60 stitches. (Leave an 8" [20.5cm] tail at the beginning, and a 12" [30cm] tail at the end.)

Securely attach the beginnings of 2 chains to the outside corner of the upper Back edge.

Securely attach the beginnings of 2 chains to the alternate outside corner of the upper Back edge. Twist chains as tightly as possible, then loosely attach the ends of them to the points at the top of the Fronts.

Try the garment on, and adjust the length of the straps by adding or removing chain stitches.

Securely attach the ends of all straps at the Front corners. Because they may stretch, you could tuck the tails inside—without securing them in—for future adjustments.

Beading (optional)

After sewing in all tails except those at the hem, work as follows.

Cut 8" (20cm) strands of MC and CC.

Thread strands onto a tapestry needle, and take one strand MC and one strand CC through the hem at all points where tails already hang.

(You are adding tails from which to hang the beads. At any points where there are no tails—side seams, for example—cut more strands to attach.)

Thread one bead through the tails at all 18 places.

(If the holes in the beads are not large enough for all tails, bring what you can through the hole of the bead and the remainder down the back of the bead.)

Overhand knot the tails at the bottom to secure the bead.

Trim tails to suit.

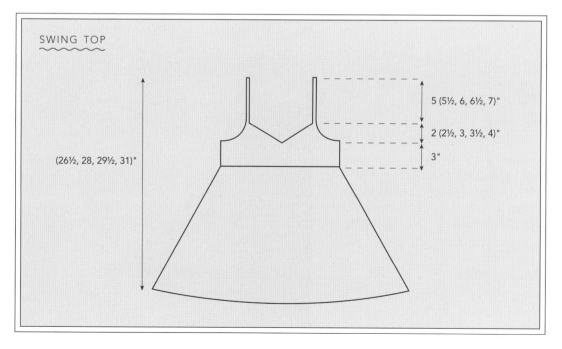

SWING TOP

5 (5½, 6, 6½, 7)"

2 (2½, 3, 3½, 4)"

3"

(26½, 28, 29½, 31)"

❧ SOPHISTICATED HOODIE ❧

Designed by Sally

WHEN I ASKED A FRIEND WHAT GARMENT SHE WOULD LIKE TO SEE IN THIS BOOK, THE ANSWER WAS IM-MEDIATE: A SHAPED HOODIE! I TRULY BELIEVE THAT THE HOODIE HAS BECOME ONE OF OUR WARDROBE BASICS, LIKE A BUTTON-DOWN SHIRT, A WHITE T-SHIRT, OR BLUE JEANS. AND JUST AS THESE OTHER GAR-MENTS CAN BE MADE IN BEAUTIFUL FABRICS AND SHAPES, SO, TOO, CAN THE HOODIE. I DID THIS ONE IN A SOFT, ALL-SEASONS YARN AND GAVE IT THE SOPHISTICATION OF WAIST-PLUS-PRINCESS SHAPING, WHICH I THINK DOES A LOVELY THING FOR A WOMAN'S HOURGLASS. IN ADDITION, IT IS WORKED IN A STITCH PATTERN THAT IS REVERSIBLE (FOR WHEN WE CAN SEE THE INSIDE OF THE HOOD) AND INTEREST-ING (AT MY TEXTURE-LOVING FRIEND'S REQUEST).

SKILL LEVEL
Experienced

SIZES
- S (M, L, 1X, 2X)
- Finished bust 37½ (42, 45½, 50, 53½)" (95 [106.5, 115.5, 127, 136]cm)
- Finished hem 40 (45, 48, 53, 56)" (101.5 (114.5, 122, 134.5, 139.5)]cm)
- Finished length 22 (22½, 23, 23½, 24)" (56 [57, 58.5, 59.5, 61]cm)
- Finished shoulder width 15" (38cm)
- Finished waist length 15½ (16, 16½, 17, 17½)" (39 (40.5, 42, 43, 44.5]cm)
- Finished sleeve length 29 (29½, 30, 30½, 31)" (73.5 [75, 76, 77.5, 78.5]cm)

MATERIALS
- 1575 (1750, 1925, 2100, 2275) yd (1420 [1575, 1735, 1890, 2050]m) / 9 (10, 11, 12, 13) balls Rowan Calmer (75% cotton, 25% acrylic/microfiber, each approximately 1¾ oz [50g] and 175 yd [160m]), in color 492 Garnet, **[3]** light/double knitting
- One pair size 6 (4mm) needles, or size needed to obtain gauge
- Stitch holder
- One pair size 4 (3.5mm) needles
- 2 Stitch markers
- Separating zipper, 18" (45cm) long
- One pair size 8 (5mm) needles

GAUGE
22 stitches and 32 rows = 4" (10cm) in stockinette or stitch pattern, over middle-size needles and after blocking

PATTERN NOTES

- This garment is hourglass-shaped so it could fall between your ideal short and mid-length sweater. It is also high-waisted. You may adjust waist length between the waist and the armhole and finished length before the waist (page 17).
- While the squares stitch pattern is reversible, the pattern demands a designation of right—and wrong-side rows.
- The second section of the squares stitch pattern starts on a wrong-side row.
- Maintain all stitch patterns as established through shaping and work even directions.

- Work all increases as lifted increases—knitwise in a knit stitch, and purlwise in a purl stitch.

STITCH PATTERN

Squares stitch pattern (over a multiple of 10 stitches)
Rows 1, 3, 5, 7 (RS) *P1, k1, p1, k1, p1, k5; repeat from *.
Row 2, 4, 6 (WS) *P5, p1, k1, p1, k1, p1; repeat from *.
Rows 8, 10, 12, 14 (WS) *K1, p1, k1, p1, k1, k5; repeat from *.
Rows 9, 11, 13 (RS) *P5, p1, k1, p1, k1, p1; repeat from *.
(See chart, page 74.)

BACK
Edging
With middle-size needles, long-tail cast on 106 (118, 128, 140, 150) stitches.
Purl 1 row, knit 1 row, then purl 2 rows.

Body
Next 6 RS rows K2, p19 (25, 30, 36, 41), k2, pm, work 10-stitch repeat of squares stitch pattern over next 60 stitches, k2, purl to last 2 stitches, k2.
Next 6 WS rows P2, k19 (25, 30, 36, 41), p2, work 10-stitch repeat of squares stitch pattern over next 60 stitches, p2, knit to last 2 stitches, p2.
End after working (WS) Row 12.
(Shorten or lengthen for finished length by changing number of rows worked even between decreases that follow, page 18.)
Decrease row (RS) K1, skp, purl to 3 stitches before marker, k2tog, k1, work 10-stitch repeat over next 60 stitches, k1, skp, purl to last 3 stitches, k2tog, k1—102 (114, 124, 136, 146) stitches.
Work 11 rows even.
Repeat decrease row.
Repeat the last 12 rows twice more—90 (102, 112, 124, 134) stitches.
(Piece measures 6½" [16.5cm]).
Work 3" (7.5cm) even.
Increase row (RS) K2, increase 1 in next stitch, purl to 2 stitches before marker, k2, work 10-stitch repeat over next 60 stitches, k2, purl to last 3 stitches, increase 1 in next stitch, k2—92 (104, 114, 126, 136) stitches.
Work 5 rows even.
Repeat increase row.
Repeat the last 6 rows 3 times more—100 (112, 122, 134, 144) stitches.
Work even until piece measures 13½" (34cm). End after working a wrong-side row.
(Shorten or lengthen for waist length here, page 18.)

SHAPE ARMHOLE
Bind off 4 (5, 7, 9, 12) stitches at the beginning of the next 2 rows—92 (102, 108, 116, 120) stitches.
Decrease row (RS) K1, skp, purl to 2 stitches before marker, k2, work 10-stitch repeat over next 60 stitches, pm, k2, purl to last 3 stitches, k2tog, k1.
Work 1 wrong-side row.
*Repeat decrease row.
Work 1 wrong-side row.
Decrease row with Princess shaping (RS) K1, skp, purl to 3 stitches before marker, k2tog, k1, increase 1 in next stitch, work squares stitch pattern to stitch before marker, increase 1 in next stitch, k1, skp, purl to last 3 stitches, k2tog, k1.
Work 1 wrong-side row.
Repeat from * until 84 stitches remain.
(Adjust shoulder width here, page 19.)
After 84 stitches remain, continue as follows.
Princess shaping (RS) Work as established to 3 stitches before marker, k2tog, k1, increase 1 in next stitch, work squares stitch pattern to stitch before marker, increase 1 in next stitch, k1, skp, work as established to end.
Repeat Princess shaping row every alternate right-side row until k4 remains at beginning and end of right-side rows.
Repeat Princess shaping row next 2 right-side rows.
Remove markers.
Following WS rows P2, work 10-stitch repeat over next 80 stitches, p2.
Following RS rows K2, work 10-stitch repeat over next 80 stitches, k2.
Work even until armhole measures 4½ (5, 5½, 6, 6½)" (11.5[12.5, 14, 15, 16.5]cm). End after working a wrong-side row.
(The stitch pattern will work best if you end after Row 8 or 14, but this is not essential.)

SHAPE SHOULDERS
Bind off 6 stitches at the beginning of the next 6 rows.
Bind off 7 stitches at the beginning of the next 2 rows.
Bind off final 34 stitches.

LEFT FRONT
Edging
With middle-size needles, long-tail cast on 56 (62, 67, 73, 78) stitches.
Purl 1 row, knit 1 row, then purl 2 rows.

Body
Next 6 RS rows K2, p19 (25, 30, 36, 41), k2, pm, work 10-stitch repeat of squares stitch pattern over next 30 stitches, k3.
Next 6 WS rows P3, work 10-stitch repeat of squares stitch pattern over next 30 stitches, p2, knit to last 2 stitches, p2.
End after working (WS) Row 12.
(Shorten or lengthen as for Back.)
Decrease row (RS) K1, skp, purl to 3 stitches before marker, k2tog, k1, work 10-stitch repeat over next 30 stitches, k3—54 (60, 65, 71, 76) stitches.
Work 11 rows even.
Repeat decrease row.

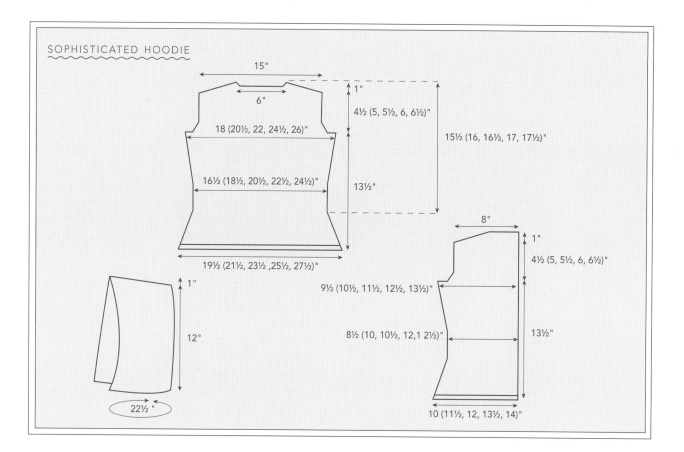

SOPHISTICATED HOODIE

15"

6"

1"

4½ (5, 5½, 6, 6½)"

18 (20½, 22, 24½, 26)"

15½ (16, 16½, 17, 17½)"

16½ (18½, 20½, 22½, 24½)"

13½"

19½ (21½, 23½ ,25½, 27½)"

1"

12"

8"

1"

4½ (5, 5½, 6, 6½)"

9½ (10½, 11½, 12½, 13½)"

8½ (10, 10½, 12,1 2½)"

13½"

22½ "

10 (11½, 12, 13½, 14)"

Repeat the last 12 rows twice more—48 (54, 59, 65, 70) stitches.

(Piece measures 6½" [16.5cm]).

Work 3" (7.5cm) even.

Increase row (RS) K2, increase 1 in next stitch, purl to 2 stitches before marker, k2, work 10-stitch repeat over next 30 stitches, k3.

Work 5 rows even.

Repeat increase row.

Repeat the last 6 rows 3 times more—53 (59, 64, 70, 75) stitches.

Work even until piece measures same length as Back to armhole. End after working a wrong-side row.

SHAPE ARMHOLE

Bind off 4 (5, 7, 9, 12) stitches at the beginning of the next row—49 (54, 57, 61, 63) stitches.

Decrease row (RS) K1, skp, purl to 2 stitches before marker, k2, work 10-stitch repeat over next 30 stitches, k3.

Work 1 wrong-side row.

*Repeat decrease row.

Work 1 wrong-side row.

Decrease row with princess shaping (RS) K1, skp, purl to 3 stitches before marker, k2tog, k1, increase 1 in next stitch, work squares stitch pattern to last 3 stitches, k3.

Work 1 wrong-side row.

Repeat from * until 45 stitches remain.

(Adjust shoulder width as for Back.)

After 45 stitches remain, continue as follows.

Princess shaping (RS) Work as established to 3 stitches before marker, k2tog, k1, increase 1 in next stitch, work squares stitch pattern to last 3 stitches, k3.

Repeat princess shaping row every alternate right-side row until k4 remains at beginning of right-side row.

Repeat princess shaping row next 2 right-side rows. Remove marker.

Following WS rows P3, work 10-stitch repeat over next 40 stitches, p2.

Following RS rows K2, work 10-stitch repeat over next 40 stitches, k3.

Work even until armhole measures same length as Back. End after working a wrong-side row.

SHAPE SHOULDER

Bind off 6 stitches at the next 3 armhole edges, and 7 stitches at the next armhole edge.

Bind off final 20 stitches.

RIGHT FRONT

Edging

With middle-size needles, long-tail cast on 56 (62, 67, 73, 78) stitches.

Purl 1 row, knit 1 row, then purl 2 rows.

Body

Next 6 RS rows K3, work 10-stitch repeat of squares stitch pattern over next 30 stitches, k2, p19 (25, 30, 36, 41), k2.

Next 6 WS rows P2, k19 (25, 30, 36, 41), p2, work 10-stitch repeat of squares stitch pattern over next 30 stitches, p3.

End after working (WS) Row 12.

(Shorten or lengthen as for Back.)

Decrease row (RS) K3, work 10-stitch repeat over next 30 stitches, k1, skp, purl to last 3 stitches, k2tog, k1—54 (60, 65, 71, 76) stitches.

Work 11 rows even.

Repeat decrease row.

Repeat the last 12 rows twice more—48 (54, 59, 65, 70) stitches.

(Piece measures 6½" [16.5cm]).

Work 3" (7.5cm) even.

Increase row (RS) K3, work 10-stitch repeat over next 30 stitches, k2, purl to last 3 stitches, increase 1 in next stitch, k2.

Work 5 rows even.

Repeat increase row.

Repeat the last 6 rows 3 times more—53 (59, 64, 70, 75) stitches.

Work even until piece measures same length as Back to armhole. End after working a right-side row.

SHAPE ARMHOLE

Bind off 4 (5, 7, 9, 12) stitches at the beginning of the next row—49 (54, 57, 61, 63) stitches.

Decrease row (RS) K3, work 10-stitch repeat over next 30 stitches, pm, k2, purl to last 3 stitches, k2tog, k1.

Work 1 wrong-side row.

*Repeat decrease row.

Work 1 wrong-side row.

Decrease row with princess shaping (RS) K3, work squares stitch pattern to stitch before marker, increase 1, k1, skp, purl to last 3 stitches, k2tog, k1.

Work 1 wrong-side row.

Repeat from * until 45 stitches remain.

(Adjust shoulder width as for Back.)

After 45 stitches remain, continue as follows.

Princess shaping (RS) K3, work squares stitch pattern to stitch before marker, increase 1 in next stitch, k1, skp, work as established to end.

Repeat princess shaping row every alternate right-side row until k4 remains at end of right-side row.

Repeat princess shaping row next 2 right-side rows. Remove marker.

Following WS rows P2, work 10-stitch repeat over next 40 stitches, p3.

Following RS rows K3, work 10-stitch repeat over next 40 stitches, k2.

Work even until armhole measures same length as Back. End after working a right-side row.

SHAPE SHOULDER

Work as Left Front, Shape Shoulder.

SLEEVES

Edging

With middle-size needles, long-tail cast on 40 (40, 46, 46, 54) stitches.

Purl 1 row, then knit 1 row, then purl 2 rows.

Body

Beginning with a knit row, work stockinette until pieces measures 1" (2.5cm). End after working a wrong-side row. Work stockinette for remainder of Sleeve.

Increase row (RS) K2, increase 1 in next stitch, knit to last 3 stitches, increase 1 in next stitch, k2.

Work 5 (5, 5, 3, 3) rows even.

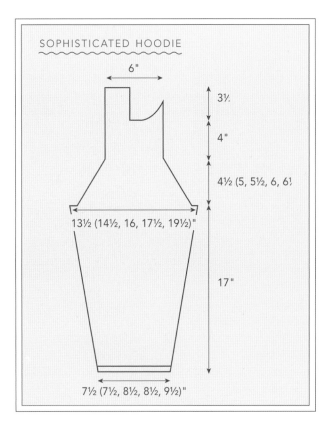

SOPHISTICATED HOODIE

6"

3¼

4"

4½ (5, 5½, 6, 6½

13½ (14½, 16, 17½, 19½)"

17"

7½ (7½, 8½, 8½, 9½)"

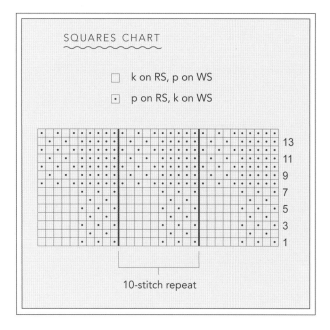

SQUARES CHART

☐ k on RS, p on WS

⊡ p on RS, k on WS

13
11
9
7
5
3
1

10-stitch repeat

Repeat the last 6 (6, 6, 4, 4) rows 16 (19, 20, 24, 26) times more—74 (80, 88, 96, 108) stitches.
Work even until piece measures 17" (43cm). End after working a wrong-side row.
(Shorten or lengthen for Sleeve length here, page 20.)

SHAPE SLEEVE CAP
Bind off 4 (5, 7, 9, 12) stitches at the beginning of the next 2 rows—66 (70, 74, 78, 84) stitches.
Decrease row (RS) K1, skp, knit to last 3 stitches, k2tog, k1.
Work 1 wrong-side row.
Repeat the last 2 rows 16 (18, 20, 22, 25) times more—32 stitches.

Right Sleeve Saddle
Work 4" (10cm) even. End after working a wrong-side row.

SHAPE FRONT NECK
Next (short) row (RS) K16. Turn.
At Front neck edge, bind off 5 stitches once, 3 stitches once, 2 stitches once, then 1 stitch until 2 stitches remain. Bind off.

SHAPE BACK NECK
Return to remaining 16 stitches, right side facing. At Back neck edge, bind off 2 stitches once, then 1 stitch twice—12 stitches.
Continue over 12 stitches until neck opening measures 3½" (9cm). Place stitches on holder.

Left Sleeve Saddle
Work 4" (10cm) even. End after working a right-side row.

SHAPE FRONT NECK
Next (short) row (WS) P16. Turn.
At Front neck edge, bind off 5 stitches once, 3 stitches once, 2 stitches once, then 1 stitch until 2 stitches remain. Bind off.

SHAPE BACK NECK
Return to remaining 16 stitches, wrong-side facing. At Back neck edge, bind off 2 stitches once, then 1 stitch twice—12 stitches.
Continue over 12 stitches until neck opening measures 3½" (9cm). Place stitches on holder.

FINISHING
Sew long edges of Sleeve saddles to top of Back.
(You may need to add or delete rows so the saddles meet at the center.)
Graft or sew live stitches together.
Sew front edges of Sleeve saddles to tops of Fronts, ending approximately 2" (5cm) from front edges.

Neck Edging
With smaller needles and right side facing, begin at Right Front neck to pick up and knit as follows:
12 stitches along tops of Fronts,
25 stitches around Front and Back neck shaping,
35 stitches along straight edge of Back neck.
—109 stitches.
Knit 1 (WS) row, purl 1 row, knit 1 row, then purl 2 rows.
Increase row (RS) K2, *increase 1 in next stitch, k3; repeat from * to last 3 stitches, increase 1 in next stitch, k2—136 stitches.
At any time during the Hood, sew this last row to the pick-up-and-knit row of the neck edging.

Hood
Change to middle-size needles.
Next row (WS) P3, beginning with Row 8, work 10-stitch repeat of squares stitch pattern over next 130 stitches, p3.
RS rows K3, work 10-stitch repeat of squares to last 3 stitches, k3.
WS rows P3, work 10-stitch repeat of squares stitch pattern to last 3 stitches, p3.
Repeat these last 2 rows until the Hood measures approximately 12" (30cm). End after working Row 8 or 14.
Next (short) row (RS) K3, work 65 stitches (to center of Hood). Turn.
Continue over this side of Hood only and as follows.

Bind off 8 stitches at the beginning of the next wrong-side row.

Work 1 right-side row.

Repeat the last 2 rows twice more—44 stitches.

Place these stitches onto a spare needle.

Return to remaining 68 stitches, right side facing.

Bind off 8 stitches at the beginning of the next right-side row.

Work 1 wrong-side row.

Repeat the last 2 rows twice more—44 stitches.

Turn the Hood to the wrong side, and work 3-needle bind-off over 44 stitches of each side.

Turn the Hood to the right side, and sew the bind-off edges together.

Front and Hood Edging

With smaller needles, right side facing, and beginning at lower Right Front edge, pick up and knit 2 stitches for every 3 rows up Right Front, around Hood, and down Left Front.

Knit 1 row, purl 1 row, knit 1 row, then bind off purlwise, leaving long tail.

With long tail, sew bind-off row of edging to selvedge. (The edging may seem like it has too few stitches, but the zipper will stretch it straight.)

Zipper

Baste the zipper into the wrong side of the Fronts (so teeth end at edge of the edging).

Cut the tab at the top of the zipper as needed (so it doesn't extend into the Hood).

With thinned yarn of project (or matching sewing thread), use a backstitch to sew the zipper.

Right Front Zipper Facing

Turn Right Front to wrong side.

Find the purl stitch at the edge of the zipper (the stitch before the squares stitch pattern).

Beginning at the top of the zipper, slip largest needle through the purl bumps of this stitch, every 2nd row, along the length of the zipper.

*Knit 1 (WS) row, purl 1 row, knit 1 row, then bind off purlwise and very loosely, leaving long tail. With the long tail, blind hem the Zipper Facing to the zipper, hiding all stitching (but not so it will interfere the with movement of the zipper).

Left Front Zipper Facing

Find the purl stitch at the edge of the zipper (the stitch before the squares stitch pattern).

Beginning at the bottom of the zipper, slip largest needle through the purl bumps of this stitch, every 2nd row, along the length of the zipper.

Work as Right Front Zipper Facing from * to end.

Sew Sleeves into armholes.

Sew side and Sleeve seams.

HOW LONG HAVE YOU BEEN KNITTING?

SALLY: I have been knitting for more than fifty years. (I knit all through university and I don't remember if that was a cool thing for a hippie to be doing, but I went to a school that was overridden with males who only wanted a warm body to drink beer with. They hardly cared what else I was doing!)

CADDY: I've been knitting furiously for five years. I guess you could say I started late. But what I've missed in years I've made up for in enthusiasm!

❧ CABLE-EDGED VEST ❧

Designed by Sally

LIKE OTHER GARMENTS OF THIS BOOK, THIS ONE WAS BASED ON A PIECE I BOUGHT AND LOVED. THE ORIGINAL HAD EXACTLY THIS SHAPE—HIGH IN THE CENTER BACK, NARROW AT THE WAIST, WITH SOFTLY-SHAPED VEST POINTS IN THE FRONT, AND WITH A NECK EDGING THAT BECOMES THE SHOULDER STRAPS. ALL OF THESE FEATURES MAKE IT AN ADVANCED PATTERN, BECAUSE THERE REALLY IS A LOT GOING ON AT ONCE. BUT THE ORIGINAL HAD ONLY A SIMPLE RIBBED BAND, AND I THOUGHT A CABLED EDGING MORE WORTHY OF AN EXPERIENCED KNITTER'S SKILLS.

EXPERIENCE LEVEL
Experienced

SIZES
- S (M, L, 1X, 2X)
- Finished bust 32 (35, 39, 43, 47)" (81 [89, 99, 109, 119.5]cm)
- Finished length (at sides) 15 (15½, 16, 16½, 17)" (38 [39, 40.5, 42, 43]cm)
- Finished shoulder width 13½" (34cm)

MATERIALS
- 450 (500, 550, 600, 650) yd (405 [450, 495, 540, 585]m) / 4 (4, 5, 5, 5) balls Filatura di Crosa Zara (100% wool, each approximately 1¾ oz [50g] and 136 yd [125m]), in color 27 light gray, (3) - (4) light/double knitting
- One circular needle, size 5 (3.75) mm, 30" (75cm) or longer
- One circular needle, any length, size 6 (4mm), or size needed to obtain gauge
- Stitch holder
- Cable needle
- Tapestry needle
- 2 Buttons, 1" (2.5cm) wide
- *Optional* 1 snap fastener

GAUGE
20 stitches and 30 rows = 4" (10cm) in stockinette stitch, over larger needle

PATTERN NOTES
- This garment is cropped and shaped. There is no formula for its finished length. But if you wish it longer, it should not extend past your waist at the sides.
- The neck edging will add 1" (2.5cm) to the length of the back and 4½" (11cm) to the length of the front.
- Work stockinette unless otherwise indicated.
- Slip all stitches with yarn to wrong side and purlwise.
- Work all increases as lifted increase.
- The reverse stockinette edging may flip up: this will be remedied by blocking.
- The fronts and back do not meet at the shoulders until the neck edging is knit.
- To continue as established means to knit the k's and purl the p's.

BACK
Edging
With smaller needle, long-tail cast on 70 (78, 88, 98, 108) stitches
Purl 1 row, knit 1 row, then change to larger needle and purl 1 row.

Body
Short row 1 (WS) P3. Turn.
Row 2 (RS) Slip 1, knit to end.
Short row 3 (WS) Purl 3 stitches past previous wrong-side row. Turn.
Repeat the last 2 rows 5 times more—21 stitches on right needle.
Row 14 (RS) Slip 1, k20.
Short row 15 (WS) Purl 4 (6, 8, 10, 12) stitches past previous wrong-side row. Turn.
Row 16 (RS) Slip 1, knit to end.

Repeat the last 2 rows once more—end with slip 1, k28 (32, 36, 40, 44)—29 (33, 37, 41, 45) stitches on right needle.

Cut yarn. Slip all stitches to other end of needle.

Short row 1 (RS) K3. Turn.

Row 2 (WS) Slip 1, purl to end.

Short row 3 (RS) Knit 3 stitches past previous right-side row. Turn.

Repeat the last 2 rows 5 times more—21 stitches on right needle.

Row 14 (WS) Slip 1, p20.

Short row 15 (RS) Knit 4 (6, 8, 10, 12) stitches past previous right-side row. Turn.

Row 16 (WS) Slip 1, purl to end.

Repeat the last 2 rows once more—end with slip 1, p28 (32, 36, 40, 44)—29 (33, 37, 41, 45) stitches on right needle.

Next row (RS) K70 (78, 88, 98, 108).

Purl 1 row.

SHAPE SIDES

Increase row (RS) K1, increase 1 in next stitch, knit to last 2 stitches, increase 1, k1.

Work 5 rows even.

Repeat the last 6 rows 4 times more—80 (88, 98, 108, 118) stitches.

Work even until side measures 7" (18cm). End with after working a wrong-side row.

(Shorten or lengthen here.)

SHAPE ARMHOLE

Bind off 3 (5, 7, 9, 11) stitches at the beginning of the next 2 rows—74 (78, 84, 90, 96) stitches.

Decrease row (RS) K1, skp, knit to last 3 stitches, k2tog, k1.

Purl 1 row.

Repeat the last 2 rows 11 (13, 16, 19, 22) times more—50 stitches.

Work even until armhole measures 4½ (5, 5½, 6½, 7)" (11.5 [12.5, 14, 16.5, 18]cm). End after working a wrong-side row.

Increase row (RS) K1, increase 1 in next stitch, knit to last 2 stitches, increase 1, k1—52 stitches.

Work 5 rows even.

SHAPE RIGHT ARMHOLE AND NECK

Next row (RS) K1, increase 1 in next stitch, knit to 15 stitches on right needle. Place remaining 38 stitches on holder. Turn.

*Bind off 6 stitches at the next neck edge, 3 stitches at the next neck edge, 2 stitches at the next neck edge—4 stitches.

Next row (RS) Work 1, increase 1 in next stitch, work to end.

Bind off 1 stitch at the next 3 neck edges.

Bind off final 2 stitches.

SHAPE LEFT ARMHOLE AND NECK

Return to remaining 38 stitches, right side facing. Place first 24 stitches on holder.

Next row (RS) Knit to last 2 stitches, increase 1 in next stitch, k1—15 stitches.

Purl 1 row.

Work as Shape Right Armhole and Neck from * to end except that increase row should be worked as follows: knit to last 2 stitches, increase 1 in next stitch, k1.

LEFT FRONT
Edging

With smaller needle, long-tail cast on 47 (51, 56, 61, 66) stitches.

Purl 1 row, knit 1 row, then change to larger needle and purl 1 row.

Cut yarn.

Body

With purl side of edging facing, slip to 21 stitches on left needle and 26 (30, 35, 40, 45) stitches on right.

Short row 1 (RS) Slip 1, k2. Turn.

Short row 2 (WS) Slip 1, p8 (7, 7, 7, 7). Turn.

Short row 3 (RS) Slip 1, knit 3 stitches past previous RS row. Turn.

Short row 4 (WS) Slip 1, purl 4 (5, 6, 7, 8) stitches past previous WS row. Turn.

Repeat the last 2 rows 4 times more. End after working a wrong-side row.

Next row (RS) K47 (51, 56, 61, 66).

Work even until side measures 2" (5cm) above edging. End after working a right-side row.

SHAPE SIDE AND NECK

Bind off 6 stitches at the beginning of the next wrong-side row—41 (45, 50, 55, 60) stitches.

Increase row (RS) K1, increase 1 in next stitch, knit to end.

Repeat increase row every 6th row 4 times more. AT THE SAME TIME, continue to bind off at neck edge as follows: 3 stitches once, 2 stitches 4 times, 1 stitch 10 times—25 (29, 34, 39, 44) stitches.

Work even until side measures same as Back. End after working a wrong-side row.

SHAPE NECK AND ARMHOLE

Bind off 3 (5, 7, 9, 11) stitches at beginning of the next right-side row—22 (24, 27, 30, 33) stitches.

Next row (WS) Bind off 1 stitch at neck edge, purl to end.

Decrease row (RS) K1, skp, knit to end.

Purl 1 row.

Repeat decrease row.

Repeat the last 4 rows 5 times more—to 12 armhole decreases and 6 stitches bound off at Neck edge—4 (6, 9, 12, 15) stitches.

Sizes M (L, 1X, 2X) only Continue with armhole edge decrease 2 (5, 8, 11) times more—4 stitches.

All sizes, next row K1, skp, k1.

Next row Bind off.

RIGHT FRONT

Edging

With smaller needle, long-tail cast on 47 (51, 56, 61, 66) stitches.

Purl 1 row, knit 1 row, then change to larger needle and purl 1 row.

Cut yarn.

Body

With knit side of edging facing, slip to 26 (30, 35, 40, 45) stitches onto right needle and 21 stitches on left.

Short row 1 (WS) Slip 1, p2. Turn.

Short row 2 (RS) Slip 1, k8 (7, 7, 7, 7). Turn.

Short row 3 (WS) Slip 1, purl 3 stitches past previous RS row. Turn.

Short row 4 (RS) Slip 1, knit 4 (5, 6, 7, 8) stitches past previous WS row. Turn.

Repeat the last 2 rows 4 times more. End after working a right-side row.

Next row (WS) P47 (51, 56, 61, 66).

Work even until side measures 1¾" (4.5cm) above edging. End with after working a wrong-side row.

Next row (RS), make two 3-stitch, 1-row buttonholes K5, *wyif, slip 1, wyib psso, (leave yarn in back until directed otherwise), slip 1, psso, slip 1, psso (3 stitches bound off). Put last slip stitch back onto left needle. Turn, wyib cable cast on 3 stitches, cable cast on 1 more stitch but, before putting stitch on left needle, bring yarn between two stitches and to front. Turn, k1, pass the final cast-on stitch over the stitch just knit, *knit to 15 stitches on right needle, repeat from * to *, then knit to end.

Work even until side measures 2" (5cm) above edging. End after working a wrong-side row.

SHAPE NECK AND SIDE

Increase row (RS) Bind off 6 stitches at neck edge, knit to last 2 stitches, increase 1 in next stitch, k1—42 (46, 51, 56, 61) stitches.

Purl 1 row.

Repeat increase row every 6th row 4 times more. AT THE SAME TIME, continue to bind off at neck edge as follows: 3 stitches once, 2 stitches 4 times, 1 stitch 10 times—25 (29, 34, 39, 44) stitches.

Work even until side measures same as Back. End after working a right-side row.

SHAPE NECK AND ARMHOLE

Bind off 3 (5, 7, 9, 11) stitches at the beginning of the next wrong-side row—22 (24, 27, 30, 33) stitches.

Decrease row (RS) Bind off 1 stitch at neck edge, knit to last 3 stitches, k2tog, k1.

Purl 1 row.

Decrease row (RS) Knit to last 3 stitches, k2tog, k1.

Purl 1 row.

Repeat the last 4 rows 5 times more—to 12 armhole decreases and 6 stitches bound off at neck edge—4 (6, 9, 12, 15) stitches remain.

Sizes M (L, 1X, 2X) only Continue with armhole edge decrease 2 (5, 8, 11) times more—4 stitches.

All sizes, next row K1, k2tog, k1.
Next row Bind off.

FINISHING
Armhole Edgings

Sew side seams.

With right-side facing and smaller needle, pick up and knit around armholes as follows:
1 stitch for each bind-off stitch at underarm,
3 stitches for every 4 rows.
—approximately 74 (82, 90, 98, 108) stitches.
Beginning with a wrong-side row, knit 1 row, purl 1 row, knit 1 row, then bind off purlwise.

Pockets (Make 2)

With smaller needle, e-wrap cast on 27 stitches.
Rows 1 & 3 (RS) K2, *p3, k2; repeat from * to end.
Row 2 P2, *k3, p2; repeat from * to end.
Row 4 (increase) P2, * k3, [p1, increase 1 in next stitch]; repeat from * to last 5 stitches, k3, p2—31 stitches.
Row 5 K2, * p3, knit into 3rd stitch on left needle, then knit first 2 stitches on left needle; repeat from * to last 5 stitches, p3, k2.
Rows 6, 8 & 10 Continue as established.
Rows 7, 9 & 11 As Row 5.

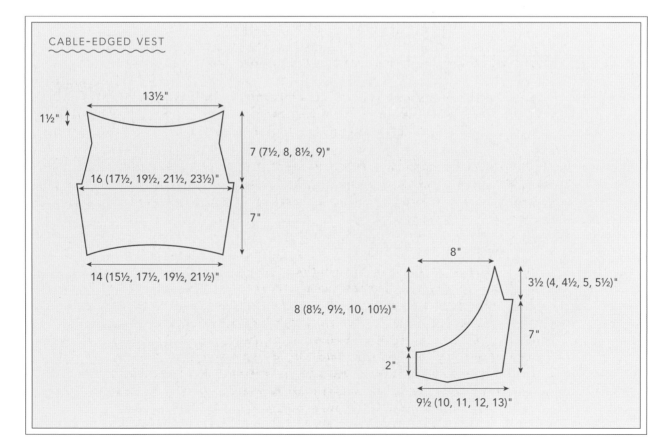

CABLE-EDGED VEST

13½"

1½"

7 (7½, 8, 8½, 9)"

16 (17½, 19½, 21½, 23½)"

7"

14 (15½, 17½, 19½, 21½)"

8 (8½, 9½, 10, 10½)"

8"

3½ (4, 4½, 5, 5½)"

7"

2"

9½ (10, 11, 12, 13)"

Row 12 (decrease) P2, *k3, p2tog, p1; repeat from * to last 5 stitches, k3, p2—27 stitches.
Row 13 (decrease, RS) [K5, k2tog] 3 times, k6—24 stitches.
Knit 1 row, purl 1 row, knit 1 row, then bind off purlwise, leaving long tail for seaming.
Taking 1 stitch at each side and cast-on edge into seam allowance, sew to Right Front as follows: place the lower left corner of the Pocket 4 stitches from the side edge and 10 rows up from the edging. (While sewing the cast-on edge of the pocket, be sure to stay on the same row of the Front.)
Sew Left Front Pocket in same manner.

Neck Edging

With right side facing, smaller needle, and beginning at Right Front, pick up and knit around neck edge as follows:
1 stitch for every bind-off stitch,
1 stitch for every 2-row step between bind-off stitches,
3 stitches for every 4-row step between bind-off stitches.
—approximately 72 (75, 79, 83, 89) stitches along Right Front curve.
Turn, and cable cast on 18 stitches. (To shorten armhole, cast on fewer stitches.)
Turn, and continue to pick up and knit around Back neck as follows:
1 stitch for every bind-off stitch,
1 stitch for every 2-row step between bind-off stitches,
1 stitch for every stitch on holder.
—approximately 77 stitches around Back neck.
Turn, and cable cast on 18 stitches. (To shorten armhole, cast on fewer stitches.)
Turn, and continue to pick up and knit around Left Front neck edge as follows:
1 stitch for every bind-off stitch,
1 stitch for every 2-row step between bind-off stitches,
3 stitches for every 4-row step between bind-off stitches.
—approximately 72 (75, 79, 83, 89) stitches along Left Front curve and 257 (263, 271, 279, 291) stitches around entire neck edge.
Count stitches on the needle before working the next row.
Next row (WS) P2, *k3, p2, repeat from * to end. AT THE SAME TIME decrease or increase across center Back so the total number of stitches is a multiple of 5 stitches + 2. Beginning with Row 3, work as Pockets to end of Row 12.
Row 13 (RS) [K5, k2tog] across row.
Knit 1 row, purl 1 row, knit 1 row, then bind off tightly and purlwise.

Sew upper corners of armhole edgings closed.

Front Edgings

With right side facing and smaller needle, pick up and knit 2 stitches for every 3 rows along front edges—approximately 24 stitches.
Knit 1 row, purl 1 row, knit 1 row, then bind off purlwise and tightly.

Sew buttons onto Left Front to correspond to buttonholes on Right Front.
Optional Sew snap to wrong-side upper corner of Right Front (and to matching point on right side of Left Front). If lower edges flip, wet edges or wash garment, then pin edges to flat surface until dry.

❧ MOTHER-OF-THE-BRIDE CARDIGAN ☙

Designed by Sally

I CALLED THIS THE "MOTHER-OF-THE-BRIDE" CARDIGAN BECAUSE IT CAN BE THAT DRESSY (AND I WORE A VERSION OF THIS TO CADDY'S WEDDING). BUT IT CAN ALSO BE DRESSED DOWN. AND DON'T LET THE "MOTHER" REFERENCE FOOL YOU: CADDY TELLS ME THAT THE BRIDE WILL WANT ONE FOR HERSELF!

THIS PIECE IS AN INTERESTING MIX OF FITTED AND SNUG VERSUS LOOSE AND FLOWING. THE CONTRAST IS APPARENT BETWEEN THE LOWER AND UPPER SLEEVE AND BETWEEN THE SOFT AND LOOSE FRONT VERSUS THE FIRM AND SNUG BACK. THE RESULT IS A GARMENT THAT BOTH FITS AND FLOATS.

SKILL LEVEL
Experienced

SIZES
- S-M (L–1X, 2X)
- Finished bust (at underarm) 36 (42, 48)" (91 [106.5, 122]cm)
- Finished length (at side) 20 (21, 22)" (51 [53.5, 56]cm)
- Finished shoulder width 12½ (12½, 14½)" (31.5 [31.5, 37]cm)
- Finished sleeve length 32 (32½, 34)" (81 [82.5, 98]cm)

MATERIALS
- 920 (1130, 1350) yd (828 [1017, 1215]m) / 5 (5, 6) balls Rowan Kidsilk Spray (70% kid mohair, 30% silk, each approximately ⅞ oz [25g] and 229 yd [210m]), in color 572 Pebbles, [2] fine/sport
- 450 (550, 660) yd (405 [495, 594]m) / 5 (5, 6) balls Skacel loft (100% merino wool, each approximately 1¾ oz [50g] and 110 yd [100m]), in color 1211 taupe, [5] bulky
- One pair size 8 (5mm) needles, or size needed to obtain gauge
- One pair size 3 (3mm) needles, or size needed to obtain gauge
- One size 3 (3mm) circular needle, 24" (60cm) long
- Tapestry needle
- H-8 (5mm) crochet hook

GAUGE
26 stitches and 36 rows = 4" in stockinette stitch, over fine yarn and smaller needles
16 stitches and 26 rows = 4" in English Lace, over heavy yarn and larger needles

PATTERN NOTES
- This garment is short and unshaped at the back, but the long collar plus tie makes the front fall longer and look shaped. You would probably choose to make the back your ideal short sweater length (page 17).
- The back is worked in the same yarn and stitch pattern as the upper sleeves.
- The sleeves are quite long so that the scallop lace extends over the hand.
- Work all increases as lifted increase.
- When one number appears, it applies to all sizes.

STITCH PATTERNS
English Lace (over a multiple of 8 stitches + 11)
(In rows 2, 4, 6, the last 7 stitches will appear as only 6 stitches on the chart.)
Row 1 (WS) Purl.
Row 2 K2, *k2, yo, sk2p, yo, k3; repeat from * to last stitch, k1.
Row 3 P1, *p2, yo, p2tog, p1, ssp, yo, p1; repeat from * to last 2 stitches, p2.
Row 4 K2, *yo, skp, yo, sk2p, yo, k2tog, yo, k1; repeat from * to last stitch, k1.
Row 5 As Row 3.
Row 6 As Row 2.
Row 7 As Row 1.
Row 8 (RS) K1, k2tog, yo, k2, *k3, yo, sk2p, yo, k2; repeat from * to last 6 stitches, k3, yo, skp, k1.
Row 9 P2, ssp, yo, p2, *p1, yo, p2tog, p1, ssp, yo, p2; repeat from * to last 5 stitches, p1, yo, p2tog, p2.
Row 10 K1, k2tog, yo, k2tog, yo, *k1, yo, skp, yo, sk2p, yo, k2tog, yo; repeat from * to last 6 stitches, k1, yo, skp, yo, skp, k1.

Row 11 As Row 9.

Row 12 As Row 8. (See chart, page 86.)

Scallop Lace (over a multiple of 10 stitches + 13)
(In Rows 1–8, the last 8 stitches will appear as only 7 stitches on the chart.) (See chart, page 86.)

Row 1 K2, yo, k3, *sk2p, k3, yo, k1, yo, k3; repeat from * to last 8 stitches, sk2p, k3, yo, k2.

All WS rows Purl.

Row 3 K3, yo, k2, *sk2p, k2, yo, k3, yo, k2; repeat from * to last 8 stitches, sk2p, k2, yo, k3.

Row 5 K4, yo, k1 *sk2p, k1, yo, k5, yo, k1; repeat from * to last 8 stitches, sk2p, k1, yo, k4.

Row 7 K5, yo, *sk2p, yo, k7, yo; repeat from * to last 8 stitches, sk2p, yo, k5.

Row 9 K1, k2tog, k3, yo, *k1, yo, k3, sk2p, k3, yo; repeat from * to last 7 stitches, k1, yo, k3, skp, k1.

Row 11 K1, k2tog, k2, yo, k1, *k2, yo, k2, sk2p, k2, yo, k1; repeat from * to last 7 stitches, k2, yo, k2, skp, k1

Row 13 K1, k2tog, k1, yo, k2, *k3, yo, k1, sk2p, k1, yo, k2; repeat from * to last 7 stitches, k3, yo, k1, skp, k1.

Row 15 K1, k2tog, yo, k3, *k4, yo, sk2p, yo, k3; repeat from * to last 7 stitches, k4, yo, skp, k1.

Fagotting Lace (over a multiple of 4 stitches + 2)

Right-side rows *K2, yo, p2tog; repeat from * to last 2 stitches, k2.

Wrong-side rows P2, *yo, p2tog, p2; repeat from *.
(See chart, page 86.)

BACK

With heavy yarn and larger needles, long-tail cast on 67 (75, 83) stitches.

Beginning with Row 1, work english lace until piece measures 12" (30cm). End after working a wrong-side row. (You may have an easier time reestablishing your pattern if you end with Row 7 or 1. If you end with Row 7, you will restart with Row 2 [8, 8]: if you end with Row 1, you will restart with Row 8 [2, 2].)

(Shorten or lengthen for finished length here, page 18.)

SHAPE ARMHOLE

Bind off 4 (6, 8) stitches at the beginning of the next 2 rows—59 (63, 67) stitches.

Decrease row (RS) K1, skp, work to last 3 stitches, k2tog, k1.

Work 1 wrong-side row.

Repeat the last 2 rows 3 (5, 3) times more—51 (51, 59) stitches.

(Adjust shoulder width here, page 19.)

Work even until armhole measures 7½ (8½, 9½)" (19, 21.5, 24]cm). End after working a wrong-side row.

SHAPE SHOULDERS

Bind off 2 stitches at the beginning of the next 4 rows—43 (43, 51) stitches.

SHAPE RIGHT BACK NECK

Bind off 2 (2, 4) stitches at the beginning of the next right-side row, work to 3 (3, 5) stitches on the right needle. Turn. Bind off 1 stitch at neck edge, work to end.

Bind off final 2 (2, 4) stitches.

SHAPE LEFT BACK NECK

Return to remaining 38 (38, 42) stitches, right side facing.

Bind off 33 stitches, work a right-side row over 5 (5, 9) stitches.

Bind off 2 (2, 4) stitches at the next armhole edge, work to end.

Bind off 1 stitch at the next neck edge, work to end.

Bind off final 2 (2, 4) stitches.

RIGHT FRONT

With smaller needles and fine yarn, long-tail cast on 93 (105, 117) stitches.

Beginning with a purl row, work 3 rows in stockinette. (Continue in stockinette to end.)

*Front edge decrease row (RS) K1, skp, knit to end.

Repeat this (RS) decrease row 2 times more.

Decrease + Increase row (RS) K1, skp, knit to last 2 stitches, increase 1 in next stitch, k1.

Repeat from * 7 times more—69 (81, 93) stitches.

Continue with Front edge decrease row, every right-side row, 22 (28, 28) times more. Then continue with Front edge decrease row, every alternate right-side row, 10 (13, 14) times more.

AT THE SAME TIME, when piece measures same length as Back to armhole (after working a right-side row), shape armhole as follows.

SHAPE ARMHOLE

Bind off 7 (10, 13) stitches at the beginning of the next row.

Armhole decrease row (RS) Knit to last 3 stitches, k2tog, k1.

Repeat armhole decrease row every right-side row 8 times more.

AT THE SAME TIME, continue Front edge decrease row every alternate right-side row until 12 (12, 20) stitches remain.

Work Front edge even until armhole measures

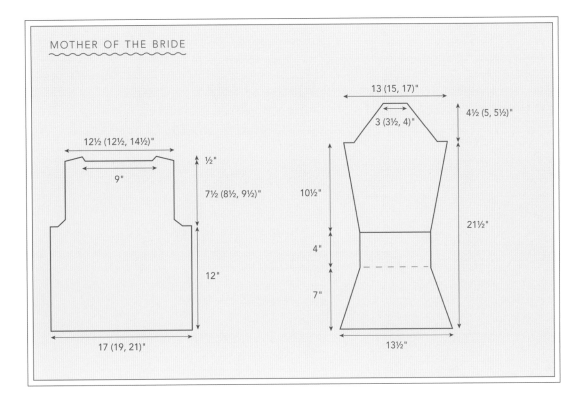

MOTHER OF THE BRIDE

same length as Back. End after working a right-side row.

SHAPE SHOULDER
Bind off 3 (3, 4) stitches at the next armhole edge, 2 (2, 4) stitches at the next armhole edge, 3 (3, 4) stitches at the next armhole edge, 2 (2, 4) stitches at the next armhole edge.
Bind off final 2 (2, 4) stitches.

LEFT FRONT
With smaller needles and fine yarn, long-tail cast on 93 (105, 117) stitches.
Beginning with a purl row, work 3 rows in stockinette. (Continue in stockinette to end.)
*Front edge decrease row (RS) Knit to last 3 stitches, k2tog, k1.
Repeat this (RS) decrease row 2 times more.
Decrease + Increase row (RS) K1, increase 1 in next stitch, knit to last 3 stitches, k2tog, k1.
Repeat from * 7 times more—69 (81, 93) stitches.
Continue with Front edge decrease row, every right-side row, 22 (28, 28) times more. Then continue with Front edge decrease row, every alternate right-side row, 10 (13, 14) times more.
AT THE SAME TIME, when piece measures same length as Back to armhole (after working a wrong-side row), shape armhole as follows.

SHAPE ARMHOLE
Bind off 7 (10, 13) stitches at the beginning of the next row.
Purl 1 row.
Armhole decrease row (RS) K1, skp, knit to end.
Repeat armhole decrease row every right-side row 8 times more.
AT THE SAME TIME, continue Front edge decrease row every alternate right-side row until 12 (12, 20) stitches remain.
Work Front edge even until armhole measures same length as Back. End after working a wrong-side row.

SHAPE SHOULDER
Work as for Right Front, Shape Shoulder.

SLEEVES
(All sizes are the same through the first two sections.)
Scallop Lace Cuff
With smaller needles and fine yarn, long-tail cast on 87 stitches.
Purl 1 row.
Row 1 (RS) K7, *sk2p, k11; repeat from * to last 10 stitches, sk2p, k7—75 stitches.
Row 2 Purl.
Row 3 K6, *sk2p, k9; repeat from * to last 9 stitches, sk2p, k6—63 stitches.
Purl 1 row, then work Rows 1–16 of scallop lace.
(Continue scallop lace until directed otherwise.)

Decrease row (RS) Work Row 1, but do not work first and last yo's—61 stitches.

Work the next 3 right-side rows without first and last yo's (as for decrease row)—55 stitches.

(Row 3, Row 5, Row 7 now begin and end with k4, k3, k2.) Work to end of Row 8, then begin again with Row 1 as follows.

Row 1 K1, work from chart to last stitch, k1.

Continue scallop lace (and with an extra k1 at the beginning and end of all right-side rows) until piece measures approximately 7" (18cm), after pressing. End after working Row 8 or 16.

Fagotting Lace Lower Arm

Increase row (RS) K2, p2, *k1, kf&b, p1; repeat from * to last 6 stitches, k2, p2, k2—70 stitches.

Beginning with a wrong-side row, work until fagotting lace section measures approximately 4" (10cm). End after working a wrong-side row. Cut fine yarn.

English Lace Upper Arm

Sizes S-M (L–1X) only, decrease row (RS) With larger needles and heavy yarn, *k1, k2tog, k2tog; repeat from * to last 5 stitches, k1, k2tog, k2—43 stitches.

Size 2X only, decrease row (RS) With larger needles and heavy yarn, *k2, k2tog, k1, k2tog; repeat from * to last 7 stitches, k2, k2tog, k3—51 stitches.

All sizes, next row Knit.

Beginning with Row 2, work english lace to end of Row 5.

Increase row (RS) K1, increase 1 in next stitch, work to last 2 stitches, increase 1 in next stitch, k1.

Repeat increase row every 6th row 3 (7, 7) times more—51 (59, 67) stitches.

Continue english lace until Sleeve measures approximately 21½" (54cm). End after working a wrong-side row.

(You may have an easier time reestablishing your pattern after the bind-off if you end with Row 7 or 1. If you end with Row 7, you will restart with Row 2 [8, 8]; if you end with Row 1, you will restart with Row 8 [2, 2].)

(Shorten or lengthen for Sleeve length here, page 20.)

SHAPE ARMHOLE

Bind off 4 (6, 8) stitches at the beginning of the next 2 rows—43 (47, 51) stitches.

Work 0 (2, 2) rows even.

Decrease row (RS) K1, skp, work to last 3 stitches, k2tog, k1.

Work 1 wrong-side row.

Repeat the last 2 rows 14 (15, 16) times more—13 (15, 17) stitches. End after working a wrong-side row.

Bind off.

FINISHING

Sew shoulder seams.

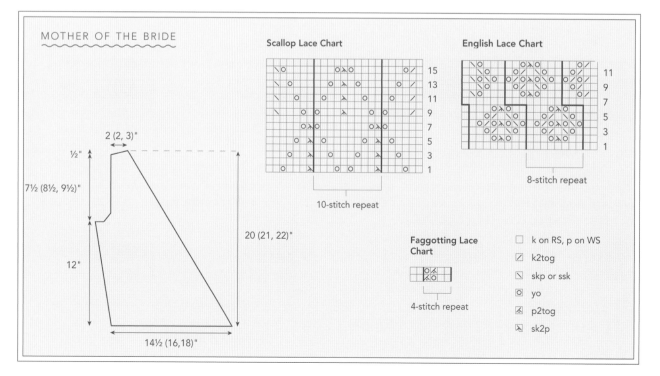

MOTHER OF THE BRIDE

Scallop Lace Chart

10-stitch repeat

English Lace Chart

8-stitch repeat

Faggotting Lace Chart

4-stitch repeat

- ☐ k on RS, p on WS
- ◢ k2tog
- ◣ skp or ssk
- ○ yo
- ◢ p2tog
- ◤ sk2p

2 (2, 3)"

½"

7½ (8½, 9½)"

12"

14½ (16,18)"

20 (21, 22)"

RIGHT FRONT COLLAR

With circular needle and fine yarn, begin at lower Right Front edge and work as follows.

Pick up and knit 1 stitch for every row up Right Front to 12" (30cm) from beginning, measuring along diagonal.

Same row, make buttonhole Turn, cast on 2 stitches. Turn, do not pick up and knit in the next 2 spaces. Continue to pick up and knit 1 stitch for every row up Right Front to shoulder seam.

[Pick up and knit 1 stitch, then make yo] in 5 places at back neck shaping and then in each bind-off stitch across the Back neck to center.

Count stitches on needle. While working the next row, make the total number of stitches a multiple of 4 stitches + 2 by increasing as follows: [yo, p1] rather than [yo, p2tog].

Next short row (WS) Beginning at center Back, *p2, yo, p2tog; repeat from * to 40 stitches, p2. (You should be close to the shoulder seam.) Turn.

Right-side rows Wyib slip 1 purlwise, k1, *yo, p2tog, k2; repeat from * to end.

Wrong-side short rows *P2, yo, p2tog; repeat from *, taking 8 more stitches into working from picked up and knit stitches. (You will always end with p2.) Turn.

**Continue until all picked up and knit stitches have been taken into working.

(Final short row will bring 8 or 4 stitches into working: it must be one or the other.)

Begin and end all following right-side rows with k2.

Continue fagotting lace until Collar measures 2" (5cm) at lower Front edge (shortest point). End after working a wrong-side row.

(Collar will measure 6½–7" ([16.5–17.5cm] at center Back.)

Next row (RS) Bind off very loosely in 2x2 rib.

LEFT FRONT COLLAR

Begin in same stitch at center back where Right Collar ends.

With circular needle and fine yarn, pick up and knit around back neck and down Left Front, as for Right Front Collar but without buttonhole.

Count stitches on needle. While working the next row, make the total number of stitches a multiple of 4 stitches + 2 by increasing as follows: [yo, p1] rather than [yo, p2tog].

Cut yarn at end of pick-up-and-knit row.

Return to center Back.

Next short row (RS) *K2, yo, p2tog; repeat from * to 40 stitches, k2—42 stitches. Turn.

Wrong-side rows Wyif slip 1 purlwise, p1, *yo, p2tog, p2; repeat from * to end.

Right-side short rows *K2, yo, p2tog; repeat from *, taking 8 more stitches into working from picked up and knit stitches. (You will always end with k2.) Turn.

Continue as for Right Front Collar from ** to end.

FINISHING

Sew center back seam of Collar.

Sew Sleeves into armholes.

Sew side and Sleeve seams.

Chains

Attach heavy yarn to the bind-off row of the Right Collar, opposite the buttonhole.

With crochet hook, chain to 18" (45cm). Cut yarn, and draw through loop.

Attach heavy yarn to the matching spot on the bind-off row of the Left Collar.

With crochet hook, chain to 24" (60cm). Cut yarn, and draw through loop.

Loop

Attach heavy yarn to the right side of the first row of the Left Collar, matching the buttonhole position of the Right Collar.

With crochet hook, chain to 1" (2.5cm). Cut yarn, and draw through loop. Sew the end of this chain to its start (to form loop).

To tie Fronts, draw Left Front chain through buttonhole on Right Front. Draw Right Front chain through loop on Left Front. Tie chains as desired.

Optional If needed, with heavy yarn, backstitch along wrong-side selvedge of Back neck to tighten.

CHAPTER THREE

❧ LIKE MOTHER, LIKE DAUGHTER...OR NOT ❧
Thoughts from an Adult Daughter

When I was growing up, my mom knew everything. It was almost as if she walked around with a light shining on her and a choir following her singing Ave Maria.

She was the grand authority on fashion, relationships, politics, history, geography, and quantum physics. I believed everything she said, and I used the information against other kids at school. My mom could do no wrong, and I wanted to be just like her when I grew up.

From thirteen to about twenty-three my mom knew nothing! She didn't understand me; she wasn't fair; she made me do everything but didn't let me do anything. And she was so embarrassing! I mean, who sings along to Guns n' Roses in a falsetto and in front of people?! If you had asked me then what I was going to do when I grew up, "writing a knitting book with my mom" would not have been my answer.

Then, at twenty-four, it hit me: I am just like my mom. I'm pretty cool, and I am just like my mom. I'm quite clever, and I am just like my mom. I'm a good friend, and I am just like my mom. I'm a good person, and I am just like my mom. I really respect my mom, and I am just like her...so that means that I really respect myself. Awesome!

I started knitting and, to my sheer astonishment, loved it. I wanted to design garments right away, and the fact that that came quite naturally to me made me realize it was definitely in my blood. I started swapping projects with my mother, and it has been so much fun seeing her knit my designs but with her own little twists. I've never heard the term two peas in a pod more in my life!

At first, the idea of being just like my mom kind of freaked me out. But it could be worse. It could be much worse. I could be nothing like her at all! ❧ —CADDY

❧ GARDEN PARTY SCARF ❧

Designed by Caddy

A LOVELY WOMAN NAMED HELEN BROUGHT ME A SCARF ONE DAY THAT SHE WANTED DUPLICATED. THE SCARF WAS SIX FEET LONG AND MADE COMPLETELY OF CROCHETED FLOWERS. NEVER ONE TO SAY "NO," I TOLD HER I WOULD MAKE MY VERSION OF IT. I CHANGED PRETTY MUCH EVERYTHING ABOUT IT, BUT SHE WAS VERY HAPPY WITH THE RESULT.

THE FLOWERS FOR THIS SCARF ARE SATISFYING TO KNIT BECAUSE THEY ARE QUICK AND CUTE. AND THE MAIN PIECES TAKE NO TIME AT ALL. THE FINISHED PRODUCT IS SOFT AND WARM BUT LOOKS MORE LIKE JEWELRY THAN A TYPICAL SCARF.

SKILL LEVEL
Easy

SIZES
- One size
- Finished length 50–54" (127–137cm)
- Finished width 3–4" (7.5–10cm)

MATERIALS
- 150 yd (135m) / 1 ball Classic Elite Princess (40% merino, 28% viscose, 15% nylon, 10% cashmere, 7% angora, each approximately 1¾ oz (50g) and 150 yd [135m]), in color 3495 Privileged Plum (MC), (4) medium/worsted weight
- 32 yd (30m) / 1 ball Classic Elite Princess, in color 3432 Majesty's Magenta (CC)
- One pair size 6 (4mm) needles
- Tapestry needle
- 8 Buttons or large beads, ½" (13mm) wide

GAUGE
20 stitches and 32 rows / 16 garter ridges = 4" in garter stitch

PATTERN NOTES
- Gauge does not matter.
- If you find that you are running out of yarn when knitting the last scarf piece, tear back from the other 2 pieces. It is important that you have 3 pieces of the same length, even if they are a little shorter than what is given in the pattern.

- Be sure to save 2 yards of MC for finishing.
- When sewing flowers to the scarf, be sure to position them so that they overlap two scarf pieces.
- Each flower takes approximately 4yd (3.6m).

SCARF
Center Piece
With MC, cast on 6 stitches.
Knit all stitches, all rows, until piece measures 50–54" (127–137cm), stretched slightly.
Bind off.

Outside Pieces (make 2)
With MC, cast on 5 stitches.
Knit to same length as Center piece.
Bind off.

FINISHING
Lay all three pieces side by side, with the Center Piece in the center. Stagger them, so that one Side Piece is 1" (2.5cm) shorter than the Center Piece and the other Side Piece is 1" (2.5cm) longer then the Center Piece. Loosely sew pieces together every 7" (17.5cm).

Flowers (Make 8)
With CC, make a slip knot.
Rows 1 & 2 K1.
Row 3 E-wrap cast on 1 stitch, k2.
Rows 4–6 K2.
Row 7 Bind off 1 stitch—1stitch.
Row 8 K1.

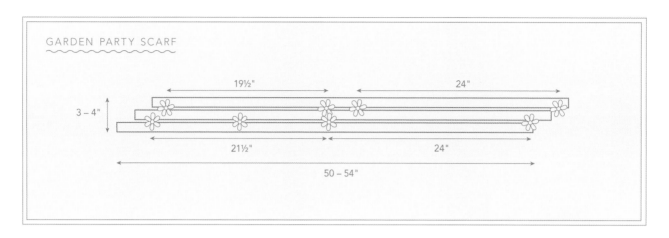

GARDEN PARTY SCARF

Row 9 K1, e-wrap cast on 1 stitch.

Leaving the first stitch from row 9 behind, repeat Rows 1–9 until there are 6 stitches on the needle.

Cut the yarn, leaving a 6" (15cm) tail.

Thread the final tail onto a tapestry needle.

Take the needle through all 6 stitches on the needle plus through the slip knot of the first petal.

Pull taut to make a circle. Sew 1 stitch at the center (to secure). Do not cut the tail.

Press to shape.

With tails, sew flowers onto scarf at 8 places shown on schematic.

Sew button or bead to the center of each flower.

HOW STEEP IS YOUR LEARNING CURVE?

SALLY: I'd say that my curve has been pretty gradual. (My first socks didn't occur until I was past fifty!) But I don't expect my curve to ever plateau, because I learn something new in every garment I design, in every piece I knit, in every class I teach.

CADDY: My friend Jen's first project was a poncho that was shown in one of my mom's books, Ali went straight to socks on #0 (2mm) double-pointed needles, Carolyn designed her own scarf after knitting for a week, and I'm writing a knitting book after knitting for only five years!

Keep in mind that knitting is in my cells. After all, I am my mother's daughter.

❖ CORSAGE CHOKER/HEADBAND ❖

Designed by Sally

I KNEW THAT CADDY WAS USING THIS YARN TO DO A SKINNY SCARF WITH FLOWERS. SO I THOUGHT, "WHAT ABOUT MAKING A SKINNY SCARF THAT BECOMES A FLOWER?" SO HERE IT IS, A SIMPLE AND SMALL STRIP OF KNITTING THAT IS RUFFLED AND THEN WRAPPED TO FORM A SORT OF FLOWER ON YOUR HEAD. THIS MAKES A GREAT CHOKER AS WELL. VERY SEX AND THE CITY!

SKILL LEVEL
Easy

SIZES
- Finished width 1¼" [3cm]
- Finished length 27 (30)" [68.5 (76)cm]

MATERIALS
Choker
- 52 yd (47m) / 1 ball Classic Elite Princess (40% merino, 28% viscose, 10% cashmere, each approximately 1¾ oz [50g] and 150 yd [135m]), in color 3458 Royal red, (4) medium/worsted weight

Headband
- 65 yd (59m) / 1 ball Berroco Suede Deluxe (85% nylon, 10% rayon, 5% polyester, each approximately 1¾ oz [50g] and 100 yd [92m]), in color 3904 Hopalong Gold, (4) medium/worsted weight

Both
- One pair size 8 (5mm) needles
- One size G-6 (4mm) crochet hook
- Tapestry needle

GAUGE
6 stitches = approximately 1¼" (3cm) in stitch pattern
6 rows = approximately 1" (2.5cm) in stitch pattern

PATTERN NOTES
- Gauge does not matter.
- The length of ruffles is the same at each end of the headband.
- The choker has fewer ruffles at one end; this creates a smaller flower that stays in place at the neck better
- The first number is for the choker, the second for the headband. When only one number is given, it applies to both versions.

CHOKER (HEADBAND)
Leaving a 15" (38cm) tail, cast on 6 stitches.
All rows P1, [yo, p2tog] twice, p1.
Continue until piece measures 48 (60)" (120 [150]cm) after stretching a little.
Bind off, leaving a 8 (15)" (20 [38]cm) tail.

MAKE RUFFLES

Measure 24" (60cm) from one end.

(You do not use new yarn to create the ruffles.)

Insert the crochet hook through the diagonal stitch at the center (to form a loop on the hook); *count 4 diagonals toward the end, draw this diagonal through the loop on the hook; repeat from * to end, then draw the cast-on or bind-off tail through the loop on the hook to secure it.

With the same tail, backstitch up the center of the ruffle on the non-hooked side, to keep it from stretching.

Measure 12" (30cm) to leave unruffled at center.

At the end of this center area, repeat the ruffle directions toward the other end.

Wrap your neck (or head) with the unruffled part of the piece. Then loosely wrap and tie the ruffles to suit and to secure.

CORSAGE CHOKER

48 (60)"

1¼"

6 (9)"   12"   9"

⤜ CORSET BELT ⤛

Designed by Caddy

BELTS ARE A PERFECT ACCESSORY TO A PLAIN DRESS OR A LONG BLOUSE: THEY REALLY SHOW OFF THE HOURGLASS. AND IT'S PROBABLY NOT OFTEN THAT WE THINK ABOUT KNITTING A BELT. BUT THE GOAL FOR THIS PATTERN WAS A BELT THAT COULDN'T BE FOUND IN A STORE, THAT IS FUN TO KNIT, AND THAT IS STRIKING ENOUGH TO TAKE THE PLACE OF JEWELRY. THE DETAIL OF WRAPPED BEADS/WASHERS, PAIRED WITH THE RIBBON, WILL BLOW PEOPLE AWAY!

SKILL LEVEL
Easy

SIZES
- XS (S, M, L, 1X)
- Finished waist (with ribbon) 23 (26, 29, 32, 35)" (58.5 [66, 73.5, 81, 89] cm)
- Finished length 17 (19, 22, 24, 26)" (43 [48.5, 56, 61, 66] cm)
- Finished height (at center) 6" (15cm)

MATERIALS
- 90 (100, 115, 130, 140) yd (80 [90, 105, 120, 130]m) / 1 (2, 2, 2, 2) skeins Prism Tulle (100% nylon, each approximately 1 oz [30g] and 96 yd [87m]), in color Fog, (4) medium/worsted weight
- One pair size 6 (4mm) needles, or size needed to obtain gauge
- Tapestry needle
- 8 plastic Washers or flat Beads with wide holes, ¾" (2cm)
- 2 yd (1.8m) Ribbon, ¾" (20mm) wide
- *Optional* 11" (28cm) boning, ¹⁄₁₆" (1mm) wide
- *Optional* Small piece of Scotch tape

GAUGE
24 stitches and 32 rows = 4" in stitch pattern

PATTERN NOTES
- The washers/beads are like flat lifesavers.
- The boning (bought at a fabric store) will come covered; cut off the cover and use only one strip— approximately ¹⁄₁₆" (1mm) wide.
- Work all increases as lifted increase.

STITCH PATTERN
(over a multiple of 8 stitches + 1)
Rows 1 and 5 *K3, p1, k1, p1, k2; repeat from * to last stitch, k1.
Rows 2 and 4 P1, *p1, k1, p3, k1, p2; repeat from *.
Row 3 *K1, p1, k1, p1, k1, p1, k1, p1; repeat from * to last stitch, k1.
Row 6 Purl. (See chart, page 96)

BELT
Cast on 29 stitches.

Next row (RS) K2, beginning with Row 1, work stitch pattern over 25 stitches, k2.

Following rows K2, work stitch pattern over 25 stitches, k2. Work even until piece measures approximately 3 (4, 5½, 6½, 7½)" (7.5 [10, 14, 16.5, 19]cm). End after working a Row 5.

First increase row (WS) K1, increase 1 in next stitch, knit to last 2 stitches, increase 1 in next stitch, k1—31 stitches. Knit 2 rows.

Following RS rows K3, beginning with Row 1, work stitch pattern over 25 stitches, k3.

Following WS rows K2, p1, work stitch pattern over 25 stitches, p1, k2.

Work even to 17 rows from increase row. End after working a Row 5.

Second increase row (WS) K1, increase 1 in next stitch, knit to last 2 stitches, increase 1 in next stitch, k1—33 stitches.

Next row (RS) Knit.

Third increase row (WS) K1, increase 1 in next stitch, knit to last 2 stitches, increase 1 in next stitch, k1—35 stitches.

Following RS rows K5, beginning with Row 1, work stitch pattern over 25 stitches, k5.

Following WS rows K2, p3, work stitch pattern over next 25 stitches, p3, k2.

Work even to 23 rows from last increase row. End after working a Row 5.

Fourth increase row (WS) K1, increase 1 in next stitch, knit to last 2 stitches, increase 1 in next stitch, k1—37 stitches.

Next row (RS) Knit.

First decrease row (WS) K2, skp, knit to last 4 stitches, k2tog, k2.

Following RS rows K5, beginning with Row 1, work stitch pattern over 25 stitches, k5.

Following WS rows K2, p3, work stitch pattern over next 25 stitches, p3, k2.

Work even to 23 rows from decrease row. End after working a Row 5.

Second decrease row (WS) K2, skp, knit to last 4 stitches, k2tog, k2—33 stitches.

Next row (RS) Knit.

Third decrease row (WS) K2, skp, knit to last 4 stitches, k2tog, k2—31 stitches.

Following RS rows K3, beginning with Row 1, work stitch pattern over 25 stitches, k3.

Following WS rows K2, p1, work stitch pattern over 25 stitches, p1, k2.

Work even to 17 rows from last decrease row. End after working a Row 5.

Fourth decrease row (WS) K2, skp, knit to last 4 stitches, k2tog, k2—29 stitches.

Knit 2 rows.

Following rows K2, beginning with Row 1, work stitch pattern over 25 stitches, k2.

Work even until piece measures 3 (4, 5½, 6½, 7½)" (7.5 [10, 14, 16.5, 19]cm) from last garter ridge. Bind off.

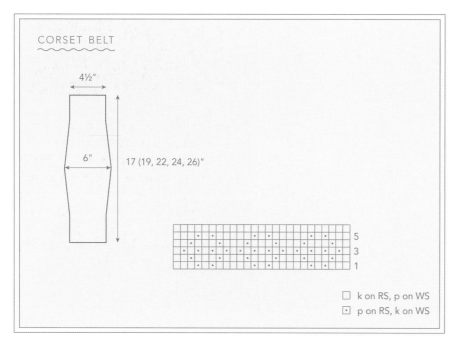

CORSET BELT

4½"

6"

17 (19, 22, 24, 26)"

5
3
1

☐ k on RS, p on WS
⊡ p on RS, k on WS

FINISHING
Lacing

Evenly space 4 washers/beads along cast-on and bind-off edges. With yarn, sew washers/beads to belt, wrapping to cover them. (Try to use the same entrance point in the center when wrapping; this will create a hole large enough to facilitate the tightening and loosening of the ribbon).

Lace the ribbon through the washers, but do not trim. (You need enough length so that you can loosen the belt to take it on and off.) Knot the ends of the ribbons.

Insert boning *(optional)*

Fold the boning so the two sharp ends meet at the center (and the boning is doubled). Join and cover the sharp ends by wrapping with tape.

With yarn, hand-sew the boning to the wrong side of the belt at center and as follows: catch a stitch, *cross over boning, catch a stitch, repeat from * to end. (Make more stitches at the top and bottom of the boning to secure and to cover the ends.)

❦ FLIRTY TOP ❧

Designed by Sally

I WANTED TO USE THE TULLE (THAT CADDY HAD CHOSEN) IN COMBINATION WITH ANOTHER YARN. BUT HOW? AS COLLAR AND CUFFS? AS FRONT BANDS? AS DETAILS? IN THE END, FOR A BOOK DEDICATED TO THE HOURGLASS SHAPE, I CHOSE TO OFFER SOMETHING THAT ENHANCES OUR FEMININE CURVES—SOMETHING FOR THE MORE ANGULAR WOMAN WITH NOT AS MUCH DIFFERENTIATION BETWEEN BUST AND WAIST AS SHE WOULD LIKE OR FOR THE WOMAN WHO IS OH-SO-PROUD OF HER CURVES. THIS ENHANCEMENT COMES THROUGH COVERAGE OF THE BUST (BECAUSE NOTHING ENHANCES AS MUCH AS COMPLETE AND UNINTERRUPTED COVERAGE), SHAPING AT THE WAIST, AND RUFFLING OVER THE HIPS.

SKILL LEVEL
Intermediate

SIZES
- XS (S, M, L, 1X)
- Finished bust 34 (39, 43, 48, 53)" 86 [99, 109, 122, 134.5]cm)
- Finished waist 27½ (32, 36½, 41, 45½)" (70 [81, 92.5, 104, 115.5]cm)
- Finished length (at center back, including ruffle) 24 (25, 25½, 26½, 27½)" (61 [63.5, 64.5, 67, 70]cm)
- Finished length (at sides, including ruffle) 21 (21½, 22, 22½, 23)" (53 [54.5, 56, 57, 58]cm)
- Finished waist length 16½ (17, 17½, 18, 18½)" (42 [43, 44, 45.5, 47]cm)
- Finished shoulder width 14½ (14½, 15, 15, 15½)" 37 [37, 38, 38, 39.5]cm)
- Finished sleeve length (including ruffle) 24 (24½, 26, 27½, 28½)" (61 [62, 66, 69.5, 72]cm)

MATERIALS
- 630 (700, 770, 850, 910) yd (570 [630, 695, 765, 820]m) / 6 (6, 7, 7, 8) skeins Prism Pebbles (MC) (100% nylon, each approximately 2 oz [60g] and 123 yd [111m]), in color Smoke, ⓘ medium/worsted weight
- 520 (575, 635, 690, 750) yd (470 [520, 570, 620, 675]m) / 6 (6, 7, 8, 8) skeins of Prism Tulle (CC) (100% nylon, each approximately 1 oz [30g] and 96 yd [86m]), in color Smoke, ⓘ medium/worsted weight
- One pair size 8 (5mm) needles, or size needed to obtain gauge

- Stitch holder
- One pair size 6 (4mm) needles
- One pair size 10 (6mm) needles
- Tapestry needle

GAUGE
14 stitches and 26 rows /13 garter ridges = 4" in garter stitch, over MC and middle-size needles

PATTERN NOTES
- This garment is hourglass-shaped. The MC side seams can match your natural waist length and the ruffle can fall to your ideal mid-length at the side (page 17).
- The main pieces are knit in MC and in garter stitch, so there is no right or wrong side until the ruffle is attached.
- The ruffle is added after and worked down, in reverse stockinette (right-side purl, wrong-side knit).

BACK
With middle-size needles and MC, e-wrap cast on 8 (12, 16, 20, 24) stitches.
Knit 1 row.
*E-wrap cast on 2 stitches, knit to end.
Repeat from * 19 (21, 23, 25, 27) times more—48 (56, 64, 72, 80) stitches.
Knit 8 rows even.
Increase row K1, kf&b, knit to last 2 stitches, kf&b, k1.
Knit 7 rows even.
Repeat from the last 8 rows 5 times more—60 (68, 76, 84, 92) stitches.

Continue garter stitch until side measures 8½" (21.5cm)
(Shorten or lengthen for waist length here, page 18.)

SHAPE ARMHOLE
Bind off 2 (3, 4, 5, 6) stitches at the beginning of the next
2 rows—56 (62, 68, 74, 80) stitches.
Decrease row K1, skp, knit to last 3 stitches, k2tog, k1.
Knit 1 row.
Repeat the last 2 rows 2 (5, 7, 10, 12) times more—50 (50,
52, 52, 54) stitches.
(Adjust shoulder width here, page 19.)
Continue garter stitch until armhole measures 7 (7½, 8,
8½, 9)" (17.5 [19, 20.5, 21.5, 23]cm).

SHAPE RIGHT SHOULDER AND BACK NECK
Bind off 3 (3, 4, 4, 4) stitches at the beginning of the next
row, knit to 8 (8, 8, 8, 9) stitches on right needle. Place
remaining 39 (39, 40, 40, 41) stitches on holder. Turn.
*Next row Wyif slip 1 purlwise, bind off 1 stitch at neck
edge, knit to end.
Bind off 3 (3, 3, 3, 4) stitches at armhole edge.
Next row Wyif slip 1 purlwise, bind off 1 stitch at neck
edge, knit to end.

Bind off final 3 stitches.

SHAPE LEFT SHOULDER AND BACK NECK
Return to remaining 39 (39, 40, 40, 41) stitches.
Bind off 28 stitches at neck edge, knit to end.
Bind off 3 (3, 4, 4, 4) stitches at armhole edge, knit to end.
Work as Shape Right Shoulder and Back Neck from * to
end.

Add Ruffle
Determine the right side of the Back.
With right side facing, smallest needle, and CC, pick up
and knit as follows:
1 stitch for every cast-on stitch, and 1 stitch for every 2-
row step (between cast-on stitches)—approximately 68
(78, 88, 98, 108) stitches.
Next row (WS) Knit.
Increase row (RS) [K1, yo, k1] in every stitch—
approximately 204 (234, 264, 294, 324) stitches.
Beginning with a wrong-side knit row, work reverse
stockinette to ¾" (2cm).
Change to middle-size needles. Continue reverse
stockinette for 4 more rows.

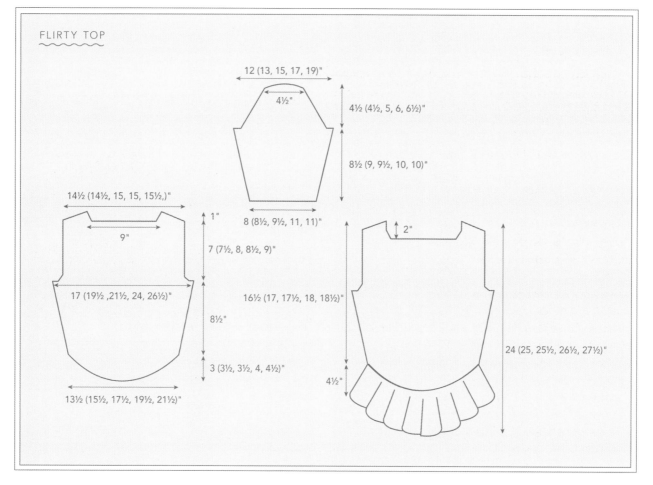

FLIRTY TOP

12 (13, 15, 17, 19)"

4½"

4½ (4½, 5, 6, 6½)"

8½ (9, 9½, 10, 10)"

14½ (14½, 15, 15, 15½,)"

1"

8 (8½, 9½, 11, 11)"

9"

7 (7½, 8, 8½, 9)"

17 (19½ ,21½, 24, 26½)"

16½ (17, 17½, 18, 18½)"

8½"

2"

3 (3½, 3½, 4, 4½)"

24 (25, 25½, 26½, 27½)"

4½"

13½ (15½, 17½, 19½, 21½)"

Change to largest needles. Continue reverse
stockinette until the ruffle measures 4½" (11.5cm). End
after working a wrong-side (knit) row.
(Shorten or lengthen for finished length here, page 18.)
Cut CC.
Next row (RS) With MC, knit.
In MC, bind off knitwise.

FRONT
Work as Back until armhole measures 6 (6½, 7, 7½, 8)"
(15 [16.5, 17.5, 19, 20.5]cm).

SHAPE RIGHT SHOULDER AND FRONT NECK
Knit to 11 (11, 12, 12, 13) stitches on right needle. Place
remaining 39 (39, 40, 40, 41) stitches on holder. Turn.
* **Next row** Wyif slip 1 purlwise, bind off 1 stitch at neck
edge, knit to end.
Knit 1 row.
Next row Wyif slip 1 purlwise, bind off 1 stitch at neck
edge, knit to end—9 (9, 10, 10, 11) stitches.
Continuing to slip 1 purlwise at neck edge, knit even
until armhole measures same length as Back.
Bind off 3 (3, 4, 4, 4) stitches at armhole edge.
Next row Wyif slip 1 purlwise, knit to end.
Bind off 3 (3, 3, 3, 4) stitches at armhole edge.
Next row Wyif slip 1 purlwise, knit to end.
Bind off final 3 stitches.

SHAPE LEFT SHOULDER AND FRONT NECK
Return to remaining 39 (39, 40, 40, 41) stitches.
Bind off 28 stitches at neck edge, knit to end.
Knit 1 row.
Work as Shape Right Shoulder and Front Neck from *
to end.
Add Ruffle as for Back.

SLEEVES
With middle-size needles and MC, e-wrap cast on 28
(30, 34, 38, 38) stitches.
Knit 8 rows.
Increase row K1, kf&b, knit to last 2 stitches, kf&b, k1.
Knit 7 (5, 5, 3, 3) rows even.
Repeat the last 8 (6, 6, 4, 4) rows 6 (7, 8, 10, 13) times
more—42 (46, 52, 60, 66) stitches.
Work even until piece measures 8½ (9, 9½, 10, 10)" (21.5
[23, 24, 25.5, 25.5]cm).
(Shorten or lengthen for Sleeve length here, page 20.)

SHAPE ARMHOLE
Bind off 2 (3, 4, 5, 6) stitches at the beginning of the next
2 rows—38 (40, 44, 50, 54) stitches.

Decrease row K1, skp, knit to last 3 stitches, k2tog, k1.
Knit 3 rows even.
Repeat the last 4 rows twice more—32 (34, 38, 44, 48)
stitches.
Decrease row K1, skp, knit to last 3 stitches, k2tog, k1.
Knit 1 row.
Repeat the last 2 rows 7 (8, 10, 13, 15) times more—16
stitches.

HOW DID YOU LEARN TO KNIT?

SALLY: I was taught in Brownies. I am so grateful for that experience that I taught a troop when my daughter attended. She didn't take to it, but I would like to think some of the other young girls have continued.

I don't think I ever stopped knitting after the Brownies experience. But I had to design early because I didn't know how to measure gauge, didn't naturally achieve gauge, and nothing fit. All this struggle was one of the universe's gifts!

CADDY: I can remember my mom teaching me multiple times when I was a kid. I never did take to it, though. Then one night when I was twenty-four, I came to her house to find my husband sitting on her couch. Do you know what he was doing? He was knitting!!!! I promptly tore the needles from his hands and started knitting. I was shocked to learn that I knew exactly what I was doing! And I haven't stopped since.

Bind of 2 stitches at the beginning of the next 2 rows. Bind off final 12 stitches.

Add Ruffle

Determine right side of Sleeve.

With right side facing, smallest needle, and CC, pick up and knit 1 stitch for every cast-on stitch—28 (30, 34, 38, 38) stitches.

Next row (WS) *K1, kf&b; repeat from * to end—42 (45, 51, 57, 57) stitches.

Increase row (RS) [K1, yo, k1] in every stitch—126 (135, 153, 171, 171) stitches.

Beginning with a wrong-side knit row, work reverse stockinette to ¾" (2cm).

Change to middle-size needles. Continue reverse stockinette for 4 more rows.

Change to largest needles. Continue reverse stockinette until the ruffle measures 4" (10cm). End after working a wrong-side (knit) row. Cut CC.

Next row (RS) With MC, knit.

In MC, bind off knitwise.

FINISHING

(Do not use textured yarn for seaming.)

Sew shoulder seams.

Sew Sleeves into armholes.

Sew side and Sleeve seams.

Sew ruffle seams.

If lower edge of ruffles roll under, work as follows. With lots of steam but without pressing the ruffle, steam gently. OR wet edges of all ruffles, pin edges of ruffles together (Back ruffles to Front ruffles), and let dry.

❧ BOX-PLEAT SKIRT ❧

Designed by Caddy

THIS SKIRT IS SO CUTE WORN HIGH ON THE WAIST AND WITH A SHORT SWEATER OR BLOUSE. I WORE IT FOR A FULL DAY, SAT IN IT FOR LONG PERIODS OF TIME, GOT A LOT OF COMPLIMENTS, AND AT THE END OF THE DAY WAS VERY EXCITED TO NOTICE THAT IT DIDN'T "SEAT." ALTHOUGH THE RIBBON IS SHOWN HERE IN A COMPLEMENTARY COLOR, IT CAN EASILY BE CHANGED TO MATCH ANY OUTFIT. FOR EXAMPLE, IF YOU FOUND SOME TEAL, LIME GREEN, AND PURPLE-STRIPED RIBBON, YOU COULD WEAR IT WITH YOUR LIME GREEN SHOES, YOUR TEAL BLOUSE, AND YOUR PURPLE TIGHTS—ALL AT THE SAME TIME! FINALLY!

SKILL LEVEL
Intermediate

SIZES
- XS (S, M, L 1X)
- Finished hem 49 (53½, 58, 63, 67½)" (124.5 [136, 147, 160, 171] cm)
- Finished waist 22 (26½, 31, 35½ , 40)" (56 [67.5, 79, 90.5, 101.5] cm)
- Finished length (including waistband) 20½ (21, 21½, 22, 22½)" (52 [53.5, 54.5, 56, 57]cm)

MATERIALS
- 865 (940, 1015, 1090, 1165) yd (780 [845, 915, 980, 1050]m) / 6 (7, 7, 8, 8) balls Classic Elite 150 (100% fine merino, each approximately 1¾ oz [50g] and 150 yd [137m]), in color 7238 Chestnut, 🔳3 light/double knitting
- One pair size 6 (4mm) needles, or size needed to obtain gauge
- One stitch holder
- Tapestry needle
- 1 (1, 1, 1.5, 1.5) yd (.9 [.9, .9, 1.4, 1.4]m) Elastic, ½" (13mm) wide
- 1.5 (2, 2, 2.5, 2.5) yd (1.4 [1.8, 1.8, 2.3, 2.3]m) Ribbon, ⅝" (16mm) wide

GAUGE
21 stitches and 28 rows = 4" in stockinette stitch.

PATTERN NOTES

- The schematic shows the skirt front with the pleats folded at top but open at bottom. This folding will take 6" (15cm) from the width of the skirt at the waist. The rib at the waistband will then make the waist a further 4" (10cm) narrower.
- The ribbon is to cover the elastic and provide a decorative element to the finished skirt.

FRONT

Cast on 140 (152, 164, 176, 188) stitches.

Set-up row (RS) K22 (26, 30, 34, 38) stitches, slip 1 purlwise (outside fold), k3, wyif slip 1 purlwise (inside fold), k30, wyif slip 1 purlwise (inside fold), k3, slip 1 purlwise (outside fold), k16 (20, 24, 28, 32), slip 1 purlwise (outside fold), k3, wyif slip 1 purlwise (inside fold), k30, wyif slip 1 purlwise (inside fold), k3, slip 1 purlwise (outside fold), knit to end.

*All WS rows Purl to first inside fold, k1, purl to next inside fold, k1, purl to next inside fold, k1, purl to next inside fold, k1, purl to end.

All RS rows Knit to first outside fold, slip 1 purlwise, k3, wyif slip 1 purlwise, knit to next inside fold, wyif slip 1 purlwise, k3, slip 1 purlwise, knit to next outside fold, slip 1 purlwise, k3, wyif slip 1 purlwise, knit to next inside fold, wyif slip 1 purlwise, k3, slip 1 purlwise, knit to end.

Repeat the last 2 rows to 7 (11, 15, 19, 23) rows. End after working a wrong-side row.

(Shorten or lengthen here by working fewer or more rows even.)

Decrease row (RS) Knit to outside fold, slip 1 purlwise, k3, wyif slip 1 purlwise, skp, knit to 2 stitches before next inside fold, k2tog, wyif slip 1 purlwise, k3, slip 1 purlwise, knit to next outside fold, slip 1 purlwise, k3, wyif slip 1 purlwise, skp, knit to 2 stitches before next inside fold, k2tog, wyif slip 1 purlwise, k3, slip 1 purlwise, knit to end.

Repeat from * 10 times more, working 11 rows (for all sizes) between decreases each time (and ignoring direction to shorten or lengthen) until 8 stitches remain between inside folds—96 (108, 120, 132, 144) stitches. End after working 11 rows even.

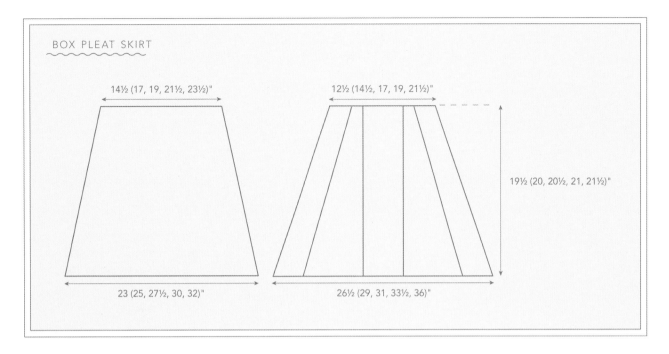

BOX PLEAT SKIRT

14½ (17, 19, 21½, 23½)"

12½ (14½, 17, 19, 21½)"

19½ (20, 20½, 21, 21½)"

23 (25, 27½, 30, 32)"

26½ (29, 31, 33½, 36)"

Piece measures approximately 19½ (20, 20½, 21, 21½)" (49.5 [51, 52, 53.5, 54.5]cm).
Bind off loosely.

Waistband

Block Front to fold pleats. With pleats folded down, right side facing, and beginning at bind-off edge, pick up and knit 1 stitch for every bind-off stitch along entire waist edge, working through all 3 layers of all pleats—62 (74, 86, 98, 110) stitches.

(You will pick up and knit 4 stitches along the folded part of each pleat and 1 stitch between the pleats.)

(You don't need to attain the number of stitches suggested, but you should be close. And you should have an even number.)

Work 1x1 rib for 1" (2.5cm). End after working a wrong-side row.

Next row (RS) Work 1x1 rib over 31 (37, 43, 49, 55) stitches. Place these stitches on a holder. Work 1x1 rib to end.

Work 1x1 rib over 31 (37, 43, 49, 55) stitches for 1" (2.5cm), then bind off in rib.

Return to stitches on holder, work 1x1 rib for 1" (2.5 cm), then bind off in rib.

BACK

Cast on 120 (132, 144, 156, 168) stitches. Work stockinette for 3 (5, 9, 13, 17) rows.

Decrease row (RS) K1, skp, knit to last 3 stitches, k2tog, k1.

Work 5 rows even.

Repeat the last 6 rows 21 times more—76 (88, 100, 112, 124) stitches.

Work even until piece measures the same length as Front to waistband. End after working a wrong-side row.

Waistband

Work 1x1 rib for 2" (5cm). Bind off in rib.

FINISHING

Block Back.

Sew side seams, leaving final 1" (2.5cm) of ribbing open at waistband.

Fold waistband over to right side, and loosely sew bind-off row to pick-up-and-knit row.

(You will have 3 vertical slits, at front and sides, for elastic and ribbon.)

Thread the elastic through the waistband. Try the skirt on, and pull the elastic tight enough to snugly fit your waist but to slide off your hips easily. Tie or pin the elastic in place. Remove the skirt, and secure the elastic.

Thread the ribbon through the waistband to cover the elastic. Tie a bow or leave the ribbon hanging in front. Trim to suit.

A GRAY CARDIGAN

Designed by Sally

A FRIEND, AND WONDERFUL KNITTER, SHARED WITH ME THAT SHE NEEDED A GRAY CARDIGAN. SHE'D SEE ONE AT THE GAP AND NOT BUY IT BECAUSE SHE COULD KNIT ONE HERSELF. BUT SHE WOULDN'T KNIT IT BECAUSE IT WAS JUST A GRAY CARDIGAN. (SHE LAUGHED AT HERSELF WHEN SHE TOLD THIS STORY.) I THINK IT'S A SHAME WHEN WE DON'T KNIT WHAT WE WILL WEAR PROUDLY AND CONSTANTLY: THE GRAY CARDIGAN THAT DEFINES CLASSIC KNITTING. SO HERE'S ONE WITH STYLING DETAILS TO KEEP YOU EN-GAGED THROUGH THE KNITTING AND THAT WILL MAKE YOU WANT TO WEAR IT OFTEN AND FOREVER.

SKILL LEVEL
Intermediate

SIZES
- S (M, L, 1X, 2X)
- Finished bust 37 (41, 46, 50, 53)" (94 [104, 116.5, 127, 134.5]cm)
- Finished length 20 (20½, 21, 21½, 22)" (50.5 (52, 53.5, 54.5, 56]cm)
- Finished shoulder width 15½" (39.5cm)
- Finished sleeve length 28½ (29, 29½, 30, 30½)" 72 [73.5, 75, 76, 77.5]cm)

MATERIALS
- 960 (1060, 1180, 1280, 1380) yd (865 [960, 1065, 1150, 1245]m) / 7 (8, 8, 9, 10) balls Classic Elite Classic One Fifty (100% merino wool, each approximately 1¾ oz [50g] and 150 yd [137m]), in color 7275 Granite, ③ light/double knitting
- One pair size 6 (4mm) needles, or size needed to obtain gauge
- One pair size 4 (3.5mm) needles
- 3 Stitch holders
- Cable needle
- Tapestry needle
- Stitch marker
- 7 Buttons, ⁵⁄₁₆" (8mm) wide

GAUGE
20 stitches and 29 rows = 4" (10cm) in stockinette stitch, over larger needles

PATTERN NOTES
- This garment is short and unshaped except for a narrowing between the bust and the waist: the more you press out the ribbing, the less apparent this narrowing will be.
- You may make this to your ideal short sweater length (page 17).
- Work all increases as lifted increases and as stitch pattern demands: knitwise in knit stitches and purlwise in purl stitches.
- The 6-stitch cable starts over 3 stitches, is increased to 6 before the first cable cross, and is decreased back to 3 after the final cable cross. (This prevents puckering.)
- To continue, or to work all stitches as established, means to continue in stockinette (knit on right side; purl on wrong side), or reverse stockinette (purl on right side; knit on wrong side), or in cable as established.

STITCH PATTERN
Cable Pattern (over 6 stitches)
Row 1 (RS) Slip 3 stitches from left needle onto cable needle, hold at back of work, k3 from left needle, k3 from cable needle.
Rows 2, 4, 6 (WS) P6.
Rows 3, 5 (RS) K6.

BACK
Edging
With larger needles, cable cast on 94 (102, 114, 122, 134) stitches.
RS rows *K2, p2; repeat from * to last 2 stitches, k2.
WS rows *P2, k2; repeat from * to last 2 stitches, p2.

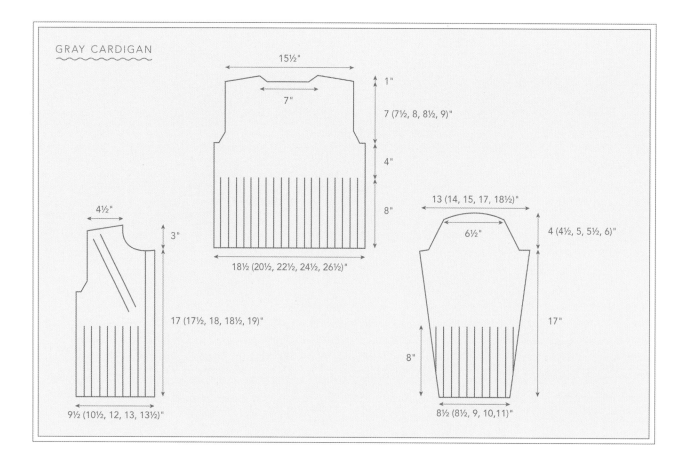

Work 2x2 rib until piece measures 8" (20.5cm). End after working a wrong-side row.
(Shorten or lengthen for finished length here, page 18.)

Body
Beginning with a knit row, work stockinette until piece measures 4" (10cm) past rib. End after working a wrong-side row.

SHAPE ARMHOLE
Bind off 4 (5, 7, 9, 11) stitches at the beginning of the next 2 rows—84 (92, 98, 104, 110) stitches.
Decrease row (RS) K1, skp, knit to last 3 stitches, k2tog, k1.
Purl 1 row.
Repeat the last 2 rows 2 (6, 9, 12, 15) times more—78 stitches.
(Adjust shoulder width here, page 19.)
Work even until armhole measures 7 (7½, 8, 8½, 9)" (17.5 [19, 20.5, 21.5, 23]cm). End after working a wrong-side row.

SHAPE RIGHT SHOULDER AND BACK NECK
Bind off 6 stitches at the beginning of the next right-side row, work to 18 stitches on right needle. Place remaining 54 stitches on holder. Turn.

*Bind off 1 stitch at the next 2 neck edges and 5 stitches at the next 2 armhole edges.
Bind off 6 stitches at the final armhole edge.

SHAPE LEFT SHOULDER AND BACK NECK.
Return to remaining 54 stitches, right side facing. Place first 30 stitches on holder. Knit 1 row over 24 stitches.
Bind off 6 stitches at the next armhole edge.
Work as Shape Right Shoulder and Back Neck, from * to end.

LEFT FRONT
Edging
With larger needles, cable cast on 48 (52, 60, 64, 68) stitches.
Row 1 (RS) K2, *p2, k2; repeat from * to last 10 stitches, p2, k3, p2, k3.
Row 2 P3, k2, increase 1 in each of the next 3 stitches, k2, *p2, k2; repeat from * to last 2 stitches, p2—51 (55, 63, 67, 71) stitches.
Next row (RS) K2, *p2, k2; repeat from * to last 13 stitches, p2, work Row 1 of cable over next 6 stitches, p2, k3.
Following WS rows P3, k2, p6, k2, *p2, k2; repeat from * to last 2 stitches, p2.

Following RS rows K2, *p2, k2; repeat from * to last 13 stitches, p2, work cable over next 6 stitches, p2, k3.
Work 2x2 rib + cable until rib is the same length as Back. End after working a wrong-side row.

Body

RS rows Knit to last 13 stitches, p2, work cable over next 6 stitches, p2, k3.
WS rows P3, k2, p6, k2, purl to end.
Continue as established to 10 rows above rib. End after working a wrong-side row.

Insert Cable

Next row (RS) Knit to last 23 stitches, pm, p1, k3, p1, k5, p2, work cable over next 6 stitches, p2, k3.
Next row P3, k2, p6, k2, p5, increase 1 in each of the next 5 stitches, purl to end—56 (60, 68, 72, 76) stitches.
Next row (RS) Knit to last 28 stitches, p2, work Row 1 of cable over next 6 stitches, p2, k5, p2, work cable over next 6 stitches, p2, k3.
Next row (WS) P3, k2, p6, k2, p5, k2, p6, k2, purl to end.
Row 1, move cable (RS) Knit to 2 stitches before marker, k2tog, p2, work cable over next 6 stitches, increase 1 in next stitch, knit into second stitch on left needle, then knit into first stitch on left needle, knit to last 13 stitches, p2, work cable over 6 stitches, p2, k3.
Rows 2 and 4 P3, k2, p6, k2, purl to 10 stitches before marker, k2, p6, k2, purl to end.
Row 3 Knit to marker, p2, work cable over next 6 stitches, p2, knit to last 13 stitches, p2, work cable over next 6 stitches, p2, k3.
Repeat the last 4 rows until piece measures the same as Back to armhole. End after working a wrong-side row.

SHAPE ARMHOLE

Continue to work the last 4 rows, moving cable every 4th row, while shaping armhole as follows.
Bind off 4 (5, 7, 9, 11) stitches at the beginning of the next right-side row—52 (55, 61, 63, 65) stitches.
Work 1 wrong-side row.
Decrease row (RS) K1, skp, work all stitches as established.
Repeat the last 2 rows 3 (6, 12, 14, 16) times more—48 stitches.
(Adjust shoulder width as for Back.)
Work even until Armhole measures 5 (5½, 6, 6½, 7)" (12.5 [14, 15, 16.5, 17.5]cm). End after working a right-side-side row.
Next row (WS) P3, k2, [p2tog] 3 times, k2, work all remaining stitches as established—45 stitches.

SHAPE NECK

Continue moving cable every 4th row, while shaping neck as follows.
Next row (RS) Work all stitches as established to last 10 stitches. Place remaining 10 stitches on holder. Turn.
Bind off 2 stitches at the next 2 neck edges and 1 stitch at the next 4 neck edges—27 stitches.
Discontinue moving cable if right-side rows begin with k3, p2.
Work even to same length as Back to shoulder. End after working a right-side row.
Next row (WS) Work all stitches as established to 10 stitches before marker, k2tog, [p2tog] 3 times across 6 stitches of cable, k2tog, purl to end—22 stitches. Remove marker.

SHAPE SHOULDER

Bind off 6 stitches at the next armhole edge, 5 stitches at the next 2 armhole edges, then 6 stitches at the final armhole edge.

RIGHT FRONT
Edging

With larger needles, cable cast on 48 (52, 60, 64, 68) stitches.
Row 1 (RS) K3, p2, k3, p2, *k2, p2; repeat from * to last 2 stitches, k2.
Row 2 P2, *k2, p2; repeat from * to last 10 stitches, k2, increase 1 in each of the next 3 stitches, k2, p3—51 (55, 63, 67, 71) stitches.
Next row (RS) K3, p2, work Row 1 of cable over next 6 stitches, p2, *k2, p2; repeat from * to last 2 stitches, k2.
Following WS rows P2 *k2, p2; repeat from * to last 13 stitches, k2, p6, k2, p3.
Following RS rows K3, p2, work cable over next 6 stitches, p2, *k2, p2; repeat from * to last 2 stitches, k2.
Work 2x2 rib + cable until rib is the same length as Back. End after working a wrong-side row.

Body

RS rows K3, p2, work cable over next 6 stitches, p2, knit to end.
WS rows Purl to last 13 stitches, k2, p6, k2, p3.
Continue as established to 10 rows above rib. End after working a wrong-side row.

Insert Cable

Next row (RS) K3, p2, work cable over next 6 stitches, p2, k5, p1, k3, p1, knit to end.
Next row Purl to last 23 stitches, increase 1 in each of the

next 5 stitches, p5, k2, p6, k2, p3—56 (60, 68, 72, 76) stitches.

Next row (RS) K3, p2, work cable over next 6 stitches, p2, k5, p2, pm, work row 1 of cable over next 6 stitches, p2, knit to end.

Next row (WS) Purl to last 28 stitches, k2, p6, k2, p5, k2, p6, k2, p3.

Row 1, move cable (RS) K3, p2, work cable over next 6 stitches, p2, knit to 3 stitches before marker, knit into back of second stitch on left needle, then knit into first stitch on left needle, increase 1 in next stitch, work cable over next 6 stitches, p2, skp, knit to end.

Rows 2 and 4 Purl to 8 stitches before marker, k2, p6, k2, purl to last 13 stitches, k2, p6, k2, p3.

Row 3 K3, p2, work cable over next 6 stitches, p2, knit to 2 stitches before marker, p2, work cable over next 6 stitches, p2, knit to end.

Repeat the last 4 rows until piece measures the same as Back to armhole. End after working a right-side row.

SHAPE ARMHOLE

Continue to work the last 4 rows, moving cable every 4th row, while shaping armhole as follows.

Bind off 4 (5, 7, 9, 11) stitches at the beginning of the next wrong-side row—52 (55, 61, 63, 65) stitches.

Decrease row (RS) Work all stitches as established to last 3 stitches, k2tog, k1.

Work 1 wrong-side row.

Repeat the last 2 rows 3 (6, 12, 14, 16) times more—48 stitches.

(Adjust shoulder width as for Back.)

Work even until armhole measures same length as Left Front to shoulder. End after working a right-side row.

Next row (WS) Work all stitches as established to last 13 stitches, k2, [p2tog] 3 times, k2, p3—45 stitches.

Work 1 right-side row.

SHAPE NECK

Continue moving cable every 4th row, while shaping the neck as follows.

Next row (WS) Work all stitches as established to last 10 stitches. Place remaining 10 stitches on holder. Turn.

Bind off 2 stitches at the next 2 neck edges and 1 stitch at the next 4 neck edges—27 stitches.

Discontinue moving cable if right-side rows end with p2, k3.

Work even to same length as Back to shoulder. End after working a right-side row.

Next row (WS) Work all stitches as established to 8 stitches before marker, k2tog, [p2tog] 3 times across

6 stitches of cable, k2tog, purl to end—22 stitches. Remove marker.

SHAPE SHOULDER

Work as Left Front, Shape Shoulder.

SLEEVES

Edging

With larger needles, cable cast on 42 (42, 46, 50, 54) stitches.

RS rows *K2, p2; repeat from * to last 2 stitches, k2.

WS rows *P2, k2; repeat from * to last 2 stitches, p2.

Work 2x2 rib until piece measures 3" (7.5cm). End after working a wrong-side row.

Increase row (RS) K2, increase 1 in next stitch, work as established to last 3 stitches, increase 1 in next stitch, k2.

(Work first 2 increases as right-side knits; work next 2 increases as right-side purls, etc.)

Work 5 rows as established.

Repeat last 6 rows until piece measures 8" (20.5cm). End after working a wrong-side row.

Body

Continue in stockinette for duration of Sleeve. AT THE SAME TIME, repeat increase row every 6th (6th, 6th, 4th, 4th) row—66 (70, 76, 84, 92) stitches.

Work even until piece measures 17" (43cm). End after working a wrong-side row.

(Shorten or lengthen for Sleeve length here, page 20.)

SHAPE SLEEVE CAP

Bind off 4 (5, 7, 9, 11) stitches at the beginning of the next 2 rows—58 (60, 62, 66, 70) stitches.

Decrease row (RS) K1, skp, work to last 3 stitches, k2tog, k1.
Purl 1 row.
Repeat the last 2 rows 11 (12, 13, 15, 17) times more—34 stitches.
Bind off 2 stitches at the beginning of the next 2 rows.
Bind off 4 stitches at the beginning of the next 2 rows.
Bind off final 22 stitches.

FINISHING
Sew shoulder seams.

Neck Edging
With smaller needles and right side facing, begin at Right Front neck to pick up and knit as follows:
k3, p2, k3, p2 from stitches on holder at Right Front neck edge, 1 stitch for every bind-off stitch and 1 stitch for every 2-row step between bind-off stitches around front and back neck shaping, 1 stitch for every stitch on holder at center back neck, 2 stitches for every 3 rows along rows worked even, p2, k3, p2, k3 from stitches on holder at Left Front neck edge.—10 stitches at edges, 86 stitches between—106 stitches in total.
(Count stitches on needle. Increase or decrease on next row to attain this number.)
Next row (WS) P3, k2, p2tog, p1, *k2, p2; repeat from * to last 10 stitches, k2, p2tog, p1, k2, p3.
Work 1 row as established, then bind off in pattern.

Left Front Button Band
With smaller needles and right side facing, begin at the top of the Left Front to pick up and knit 5 stitches for every 6 rows along the Front edge.
Count stitches on needle. While working the next row, increase or decrease to make a multiple of 4 stitches + 2.
Next row (WS) P2, *k2, p2; repeat from * to end.
Work 2 more rows rib, then bind off in pattern.
Mark spaces for 7 evenly spaced buttons. (Place the first one ½–1" [1.5–2.5cm] from the upper edge and the final one 1–2" [2.5–5cm] from the lower edge.)

Right Front Buttonhole Band
With smaller needle and right side facing, begin at bottom of Right Front to pick up and knit 5 stitches for every 6 rows along Front edge.
Count stitches on needle. While working next row, increase or decrease to make a multiple of 4 stitches + 2.
Next row (WS), make buttonholes P2, *k2, p2; repeat from * to end. AT THE SAME TIME, make 7 buttonholes at marked spots by [k2tog, yo].
Work 2 more rows in rib, then bind off in pattern.
Sew buttons onto Left Front band to correspond to buttonholes on Right Front band.
Sew Sleeves into armholes.
Sew side and Sleeve seams.
If waistband rib is tight, steam-press open to desired shape.

WHAT DO YOU LIKE TO KNIT?

SALLY: My favorite thing to do is to take something from my closet that I love and then to reinterpret it into knitting.

Otherwise I'd say that my favorite knitting is textural: this is what knitting does beautifully...and no other craft does as well.

CADDY: I love attempting to invent. When I was little I used to make outfits by taking sheets and wrapping them around me (or my poor niece!). Keeping it simple but interesting in the construction and the way that a garment can be worn is my favorite way to knit.

⋊ INSIDE-OUT PANEL SUIT ⋉

Designed by Sally

I BASED THIS OUTFIT ON A SUIT I BOUGHT RATHER IMPULSIVELY IN AN AIRPORT. THE SUIT'S SKIRT HAD BLACK-EDGED PANELS WITH SEAMS TO THE OUTSIDE. IT TOOK SOME EXPERIMENTATION, BUT IT WAS GREAT FUN TO FIND THIS METHOD FOR KNITTING A SIMILAR EFFECT. AND WHILE THE VEST IS CERTAINLY MORE COMPLEX THAN THE SKIRT (DUE TO ALL ITS SHAPING), THE TECHNIQUE IS NOT DIFFICULT TO EXECUTE. IF YOU ARE A LESS EXPERIENCED KNITTER, THEN MAKE ONLY THE SKIRT! ITS PANELS ARE PERFECT TAKE-ALONG KNITTING.

SKILL LEVEL

Skirt
Intermediate

Vest
Experienced

SIZES

- S (M, L, 1X, 2X)

Skirt
- Finished waist (before elastic) 27½ (31½, 35½, 40, 44)" (70 [80, 90, 101.5, 111.5]cm)
- Finished hem 57 (61, 65, 69½, 73½)" (145 [155, 165, 176.5, 186.5]cm)
- Finished length (with waistband) 25 (25½, 26, 26½, 27)" (63.5 [65, 66, 67, 68.5]cm)

Vest
- Finished hem 37 (40, 43, 47, 51)" (94 [101.5, 109, 119, 129.5[cm)
- Finished bust 34½ (38, 41½, 46, 50½)" (87.5 [96.5, 105, 117, 128]cm)
- Finished waist 32 (35, 38, 42, 46)" (81 [89, 96, 106.5, 116.5]cm)
- Finished length 20 (20½, 21, 21½, 22)" (50.5 [52, 53, 54.5, 56]cm)
- Finished shoulder width 15"
- Finished waist length 15 (15½, 16, 16½, 17)"

MATERIALS

Skirt
- 790 (880, 970, 1055, 1190) yd (711 [792, 873, 950, 1071]m) / 5 (6, 6, 7, 7) skeins Lanaknits Hemp for Knitting All Hemp 6 (100% long fiber hemp, each approximately 3½ oz [100g] and 165 yd [150m]), in color 015 teal (MC), **3** light/double knitting
- 150 yd (135m) / 1 skein of Lanaknits Hemp for Knitting All Hemp 6, in color 029 black (CC)
- 1yd (1m) Elastic, ¾" (19mm) wide
- *Optional* small crochet hook

Vest
- 570 (640, 715, 815, 900) yd (513 [576, 644, 734, 810]m) / 4 (4, 5, 5, 6) skeins Lanaknits Hemp for Knitting All Hemp 6), in color 015 teal (MC), **3** light/double knitting
- 140 yd (126m) / 1 skein of Lanaknits Hemp for Knitting All Hemp 6, in color 029 black (CC)
- Cable needle (cn)
- 2 Stitch holders
- 3 Buttons, 1" (25mm) wide
- *Optional* 3 Buttons, ½" (13mm) wide

Skirt and Vest
- One pair size 5 (3.75 mm) needles, or size needed to obtain gauge
- One size 3 (3.25mm) circular needle, 16–20" (40–50cm)
- Tapestry needle

GAUGE
19 stitches and 26 rows = 4" in stockinette stitch, over larger needles and before washing.

PATTERN NOTES

For both patterns
- Use larger needles until finishing.
- The knitted cast-on works best.
- Work all increases as lifted increase.

For the skirt only
- The skirt is made in 10 panels that are seamed.

For the vest only
- This garment is short with a little waist shaping. You could make it to your ideal short sweater length, or your ideal mid-length, or between (page 17).
- It is also high-waisted. You may adjust waist length between the waist and the armhole and finished length before the waist (page 17).
- Each front is two pieces to the bust, and the back is four pieces to the bust and has a center seam. The schematics show the front and back measurements after seaming.
- The purl side is the right side of the finished piece; if you forget this, it may seem as if the directions are reversed. (The Right Front refers to what sits on the right when worn.)
- Slip all stitches purlwise and with yarn on the purl side.

STITCH PATTERN

Knit rows K1 in CC; knit in MC to last stitch; k1 in CC.
Purl rows K1 in CC; purl in MC to last stitch; k1 in MC.
Always cross yarns at the color change by taking the previous color over the next color. And always cross on the purl side of the piece. (Even though the purl side is the right side of the garment, this color cross will tuck behind the seam allowance.)

SKIRT PANELS (Make 10)

With CC, cast on 1 stitch; with MC, cast on 15 (17, 19, 21, 23) stitches; with CC, cast on 1 stitch—17 (19, 21, 23, 25) stitches.
Work stitch pattern to 10 rows from beginning. End after working a purl row.
Increase row K1 in CC; in MC, k1, increase 1 in next stitch, knit to last 3 stitches, increase 1 in next stitch, k1; k1 in CC.
Continue with purl and knit rows for 19 more rows.
Repeat the last 20 rows 7 times more—31 (33, 35, 37, 39) stitches.
(Shorten or lengthen by working fewer or more rows between increases each time.)
Work 16 (19, 22, 25, 28) more rows.
Bind off, leaving long MC tail for seaming.

FINISHING

Steam-press pieces.
With knit side facing, and taking 1 CC and 1 MC stitch from each side into each seam allowance, sew pieces together.
Turn piece so purl side is facing; steam-press seams flat.

Waistband

With purl side facing, and with smaller needle, pick up and knit 1 stitch in every stitch around waist of skirt—approximately 130 (150, 170, 190, 210) stitches.
(In overlap of seams, pick up and knit 1–2 stitches for each seam, through both layers. Use a crochet hook to make this easier.)
Count stitches.
Next round Turn, slip 1, knit remaining stitches and decrease evenly to 120 (140, 160, 180, 200) stitches.
Knit in rounds to 1½" (3.8cm)—twice the height of the elastic.
Bind off very loosely, leaving a long tail for seaming.
Turn the waistband over so the purl side of the waistband is the right side, inserting the elastic between the layers.
Loosely sew the bind-off edge to the waistband selvedge, over the elastic, and leaving a small hole open for the remaining elastic.
Tie or pin the elastic ends together. Try the skirt on, and pull the elastic to fit.
Sew the ends of the elastic securely together, and trim the excess. Tuck the ends inside the waistband.
Sew the small hole closed.
To soften the fabric, wash in warm water and dry flat.

VEST

Right Back Side Piece

Cut 6½ yd (6m) and 2 yd (1.8m) strands of CC.
(For larger sizes, cut slightly more CC here and in all following directions.)
With longer strand of CC, cast on 1 stitch; with MC, cast on 27 (29, 31, 34, 37) stitches; with shorter strand of CC, cast on 1 stitch—29 (31, 33, 36, 39) stitches.
*Beginning with a knit row, work, stitch pattern for 2 rows. (Lengthen for finished length here by working more rows before decrease row, page 18.)
Decrease (knit) row K1 in CC; in MC, k1, skp, knit to last 4 stitches, k2tog, k1; k1 in CC.
Work 13 rows even.
Repeat the last 14 rows twice more—23 (25, 27, 30, 33) stitches. End after working 13 rows even.
Increase (knit) row K1 in CC; in MC, k1, increase 1 in next stitch 1, knit to last 3 stitches, increase 1 in next stitch, k1; k1 in CC.
Work 11 (13, 15, 17, 19) rows even.
(Shorten or lengthen for waist length here by changing the number of rows worked even between increases, page 18.)
Repeat increase row—27 (29, 31, 34, 37) stitches.
Work 2 rows even. End after working a knit row.
Do not cut MC or long strand of CC.

Place stitches on holder.

Right Back Center Piece
Cut 5 yd (4.5m) and 2 yd (1.8m) strands of CC.
With shorter strand of CC, cast on 1 stitch; with MC, cast on 20 (22, 24, 26, 28) stitches; with longer strand of CC, cast on 1 stitch—22 (24, 26, 28, 30) stitches.
**Work stitch pattern to same number of rows as Side piece. End after working a knit row.
Cut MC, leaving long tail for seaming. Do not cut long strand of CC.

JOIN RIGHT BACK PIECES
With knit side facing, use MC tail to sew side and center pieces together, taking 1 CC and 1 MC stitch from each edge into seam allowance.
Next (purl) row K1 in CC; in MC, purl to 4 stitches before seam, slip next 2 stitches from the left needle onto the right, slip next 2 stitches onto cn and hold at front, return previous 2 stitches to the left needle, turn cn to its own wrong side, [p2tog—1 stitch from left needle and 1 stitch from cn] twice, slip next 2 stitches onto cn and hold at front, turn cn to its own wrong side, [p2tog—1 stitch from left needle and 1 stitch from cn] twice, purl to last stitch; k1 in CC—45 (49, 53, 58, 63) stitches.
Work knit and purl rows for 6 rows.

Increase (knit) row K1 in CC; in MC, knit to last 3 stitches, increase 1 in next stitch, k1; k1 in CC.
Work 7 rows even.
Repeat last 8 rows once more—47 (51, 55, 60, 65) stitches.
Work even in knit and purl rows until piece measure 11½" (29cm). End after working a knit row.

SHAPE RIGHT BACK ARMHOLE
Next (purl) row In CC, bind off 4 (5, 7, 9, 11) stitches; in MC, purl to last stitch; k1 in CC. (First and last stitch of row are in CC.)
Decrease (knit) row K1 in CC; in MC, knit to last 4 stitches, k2tog, k1; k1 in CC.
Repeat decrease row every knit row 3 (6, 8, 11, 14) times more—39 stitches. Adjust shoulder width here. (See page 19.)
Work even in knit and purl rows until armhole measures 7 (7½, 8, 8½, 9)" (18 [19, 20, 21.5, 22.5]cm). End after working a purl row.

SHAPE RIGHT BACK SHOULDER AND NECK
Discontinue using CC's, but do not cut CC at armhole edge. Shape by short-rowing as follows and in MC only.
Next row Knit to last 5 stitches. Turn.
Next row Slip 1, purl to last 16 stitches. Place these 16 stitches onto holder for neck. Turn.

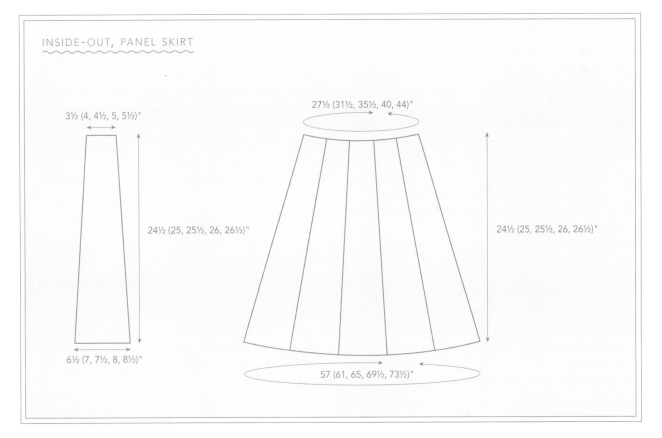

INSIDE-OUT, PANEL SKIRT

3½ (4, 4½, 5, 5½)"

27½ (31½, 35½, 40, 44)"

24½ (25, 25½, 26, 26½)"

24½ (25, 25½, 26, 26½)"

6½ (7, 7½, 8, 8½)"

57 (61, 65, 69½, 73½)"

Next row Bind off 1 stitch at neck edge, knit to last 5 stitches. Turn—10 stitches left at armhole edge.
Next row Slip 1, p11.
Next row Bind off 1 stitch at neck edge, knit to last 5 stitches. Turn—15 stitches left at armhole edge.
Next row Slip 1, p5.
Cut MC. Slip 21 stitches, ready to work a purl row.
Next row In CC, bind off 2, p19.
Next row In CC, bind off purlwise.

Left Back Side Piece

Cut 6½ yd (6m) and 2 yd (1.8m) strands of CC.
With shorter strand of CC, cast on 1 stitch; with MC, cast on 27 (29, 31, 34, 37) stitches; with longer strand of CC, cast on 1 stitch—29 (31, 33, 35, 39) stitches.
Work as Right Back Side Piece from * to end, but cut MC, leaving long tail for seaming.

Left Back Center Piece

Cut 5 yd (4.5m) and 2 yd (1.8m) strands of CC.
With longer strand of CC, cast on 1 stitch; with MC, cast on 20 (22, 24, 26, 28) stitches; with shorter strand of CC, cast on 1 stitch—22 (24, 26, 28, 30) stitches.
Work as Right Back Center Piece from ** to end, but do not cut MC.

JOIN LEFT BACK PIECES
Work as for Join Right Back Pieces to increase row, then work as follows.
Increase (knit) row K1 in CC; in MC, k1, increase 1 in next stitch, knit to last stitch; k1 in CC.
Work 7 rows even.
Repeat last 8 rows once more—47 (51, 55, 60, 65) stitches.
Work knit and purl rows until piece measure same length as Right Back to armhole. End after working a purl row.

SHAPE LEFT BACK ARMHOLE
Next row In CC, bind off 4 (5, 7, 9, 11) stitches; knit in MC to last stitch; k1 in CC. (First and last stitch of row are in CC.)
Work 1 purl row.
Decrease (knit) row K1 in CC; in MC, k1, skp, knit to last stitch; k1 in CC.
Repeat decrease row every knit row 3 (6, 8, 11, 14) times more—39 stitches.
Work knit and purl rows until armhole measures same length as Right Back. End after working a knit row.

SHAPE LEFT BACK SHOULDER AND NECK
Discontinue using CC's, but do not cut CC at armhole edge.

Shape by short-rowing as follows and in MC only.
Next row Purl to last 5 stitches. Turn.
Next row Slip 1, knit to last 16 stitches. Place these 16 stitches onto holder for neck. Turn.
Next row Bind off 1 stitch at neck edge, purl to last 5 stitches. Turn—10 stitches left at armhole edge.
Next row Slip 1, k11.
Next row Bind off 1 stitch at neck edge, purl to last 5 stitches. Turn—15 stitches left at armhole edge.
Next row Slip 1, k5.
Cut MC. Slip 21 stitches, ready to work a knit row.
Next row In CC, bind off 2, k19.
Next row In CC, bind off knitwise.

Left Front Side Piece

Cut 6½ yd (6m) and 2 yd (1.8m) strands of CC.
With longer strand of CC, cast on 1 stitch; with MC, cast on 29 (31, 33, 36, 39) stitches; with shorter strand of CC, cast on 1 stitch—31 (33, 35, 38, 41) stitches.
Continue as Right Back Side Piece, from * to end—29 (31, 33, 36, 39) stitches.

Left Front Center Piece

Cut 5 yd (4.5m) and 2 yd (1.8m) strands of CC.
With shorter strand of CC, cast on 1 stitch; with MC, cast on 23 (25, 27, 29, 31) stitches; with longer strand of CC, cast on 1 stitch—25 (27, 29, 31, 33) stitches.
Continue as Right Back Center Piece, from ** to Join Pieces, but work the last knit row as follows.
Increase row K1 in CC; in MC, knit to last 3 stitches, increase 1 in next stitch, k1; k1 in CC—26 (28, 30, 32, 34) stitches.

JOIN LEFT FRONT PIECES
Work as for Join Right Back Pieces—51 (55, 59, 64, 69) stitches.
Continue working through Join Right Back Pieces to armhole—53 (57, 61, 66, 71) stitches.

SHAPE LEFT FRONT ARMHOLE
Next (purl) row In CC, bind off 5 (7, 9, 11, 13) stitches, work as established to end.
Decrease (knit) row K1 in CC; in MC, knit to last 4 stitches, k2tog, k1; k1 in CC.
Repeat decrease row every knit row 2 (4, 6, 9, 12) times more—45 stitches.
Work even in knit and purl rows until armhole measures 4½ (5, 5½, 6, 6½)" (11.5 [12.5, 14, 15, 16.5]cm). End after working a purl row.

SHAPE LEFT FRONT NECK

While working armhole edge even, cut CC at neck edge and shape neck edge as follows.

Bind off 12 stitches once, 3 stitches once, 2 stitches twice, 1 stitch 5 times—21 stitches.

Work until armhole measures same length as others. End after working a purl row.

SHAPE LEFT FRONT SHOULDER

Discontinue using CC at armhole edge, but do not cut CC. Work MC short rows as follows.

On knit rows, leave 5 stitches behind 3 times—6 stitches remain.

On purl rows, slip 1, purl to end.

(End with slip 1, p5.)

Cut MC. Slip 21 stitches, ready to work a purl row.

Next row In CC, bind off 2, p19.

Next row In CC, bind off purlwise.

Right Front Side Piece

Cut 6½ yd (6m) and 2 yd (1.8m) strands of CC.

With shorter strand of CC, cast on 1 stitch; with MC, cast on 29 (31, 33, 36, 39) stitches; with longer strand of CC, cast on 1 stitch—31 (33, 35, 38, 41) stitches.

Continue as Right Back Side piece, from * to end, but cut MC, leaving long tail for seaming.

Right Front Center Piece

Cut 5 yd (4.5m) and 2 yd (1.8m) strands of CC.

With longer strand of CC, cast on 1 stitch; with MC, cast on 23 (25, 27, 29, 31) stitches; with shorter strand of CC, cast on 1 stitch—25 (27, 29, 31, 33) stitches.

Continue as Right Back Center Piece, from ** until piece measures 4" (10cm). End after working a purl row. (If you lengthened or shortened other pieces, add or subtract length here.)

Next row, make 3-stitch, 1 row buttonhole, Work to last 7 stitches, k5, wyif slip 1, wyib psso, (leave yarn in back until directed otherwise), slip 1, psso, slip 1, psso (3 stitches bound off), put last slip stitch back onto left needle. Turn, wyib cable cast on 3 stitches, cable cast on 1 more stitch but, before putting stitch on left needle, bring yarn between two needles and to front, now put 4th cast-on stitch onto left needle.

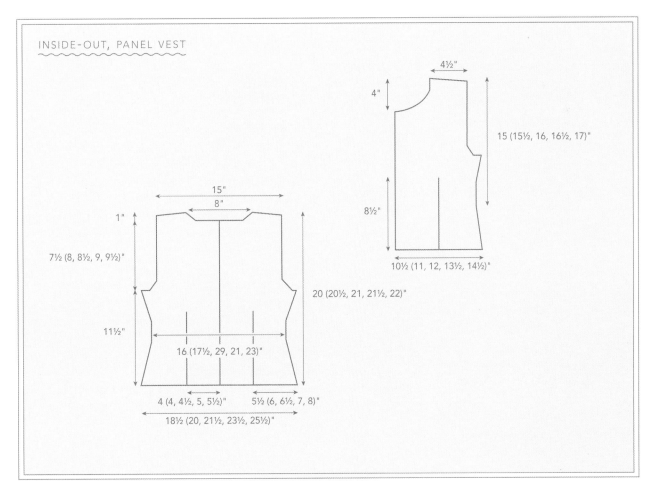

INSIDE-OUT, PANEL VEST

Turn, k1, pass the final cast-on stitch over the stitch just knit, work to end of row.
Continue as Right Back Center Piece until piece measures 3½" (9cm) above previous buttonhole. End after working a purl row.
Make second buttonhole (as above).
Continue as Right Back Center Piece to Join Pieces, but work the last knit row as follows.
Increase row K1 in CC; in MC, k1, increase 1 in next stitch, knit to last stitch; k1 in CC—26 (28, 30, 32, 34) stitches.

JOIN RIGHT FRONT PIECES
Work as for Join Right Back Piece—over 51 (55, 59, 64, 69) stitches—to increase row, then work as follows.
Increase (knit) row K1 in CC; in MC, k1, increase 1 in next stitch, knit to last stitch; k1 in CC—53 (57, 61, 66, 71) stitches.
Work 7 rows even.
Repeat last 8 rows once more—55 (59, 63, 68, 73) stitches.
AT THE SAME TIME, when piece measures 3½" (9cm) above previous buttonhole, make a third buttonhole (as above).
Work knit and purl rows until piece measure same length as Right Back to armhole. End after working a purl row.

SHAPE RIGHT FRONT ARMHOLE
Next (knit) row In CC, bind off 5 (7, 9, 11, 13) stitches, work as established to end.
Work 1 purl row.

Decrease (knit) row K1 in CC; in MC, k1, skp, knit to last stitch; k1 in CC.
Repeat decrease row every knit row 2 (4, 6, 9, 12) times more—45 stitches.
Work even in knit and purl rows until armhole measures 4½ (5, 5½, 6, 6½)" (11.5 [12.5, 14, 15, 16.5]cm). End after working a knit row.

SHAPE RIGHT FRONT NECK
Work as for Shape Left Front Neck.

SHAPE RIGHT FRONT SHOULDER
Discontinue using CC at armhole edge, but do not cut CC.
Work MC short rows as follows.
On purl rows, leave 5 stitches behind 3 times—6 stitches remain.
On knit rows, slip 1, knit to end.
End with slip 1, k5.
Cut MC. Slip 21 stitches, ready to work a purl row.
Next row In CC, bind off 2, k19.
Next row In CC, bind off knitwise.

FINISHING
Sew center Back seam (in same manner as other seams).
With knit sides facing, sew deep shoulder seams (so seam allowances are big enough to be pressed flat).
Sew side seams (in same manner as other seams).
Press all seams open.

Armhole Edgings
Turn 1 CC and 1 MC stitch to the purl side where possible around the armhole (to mimic seam allowances).
With purl side facing and beginning at the underarm, use smaller needle to pick up and knit in CC as follows:
1–2 stitches in underarm and shoulder seam allowances (and through both layers),
1 stitch in every bind-off stitch,
3 stitches for every 4 rows along diagonals,
2 stitches for every 3 rows along rows worked even.
—approximately 75 (80, 85, 95, 105) stitches.
(Along the rows of the armhole edgings, you will be picking up and knitting between the first and second MC stitches—and almost as if picking up and knitting through a small fold line.)
At the beginning of the row, turn. Knit 3 rounds. Bind off.
Leave long tail, then sew bind-off edge to selvedge.

Neck Edging
Turn 1 CC and 1 MC stitch of Front edge to purl side (to mimic seam allowances).

With purl side facing and beginning at the Right Front neck, use smaller needle to pick up and knit in CC and as follows:
1–2 stitches in front and center back seam allowances (and through both layers),
1 stitch in every bind-off stitch and 1 stitch for every 2-row step between bind-off stitches around front and back neck shaping,
2 stitches for every 3 rows along rows worked even,
1 stitch for every stitch on holder.
—approximately 110 stitches.
Knit 1 (WS) row, purl 1 row, then knit 1 row. Bind off purlwise (and tightly across the Back neck).
Leave long tail, then sew bind-off edge to selvedge.

Lower Edging

Turn 1 CC and 1 MC stitch of Front edge to purl side (to mimic seam allowances).
With purl side facing and beginning at lower Left Front edge, use smaller needle to pick up and knit in CC and as follows: 1–2 stitches in all seam allowances (and through both layers), and 1 stitch in every cast-on stitch—approximately 184 (200, 216, 236, 256) stitches
Knit 1 (WS) row, purl 1 row, then bind off.

Front Edgings

With purl side facing, turn 1 CC and 1 MC stitch to right side along Front edges (to mimic seam allowances).
With purl side facing, smaller needle, and CC, pick up and knit 2 stitches for every 3 rows and between first and second MC stitches up Front edges.
Knit 1 (WS) row, purl 1 row, then bind off. Leave long tail, then sew bind-off edge to selvedge.

Sew buttons onto Left Front to correspond to buttonholes on Right Front.
To soften fabric, wash in warm water and dry flat.
Optional Match placement of right-side buttons with smaller buttons on wrong side, then sew through both buttons.

HOW DID YOUR SENSE OF STYLE DEVELOP?

SALLY: Painfully and slowly! It took years for me to learn to really look in the mirror! (I shudder with the memory of things I have worn.) I also think that if you lived through a period, and worn its more eccentric fashions, you might not want to revisit them?

Now I am influenced by what is timeless and universally attractive. I want what I create to be somehow real enough that you'd look at my designs and say, "I can wear that!"

CADDY: Playing dress-up with my mom's old clothes had a big influence on my style. I wanted those minidresses to fit so badly, but of course everything was too big. So I took her skirts and wore them as dresses; I took her shirts and forced them to be minidresses. I made my mom's clothes fit me by tying or draping them in interesting ways. Always a show-off, I would parade these fashions in front of my mom, and she would encourage me by saying how nice I looked and how creative I was. So of course I thought I was pretty darn cool in my creations, and I've had a soft spot for clothes that fit and the styles of the '60s and '70s ever since.

❧ ECO-TOTE ❧

Designed by Caddy

IF YOU HAVEN'T YET SWITCHED TO REUSABLE SHOPPING BAGS, NOW'S THE TIME. SOON PLASTIC AND PA-PER BAGS WILL BE UNAVAILABLE, BANNED, OR NO LONGER FREE. AND WHAT'S MORE ECO-FRIENDLY THAN NOT ONLY USING A REUSABLE BAG BUT MAKING YOUR OWN!?

  THIS BAG IS INCREDIBLY STRONG BECAUSE IT IS MADE OF HEMP AND BECAUSE THE STRAPS AND THE SEAMS ARE AN UNBROKEN LINE. SO, FEEL FREE TO FILL IT TO THE BRIM WITH DELICIOUS GOODIES!

SKILL LEVEL
Easy

SIZES
- One size
- Finished circumference 31"(79cm)
- Finished length (from top of strap to base) 17½" (44.5cm)

MATERIALS
- 370 yd (335m) / 3 skeins of Lanaknits Hemp for Knitting, All Hemp 6 (100% long fiber hemp, each approximately 3½ oz [100g] and 165yd [150m]), in color 018 Sapphire, ③ light/double knitting
- One size 10 (6mm) circular needle, 16–24" (40.5–61cm) long
- One pair size 6 (4mm) needles, or size needed to obtain gauge
- 20 yd (18m) Ribbon, ¼" (6mm) wide
- Two double-pointed needles, size 10 (6mm) (for I-cord)
- 1 Sheet of plastic, needlepoint mesh at least 18" x 13" (45.5cm x 30.5cm)
- One size H-8 or J-10 (5 or 6mm) crochet hook

GAUGE
20 stitches and 24 rows = 4" in stockinette stitch, over smaller needles

PATTERN NOTES
- This tote is knit in two pieces: the first piece is the Front + Base + Back; the second is the Side + Base + Side.
- Work all increases as lifted increase.
- The long tails left at each end of the I-cords are used to seam the sides.

- The bag may look small, but it will stretch extensively when filled.

STITCH PATTERN
Purse stitch (over a multiple of 2 stitches + 4)
All rows P2, *yo, p2tog; repeat from * to last 2 stitches, p2.

FRONT + BASE + BACK
With long-tail cast on, larger needles, and using ribbon plus yarn, cast on 42 stitches. Cut ribbon, leaving a 4" (10cm) tail.
With yarn only, work purse stitch until piece measures 9" (23cm).
With smaller needles, work stockinette stitch to 6" (15cm).
With larger needles, work purse stitch until this section measures the same as the first section—24" (61cm) from beginning.
With ribbon plus yarn, bind off knitwise, leaving 4" (10cm) tails.

SIDE + BASE + SIDE
With long-tail cast on, larger needles, and using ribbon plus yarn, cast on 14 stitches. Cut ribbon, leaving a 4"(10cm) tail.
With yarn only, work purse stitch until piece measures 8¾" (22cm).
Increase row P2, *yo, p1; repeat from * to last 2 stitches, p2—25 stitches.
With smaller needles, knit 1 row, then purl 1 row.
Increase row (RS) *K1, increase 1 in next stitch; repeat from * twice more, knit to last 4 stitches, **increase 1 in next stitch, k1; repeat from ** once—30 stitches.
Continue in stockinette to 8" (20.5cm). End after working a wrong-side row.

Decrease row (RS) K1, *k2tog, k1; repeat from * to last 2 stitches, k2tog—20 stitches.

Decrease row (WS) *P1, ssp; repeat from * to last 2 stitches, p2—14 stitches.

With larger needles, work purse stitch until this section measures the same as the first section—26½" (67cm) from beginning.

With ribbon plus yarn, bind off knitwise, leaving 4" (10cm) tails.

FINISHING

Press both pieces.

I-cord Handles (Make 2)

With ribbon plus yarn, larger needles, and leaving 2 yd (1.8m) tails, cast on 2 stitches. Work I-cord over 2 stitches until cord measures 17" (44.5cm). Bind off, leaving 2 yd (1.8m) tails.

Base

Cut mesh into two pieces, each 8½" x 6" (21.5cm x 15cm). Trim to round off the corners.

Lay mesh pieces on top of each other, and sew them together around the circumference with yarn (sewing through the holes along the edge).

Assembly

Lay the Front + Base + Back piece on a surface, wrong side facing.

Lay the Side + Base + Side piece on top of the first piece, right side facing and so the stockinette Bases are on top of each other but the Sides are perpendicular to the Front and Back.

Sew three edges of the stockinette Bases together. Slide the mesh through the opening, and sew the fourth edge. Designate one larger purse-stitch section the Front. Hold an adjacent Side piece to this Front piece with edges meeting and wrong sides together.

Hold the cast-on of one I-cord Handle to where the Front and Side meet at the top.

With the tails from the cast-on edge of this I-cord, and beginning at the cast-on row of the I-cord, work one row of slip-stitch crochet from top to base, attaching the Handle while joining the Side to the Front. (Make sure to crochet through both layers.)

Hold the second Side to this Front, with edges meeting and wrong sides together.

Carry the same piece of I-cord to where this Front and this Side meet at the top.

With the tails from the end of this I-cord, and beginning at the end of the I-cord, work one row of slip-stitch crochet from top to base, attaching the Handle while joining this Side to this Front.

Repeat for the Back and with the second I-cord Handle.

With the 2 remaining tails of ribbon, make a bow at the base of one Handle.

Secure all remaining tails.

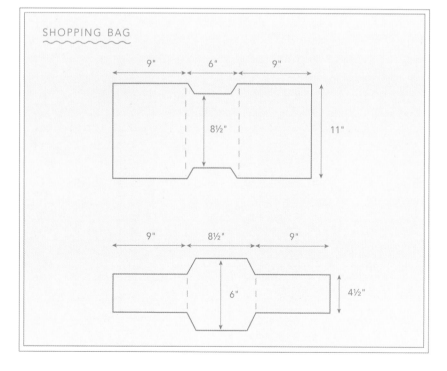

SHOPPING BAG

❧ REVERSIBLE TANK TOP ❧

Designed by Caddy

CHOICES ARE GREAT, AND WITH THIS TOP YOU CAN CHOOSE TO WEAR THE SCOOP NECK IN THE FRONT OR IN THE BACK DEPENDING ON WHAT PART OF YOU WANTS MORE EXPOSURE THAT DAY. SOMETIMES THE CHEST WANTS A LITTLE EXTRA AIRTIME, AND SOMETIMES THE BACK WANTS TO BE THE SHOW OFF. BECAUSE IT'S MADE OF COTTON, IT IS VERY SUMMER-FRIENDLY, BUT TRY WEARING IT LAYERED OVER A TURTLENECK IN THE COLDER MONTHS.

SKILL LEVEL
Easy

SIZES
- XS (S, M, L, 1X)
- Finished bust 27 (31, 35, 39, 43)" (68.5 [79, 89, 99, 109] cm)
- Finished length 20 (20½, 21, 21½, 22)" (51 [52, 53.5, 54.5, 56]cm)
- Finished shoulder width 12½ (13½, 14, 14½, 15)" (32 [34.5, 35.5, 37, 38]cm)

MATERIALS
- 530 (590, 650, 710, 770) yd (480 [530, 585, 640, 695]m) / 5 (6, 7, 7, 8) balls Needful Yarns Kim (55% cotton, 45% acrylic, each approximately 1¾ oz (50g) and 107 yd [96m]), in color 340 ivory, (4) medium/worsted weight
- One pair size 10 (6mm) needles, or size needed to obtain gauge
- One size J-10 (6mm) crochet hook
- Stitch holder
- Tapestry needle

GAUGE
16 stitches and 20 rows = 4" in stockinette stitch.

PATTERN NOTES
- This garment is short and unshaped; you might make it to your ideal short-sweater length (page 17).
- It is also very close fitting but will stretch 3" (7.5cm) in circumference when worn.
- This pattern is written for the deeper scoop to the back.

FRONT
Long-tail cast on 56 (64, 72, 80, 88) stitches.

Knit 2 rows, then purl 1 (WS) row.

Work stockinette until piece measures 2" (5cm). End after working a wrong-side row. Purl 2 rows.

Starting with a (RS) knit row, continue in stockinette until piece measures 13" (33cm). End after working a wrong-side row.

(Shorten or lengthen for finished length here: see page 18.)

SHAPE ARMHOLE
Bind off 2 (3, 4, 5, 6) stitches at the beginning of the next

2 rows—52 (58, 64, 70, 76) stitches.

Decrease row (RS) K1, skp, knit to last 3 stitches, k2tog, k1.

Purl 1 row.

Repeat the last 2 rows 0 (1, 3, 5, 7) times more—50 (54, 56, 58, 60) stitches.

(Adjust for shoulder width here, page 19.)

Continue in stockinette until armhole measures 3 (3½, 4, 4½, 5)" (7.5 [9, 10, 11.5, 12.5] cm). End after working a wrong-side row.

SHAPE NECK

Next row (RS) K6 (8, 9, 10, 11), place these stitches on a holder, bind off center 38 stitches (for front neck), knit to end.

*Beginning with a wrong-side row, work stockinette until armhole measures 7 (7½, 8, 8½, 9)" (18 [19, 20.5, 21.5, 23]cm). End after working a wrong-side row. Bind off. Return to 6 (8, 9, 10, 11) stitches on holder. Repeat from *.

BACK

Work as Front to Shape Armhole.

Bind off 2 (3, 4, 5, 6) stitches at the beginning of the next 2 rows—52 (58, 64, 70, 76) stitches.

Decrease row (RS) K1, skp, knit to last 3 stitches, k2tog, k1.

Purl 1 row.

Repeat the last 2 rows 0 (1, 3, 5, 7) times more—50 (54, 56, 58, 60) stitches.

(Adjust for shoulder width as for Front.)

Continue in stockinette until armhole measures ½ (1, 1½, 2½, 3½)" (1.5 [2.5, 4, 6.5, 9]cm). End after working a wrong-side row.

Work as Front from Shape Neck to end.

FINISHING

Block both pieces.

Sew right shoulder seam.

Neck Edging

With right side facing, and beginning at left shoulder, pick up and knit 1 stitch for every row, and 1 stitch for every bound-off stitch around entire neck edge—approximately 180 (180, 180, 176, 172) stitches.

Beginning with a (WS) knit row, work reverse stockinette stitch for 2" (5cm). End after working a right-side row. Bind off.

Sew left shoulder and edging seam.

Block neck edging.

Fold neck edging over to the right side. Sew center 3" (7.5cm) of neck edging down to the Front.

Repeat for the Back.

Armhole Edgings

With right side facing, and beginning at underarm seam, pick up and knit 1 stitch for every bound-off stitch, and 1 stitch for every row around entire armhole edge—approximately 74 (80, 88, 94, 102) stitches.

Knit 1 (WS) row, purl 1 row, then bind off loosely.

Sew side and edging seams.

Using a crochet hook, work one row of slip-stitch crochet along purl row (at 2" [5cm] from lower edge) of Front and Back.

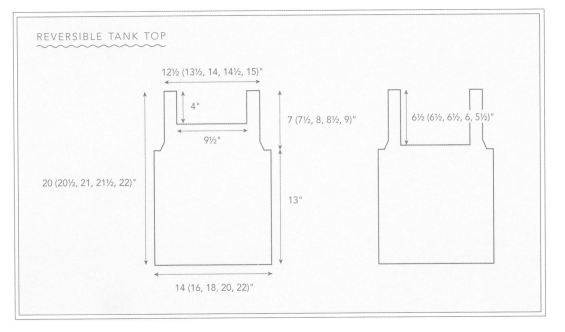

REVERSIBLE TANK TOP

12½ (13½, 14, 14½, 15)"

4"

9½"

7 (7½, 8, 8½, 9)"

6½ (6½, 6½, 6, 5½)"

20 (20½, 21, 21½, 22)"

13"

14 (16, 18, 20, 22)"

❦ FEMME TIE ❦

Designed by Sally

I LEARNED 2 YEARS AGO THAT A SHORT, FLIRTY TIE WORN BY A WOMAN, IS A "FEMME" TIE. FROM THE FIRST MOMENT I WORE ONE, I WAS HOOKED! EVEN THOUGH I HAVE ALWAYS LOVED WEARING TIES, I PREFER NOT HAVING QUITE SO MUCH FABRIC AT MY CHEST—OR TO KNIT! SO HERE'S A VERSION OF THE FEMME TIE, KNIT IN A LIGHTLY-VARIEGATED YARN AND A DIAGONAL GARTER STITCH PATTERN—EASY, BUT STILL INTERESTING.

SKILL LEVEL
Easy

SIZES
- One size
- Finished length 33" (84cm)
- Finished width (at hem) 2" (5cm)

MATERIALS
- 50 yd (45m) / 1 ball Needful Yarns Kelly (55% cotton, 45% acrylic, each approximately 1¾ oz [50g] and 107 yd [98m]), in color 64 taupe, (4) medium/worsted weight
- One pair size 6 (4mm) needles, or size needed to obtain gauge
- Tapestry needle

GAUGE
10 stitches and 12 rows / 6 garter ridges = approximately 2" (5cm) in bias garter stitch pattern

STITCH PATTERN
Bias Garter
Row 1 (WS) Wyif slip 1 purlwise, knit to last stitch, slip 1.
Row 2 (RS) K1, kf&b, knit to last 3 stitches, k2tog, k1.

TIE
Cast on 12 stitches.
Begin bias garter stitch pattern, and work even until piece measures 3" (7.5cm). End after working a wrong-side row.
Decrease row (RS) With right side facing, knit to last 3 stitches, k2tog, k1—11 stitches.

Work even until piece measures 6" (15cm). End after working a wrong-side row.
Repeat Decrease row—10 stitches.
Work even until piece measures 10" (25.5cm). End after working a wrong-side row.
Repeat Decrease row—9 stitches.
Work even until piece measures 14" (35.5cm). End after working a wrong-side row.

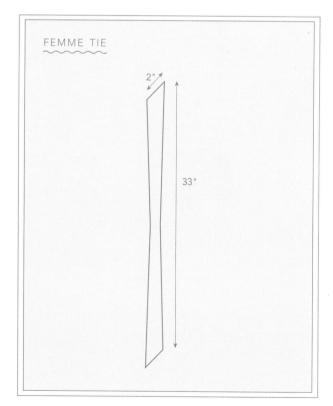

FEMME TIE

2"

33"

Repeat Decrease row—8 stitches.

Work even until piece measures 19" (48.5cm). End after working a wrong-side row.

Increase row (RS) K1, kf&b, knit to end—9 stitches.

Work even until piece measures 23" (58.5cm). End after working a wrong-side row.

Repeat Increase row—10 stitches.

Work even until piece measures 27" (68.5cm). End after working a wrong-side row.

Repeat Increase row—11 stitches.

Work even until piece measures 30" (76cm). End after working a wrong-side row.

Repeat Increase row—12 stitches.

Work even until piece measures 33" (84cm). End after working a wrong-side row.

Bind off.

FINISHING

Steam-press to measurements.

ALTERED AUSTEN JACKET

Designed by Caddy

YOU GOTTA LOVE THE EMPIRE WAIST! JANE AUSTEN MOVIES MAKE THEM LOOK SOOOOO GOOD! I KNOW MANY WOMEN GROAN AT THE IDEA OF WEARING EMPIRE-WAIST GARMENTS, BUT THEY TRULY DO AMAZING THINGS—ESPECIALLY FOR THOSE WHO ARE VERY LONG IN THE TORSO OR SHORT IN THE LEG. IT'S ALL ABOUT BALANCE, RIGHT? THE FACT THAT THIS JACKET IS SHORT AVOIDS WHAT MANY WOMEN DON'T LOVE ABOUT A FULL EMPIRE WAIST—LOOKING LIKE A LITTLE GIRL OR PREGNANT! ALSO, THE USE OF ELASTIC IN THE BACK CREATES A GORGEOUS PLEATING EFFECT, WHILE THE FRONT LIES FLAT AND HAS A MORE SUBTLE EMPIRE SHAPE.

SKILL LEVEL
Intermediate

SIZES
- XS (S, M, L, 1X)
- Finished hem 48 (53, 57½, 63½, 68)" (122 [134.5, 146, 162, 172.5]cm)
- Finished bust 31½ (35½, 39½, 43½ , 47½)" (80 [90, 100, 110.5, 121]cm)
- Finished shoulder width 13½ (14, 14½, 15, 15½)" (34.5 [35.5, 37, 38, 39.5]cm)
- Finished length 19½ (20, 20½, 21, 21½)" (49.5 [51, 52, 53.5, 54.5]cm)
- Finished sleeve length 12¼ (13, 13¾, 14½, 15¼)" (31 [33, 35, 37, 39]cm)

MATERIALS
- 660 (735, 810, 875, 955) yd (595 [660, 730, 790, 860] m) / 8 (8, 9, 10, 11) balls Needful Yarn London Tweed (95% wool, 5% viscose, each approximately 1¾ oz [50g] and 92 yd [85m], in color 10 green, 〔4〕 medium/worsted weight
- One pair size 8 (5mm) needles, or size needed to obtain gauge
- One pair size 9 (5.5mm) needles
- 2 Stitch holders
- 2¼ yards (2m) Ribbon, ½" (13mm) wide
- 24–36" (61–91.5cm) Elastic (to fit waist), ¼" (6mm) wide
- Tapestry needle
- 4 Buttons, 1" (25mm) wide

GAUGE
16 stitches and 20 rows = 4" in stockinette stitch, over smaller needles

PATTERN NOTES
- This short, empire-waist garment is meant to fall to your ideal short sweater length (page 17). But because it is so full, it could be worn with something straight or slim on the lower half.
- Use smaller needles unless directed otherwise.
- The sleeves are picked up around the armhole and knit down.

BACK
Cast on 89 (100, 111, 122, 133) stitches.
Knit 2 rows.
Beginning with a knit row, work stockinette until piece measures 9" (23cm). End after working a wrong-side row. (Shorten or lengthen for finished length here, page 18.)
Decrease row (RS) K4 (5, 6, 7, 8), *k1, k2tog; repeat from * to last 4 (5, 6, 7, 8) stitches, knit to end—62 (70, 78, 86, 94) stitches.

Lace Stripe
Next row (WS) P1, *yo, p2tog; repeat from * to last stitch, p1.
Next row (RS) P1, *yo, p2tog; repeat from * to last stitch, p1.
Repeat the last 2 rows once more, then work 1 more wrong-side row.

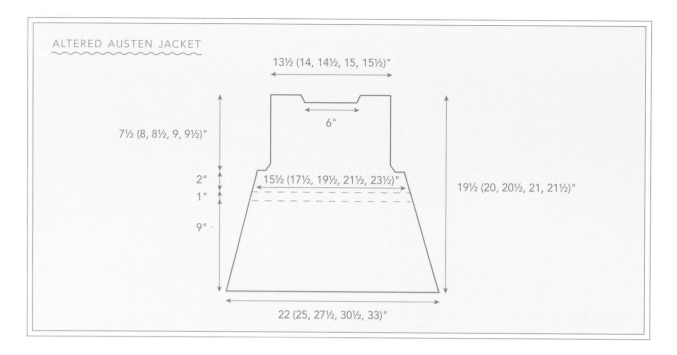

ALTERED AUSTEN JACKET

13½ (14, 14½, 15, 15½)"

6"

7½ (8, 8½, 9, 9½)"

2"
1"
9"

15½ (17½, 19½, 21½, 23½)"

19½ (20, 20½, 21, 21½)"

22 (25, 27½, 30½, 33)"

Beginning with a knit row, work stockinette until piece measures 12" (30cm). End after working a wrong-side row.

SHAPE ARMHOLE
Bind off 2 (4, 6, 7, 8) stitches at the beginning of the next 2 rows—58 (62, 66, 72, 78) stitches.
Decrease row (RS) K1, skp, knit to last 3 stitches, k2tog, k1.
Purl 1 row.
Repeat the last 2 rows 1 (2, 3, 5, 7) times more—54 (56, 58, 60, 62) stitches.
(Adjust shoulder width here: see page 19.)
Work stockinette until armhole measures 6½ (7, 7½, 8, 8½)" (16.5 [18, 19, 20.5, 21.5]cm). End after working a wrong-side row.

SHAPE NECK
Next row (RS) K15 (16, 17, 18, 19) stitches, place these stitches on a holder. Bind off next 24 stitches (for back neck), k15 (16, 17, 18, 19).
*Beginning with a purl row, work 5 rows in stockinette, then bind off.
Return to 15 (16, 17, 18, 19) stitches on holder, ready to work a wrong-side row.
Repeat from *.

LEFT FRONT
Cast on 53 (58, 63, 68, 73) stitches.
Knit 2 rows.
Next row (RS) Knit.

Next row (WS) K1, purl to end.
Repeat the last 2 rows until piece measures 3" (7.5cm). End after working a wrong-side row.

Pocket Front
Next row (RS) K36 (39, 42, 45, 48), place remaining 17 (19, 21, 23, 25) stitches on a holder.
Next row (WS) P19 (20, 21, 22, 23), place remaining 17 (19, 21, 23, 25) stitches on a holder.
Knit 1 row, then purl 1 row (over center stitches).
Decrease row (RS) K1, skp, knit to last 3 stitches, k2tog, k1.
Work 7 rows even.
Repeat decrease row, then purl 1 row.
Repeat decrease row—13 (14, 15, 16, 17) stitches.
Knit 1 (WS) row, purl 1 row, then bind off.

JOIN POCKET
With right side facing, k17 (19, 21, 23, 25) from first holder, pick up and k19 (20, 21, 22, 23) from the purl bumps along the first (WS) row of the pocket front, k17 (19, 21, 23, 25) from second holder.
Next row (WS) K1, purl to end.
Next row (RS) Knit.
Repeat the last 2 rows until piece measures same length as Back to Lace stripe. End after working a wrong-side row.
Decrease row (RS) K4 (5, 6, 7, 8), *k1, k2tog; repeat from * to last 4 (5, 6, 7, 8) stitches, knit to end—38 (42, 46, 50, 54) stitches.

Lace Stripe

Next row (WS) K1, *yo, p2tog; repeat from * to last stitch, p1.

Decrease row (RS) P1, p2tog, *yo, p2tog; repeat from * to last 3 stitches, p2tog, k1—36 (40, 44, 48, 52) stitches.

Next row (WS) K1, *yo, p2tog; repeat from * to last stitch, p1.

Next row (RS) P1, *yo, p2tog; repeat from * to last stitch, k1.

Next row (WS) K1, *yo, p2tog; repeat from * to last stitch, p1.

Next row (RS) Knit.

Next row (WS) K1, purl to end.

Repeat the last 2 rows until piece measures same length as Back to armhole. End after working a wrong-side row.

SHAPE ARMHOLE

Bind off 2 (4, 6, 7, 8) stitches at the beginning of the next right-side row, knit to end—34 (36, 38, 41, 44) stitches.

Next row (WS) K1, purl to end.

Decrease row (RS) K1, skp, knit to end.

Repeat the last 2 rows 1 (2, 3, 5, 7) times more—32 (33, 34, 35, 36) stitches.

(Adjust shoulder width as for Back.)

Work even (in stockinette, but with k1 at the beginning of wrong-side rows) until armhole measures 3 (3½, 4, 4½, 5)" (7.5 [9, 10, 11.5, 12.5]cm).

SHAPE NECK

Decrease row (RS) Knit to last 3 stitches, k2tog, k1.

Decrease row (WS) P1, p2tog, purl to end.

Repeat the last 2 rows 6 times more—18 (19, 20, 21, 22) stitches. End after working a wrong-side row.

Decrease row (RS) Knit to last 3 stitches, k2tog, k1.

Next row (WS) Purl.

Repeat the last 2 rows twice more—15 (16, 17, 18, 19) stitches.

Work stockinette until armhole measures same length as Back, then bind off.

RIGHT FRONT

Cast on 53 (58, 63, 68, 73) stitches.

Knit 2 rows.

Next row (RS) Knit.

Next row (WS) Purl to last stitch, k1.

Repeat the last 2 rows until piece measures 3" (7.5cm). End after working a wrong-side row.

Pocket Front

Work as for Left Front, Pocket Front.

JOIN POCKET

With right side facing, join yarn and k17 (19, 21, 23, 25) from first holder, pick up and knit 19 (20, 21, 22, 23) from the purl bumps along the first (wrong-side) row of the pocket front, k17 (19, 21, 23, 25) from second holder.

Next row (WS) Purl to last stitch, k1.

Next row (RS) Knit.

Repeat the last 2 rows until piece measures same length as Back to lace stripe. End after working a wrong-side row.

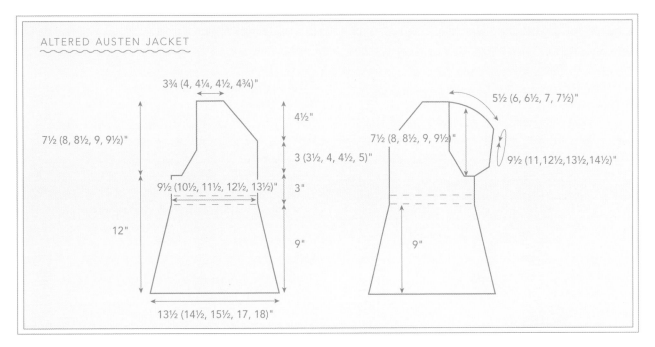

ALTERED AUSTEN JACKET

3¾ (4, 4¼, 4½, 4¾)"

4½"

7½ (8, 8½, 9, 9½)"

3 (3½, 4, 4½, 5)"

9½ (10½, 11½, 12½, 13½)"

3"

12"

9"

13½ (14½, 15½, 17, 18)"

5½ (6, 6½, 7, 7½)"

7½ (8, 8½, 9, 9½)"

9½ (11, 12½, 13½, 14½)"

9"

Decrease row (RS) K4 (5, 6, 7, 8), *k1, k2tog; repeat from * to last 4 (5, 6, 7, 8) stitches, knit to end—38 (42, 46, 50, 54) stitches.

Lace Stripe

Next row (WS) P1, *yo, p2tog; repeat from * to last stitch, k1.

Decrease row (RS) K1, p2tog, *yo, p2tog; repeat from * to last 3 stitches, p2tog, p1—36 (40, 44, 48, 52) stitches.

Next row P1, *yo, p2tog; repeat from * to last stitch, k1.

Next row (RS) K1, *yo, p2tog; repeat from * to last stitch, p1.

Next row P1, *yo, p2tog; repeat from * to last stitch, k1.

Next row (RS) Knit.

Next row Purl to last stitch, k1.

Repeat the last 2 rows until piece measures 1½" (4cm) or 8 rows short of Back length to armhole. End after working a wrong-side row.

Next row (RS), make buttonhole K5, yo, k2tog, knit to end.

Next row Purl to last stitch, k1.

Next row (RS) Knit.

Repeat the last 2 rows twice more. End after working a right-side row.

SHAPE ARMHOLE

Bind off 2 (4, 6, 7, 8) stitches at the beginning of the next wrong-side row, purl to last stitch, k1—34 (36, 38, 41, 44) stitches.

Decrease row (RS), make buttonhole K5, yo, k2tog, knit to last 3 stitches, k2tog, k1.

Next row (WS) Purl to last stitch, k1.

Decrease row (RS) Knit to last 3 stitches, k2tog, k1.

Repeat the last 2 rows 0 (1, 2, 4, 6) times more—32 (33, 34, 35, 36) stitches.

(Adjust for shoulder width as for Back.)

AT THE SAME TIME, make 3rd buttonhole 8 rows after 2nd, and make 4th buttonhole 8 rows after 3rd.

Work even (in stockinette, but with k1 at the end of wrong-side rows) until armhole measures 3 (3½, 4, 4½, 5)" (7.5 [9, 10, 11.5, 12.5]cm). End after working a wrong-side row.

SHAPE NECK

Decrease row (RS) K1, skp, knit to end.

Decrease row (WS) Purl to last 3 stitches, ssp, p1.

Repeat the last 2 rows 6 times more—18 (19, 20, 21, 22) stitches. End after working a wrong-side row.

Decrease row (RS) K1, skp, knit to end.

Next row (WS) Purl.

Repeat the last 2 rows twice more—15 (16, 17, 18, 19) stitches.

Work stockinette until armhole measures same length as Back, then bind off.

FINISHING

Block all three pieces.

Sew shoulder seams.

Collar

(The Collar will turn to the right side when worn.)

With right side facing, and beginning at Right Front, pick up and knit 1 stitch for every row, and 1 stitch for every bind-off stitch around the entire neck edge—approximately 78 stitches.

Beginning with a knit row, work reverse stockinette stitch for 2½" (6.5cm). End after working a purl row.

Decrease row K1, skp, knit to last 3 stitches, k2tog, k1.

Next row Purl.

Repeat the last 2 rows twice more—72 stitches.

Bind off.

COLLAR EDGING

With stockinette side of Collar facing, and beginning at the corner where the Collar meets the Left Front, pick up and knit 1 stitch for every row, and 2 stitches for every bind-off stitch along the entire Collar edge—approximately 180 stitches.
Knit 2 rows, then bind off.

Sleeves

With larger needles, right side facing, and beginning at an underarm, pick up and knit 1 stitch for every bind-off stitch, and 3 stitches for every 4 rows around the entire armhole edge—60 (68, 76, 82, 88) stitches.
(If needed, increase or decrease on next row to attain this number.)
Beginning with a (WS) purl row, work stockinette for 5 rows.
Decrease row (RS) *K1, k2tog; repeat from * 4 times more, knit to last 15 stitches, *k2tog, k1; repeat from * to end—50 (58, 66, 72, 78) stitches.
Work stockinette until Sleeve measures 3½ (4, 4½, 5, 5½)" (9 [10, 11.5, 12.5, 14]cm). End after working a wrong-side row.
(Shorten or lengthen for Sleeve length here.)
Decrease row (RS) *K2, k2tog; repeat from * to last 2 (2, 2, 4, 2) stitches, knit to end—38 (44, 50, 55, 59) stitches.
Next row (WS) Purl, decreasing 0 (0, 0, 1, 1) stitches in next row—38 (44, 50, 54, 58) stitches.
Work 1x1 rib for 1½" (4cm), then bind off in rib.

FINISHING

Sew Sleeve and side seams.
Fold Collar down, and block lightly.
Sew buttons onto Left Front to correspond to buttonholes.
Beginning at a side seam, with wrong side facing, and just below the Lace Stripe, thread elastic under 2 stitches and then over 4 stitches along entire Back. End at opposite side seam and on the wrong side. Tighten the elastic from both ends to desired pleated effect. Across wrong side, tie ends of elastic to each other, and trim.
Sew pockets down at sides.
Cut ribbon into 4 even lengths. Wrap pocket seams, moving about ½" (13mm) at a time. Secure by tying the ribbon to itself on the inside of the jacket.

HOW IS YOUR SENSE OF STYLE DIFFERENT FROM YOUR DAUGHTER/MOM?

SALLY: I believe that when I was young I thought I could wear anything! But as I've aged, I've become more self-conscious about my body. I'm sorry to hear myself say that, because while I think it's fine to know what body parts should be covered, I would love us older girls to be proud of our womanly curves—earned through childbirth, years of living, and chocolate!

Having said all that, I also know that you never look so old as when you dress too young. No more short skirts for me!

CADDY: My mom is way funkier than me! She has a way of putting an outfit together that stops traffic—She's the one getting stared at when we're walking down the street!—and in a really good way, not the "What was that woman wearing!?" sort of way.

⚔ LACE-AND-CABLE JUMPER ⚔

Designed by Sally

I LOVE LACE, AND I LOVE TO SEE IT USED IN UNEXPECTED WAYS. HERE IT IS IN A HEAVIER YARN THAN YOU MIGHT EXPECT, WITH A BIT OF TWEED TO ITS TEXTURE. THE LACE IS PAIRED WITH CABLES WHOSE MOVEMENTS PARALLEL THE JUMPER'S A-LINE SHAPE. AND HERE, AGAIN, IS THE EMPIRE WAIST WE ALL LOVE, EXPRESSED AS IT ORIGINALLY WAS, WITH A VERY LOW FRONT NECK. THIS SHAPE IS WONDERFUL ON THOSE OF US WHO'D LIKE TO MINIMIZE A LARGER BUST. AND IF YOU AREN'T IN THAT PARTICULAR GROUP, THEN TURN IT AROUND TO WEAR THE HIGHER BACK NECKLINE TO THE FRONT.

SKILL LEVEL
Experienced

SIZES
- S (M, L, 1X, 2X)
- Finished bust 33½ (36, 41, 44, 47)" (85 [91, 104, 112, 119]cm)
- Finished hem 78 (83, 85, 92, 97)" (198 [211, 216, 234, 246]cm)
- Finished length 36½ (37½, 38½, 39½, 40½)" (93 [95, 98, 100, 103]cm)
- Finished shoulder width 12–13" (30–33cm)

MATERIALS
- 1360 (1480, 1650, 1780, 1925) yd (1225 [1330, 1485, 1600, 1730]m) / 15 (16, 18, 19, 21) balls Needful Yarns London Tweed (95% wool, 5% viscose, each approximately 1¾ oz [50g] and 92 yd [83m]), in color #10 green, ④ medium/worsted weight

Different sized needles are used to attain the various sizes.
- One size 5 (6, 5, 6, 7) (3.75 [4, 3.75, 4, 4.5] mm) circular needle, 24" (60cm) long
- One size 5 (6, 5, 6, 7) (3.75 [4, 3.75, 4, 4.5] mm) circular needle, 60" (150cm) long
- One pair size 8 (9, 8, 9, 10) (5 [5.5, 5, 5.5, 6] mm) needles, or size needed to obtain gauge
- Cable needle (cn)
- 2 Stitch holders
- Tapestry needle

GAUGES
(All gauges are in stockinette stitch using larger needles.)

Small: 16 stitches and 22 rows = 4" (10cm)
Medium: 15 stitches and 22 rows = 4" (10cm)
Large: 16 stitches and 22 rows = 4" (10cm)
1X: 15 stitches and 22 rows = 4" (10cm)
2X: 14 stitches and 21 rows = 4" (10cm)

PATTERN NOTES
- This garment is a long, empire-waist A-line. It is meant to fall to a dress length. To shorten, begin the chart higher; to lengthen, extend the chart down. Cast on accordingly.
- This garment may stretch 2" (5cm) in length when worn.
- To center stitch patterns, the Front is wider than the back. Therefore, there are no stitches bound off at the underarm of the Back, and the side seams are toward the back.
- Work all increases as lifted increase—knitwise in knit stitches, purlwise in purl stitches.

FRONT
Skirt
With larger needles, long-tail cast on 188 (188, 205, 205, 205) stitches.

(Shorten or lengthen here by starting the chart where desired and casting on accordingly: the set-up row will change.)

Set-up Row (WS) *P2, k2 (2, 3, 3, 3), p6, k2 (2, 3, 3, 3), p2, k1 (1, 2, 2, 2), p2, k16, p2, k2 (2, 3, 3, 3), p2, k16, p2, k1 (1, 2, 2, 2); repeat from * twice more and to last 14 (14, 16, 16, 16) stitches, p2, k2 (2, 3, 3, 3), p6, k2 (2, 3, 3, 3), p2.

Beginning with Row 1, work skirt chart (page 139) from A to B once, then from E to B twice, then from E to C once.

(Note that the darker dots mean different things for different sizes.)

Work through the last (RS) row of the skirt chart.

Under-bust Band

Decrease Row (WS) With smaller needles, work in stitch pattern as established, and AT THE SAME TIME p2tog twice across all cables (4 stitches become 2), and k2tog once in center of lace panels (6 stitches become 5)—65 (65, 82, 82, 82) stitches.

Continuing on smaller needles, knit 1 (RS) row, then work 4 rows reverse stockinette (beginning with a knit row and ending with a purl row), then purl 1 row.

TOP

Next row (RS) With larger needles, k2, p1 (1, 2, 2, 2), *k5, p1 (1, 2, 2, 2), [k2, p1 (1, 2, 2, 2)] 4 times; repeat from * twice more, then k5, p1 (1, 2, 2, 2), k2.

Set up, increase row (WS) P2, k1 (1, 2, 2, 2), *p2, increase in p1, p2, k1 (1, 2, 2, 2), p2, k1 (1, 2, 2, 2), [increase in p1] twice, k1 (1, 2, 2, 2), [increase in p1] twice, k1 (1, 2, 2, 2), p2, k1 (1, 2, 2, 2), repeat from * twice more, p2, increase in p1, p2, k1 (1, 2, 2, 2), p2—81 (81, 98, 98, 98) stitches.

Beginning with Row 1, work top chart from F to H once, then from F to L once.

Continue top chart for 5 more rows.

Increase row (RS) K2, increase 1 in next stitch, work to last 3 stitches, increase 1 in next stitch, k2—83 (83, 100, 100, 100) stitches.

Continue top chart, with extra purl stitches at sides, to 3 (3½, 4, 4½, 5)" (7.5 [9, 10, 11.5, 12.5]cm) above under-bust band. End after working a wrong-side row.

SHAPE ARMHOLE AND NECK

Bind off 8 (8, 11, 11, 11) stitches at the beginning of the next 2 rows—67 (67, 78, 78, 78) stitches.

Left Front Armhole and Neck

Decrease row (RS) K1, skp, work to 24 (24, 27, 27, 27) stitches on the right needle. Place center 17 (17, 22, 22, 22) stitches on holder. Turn.

Next row (WS) Bind off 3 (3, 4, 4, 4) stitches, work to end.

Decrease row (RS) K1, skp, work to end.

Next (WS) row Bind off 2 stitches, work to end.

Next 4 (4, 6, 6, 6) decrease rows (RS) K1, skp, work to end.

Next 3 (WS) rows Bind off 1 stitch, work to end.

(Work remaining wrong-side rows even.)

Special decrease instructions When 2 stitches remain outside the first cable, cross this cable on the right-side row, then p2tog twice across this cable on the next wrong-side row.

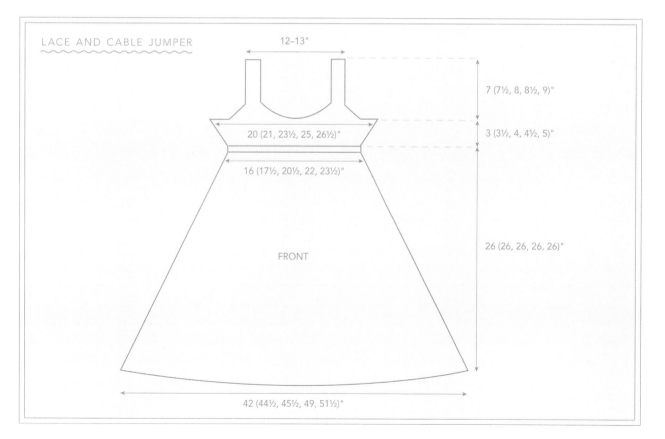

LACE AND CABLE JUMPER

12–13"

20 (21, 23½, 25, 26½)"

16 (17½, 20½, 22, 23½)"

FRONT

7 (7½, 8, 8½, 9)"

3 (3½, 4, 4½, 5)"

26 (26, 26, 26, 26)"

42 (44½, 45½, 49, 51½)"

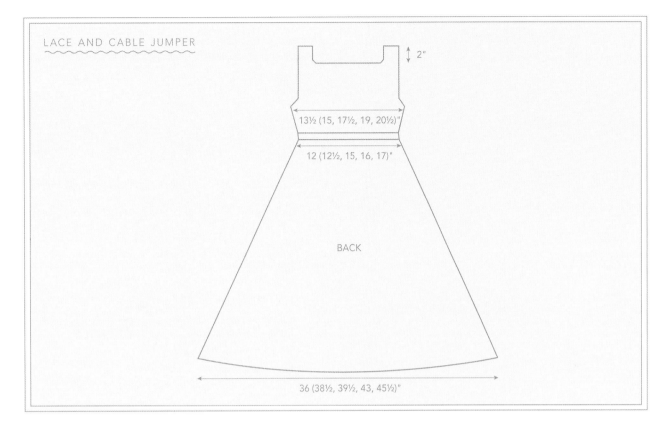

LACE AND CABLE JUMPER

2"

13½ (15, 17½, 19, 20½)"

12 (12½, 15, 16, 17)"

BACK

36 (38½, 39½, 43, 45½)"

Final decrease row (RS) K1, p2tog, work next 6 stitches as established—8 stitches.

Continue as established (crossing cable as indicated every alternate right-side row) to approximately 7 (7½, 8, 8½, 9)" (18 [19, 20.5, 21.5, 23]cm) above armhole. End after working a cable cross row.

Next row (WS) P1, k1, [p2tog] twice, k1, p1.

Bind off.

Right Front Armhole and Neck

With right side facing, return to remaining 25 (25, 28, 28, 28) stitches. Work 2 rows from Top chart as established.

Decrease row (RS) Bind off 3 (3, 4, 4, 4) stitches at neck edge, work to last 3 stitches, k2tog, k1.

Work 1 wrong-side row.

Following 5 (5, 7, 7, 7) decrease rows (RS) Shape neck by binding off 2 stitches once, then 1 stitch 3 times. AT THE SAME TIME, work to last 3 stitches, k2tog, k1.

(Work remaining wrong-side rows even.)

Special decrease instructions When 2 stitches remain outside the last cable, cross this cable on the right-side row, then p2tog twice across this cable on the next wrong-side row.

Final decrease row (RS) Work to last 3 stitches, p2tog, k1—8 stitches.

Continue as established (crossing cable as indicated

every alternate right-side row) until armhole measures same length as Left Front. End after working a cable cross row.

Next row (WS) P1, k1, [p2tog] twice, k1, p1.

Bind off.

BACK

Skirt

With larger needles, long-tail cast on 164 (164, 177, 177, 177) stitches.

(Shorten of lengthen as for Back.)

Set-up row (WS) *P2, k1 (1, 2, 2, 2), p2, k16, p2, k2 (2, 3, 3, 3), p2, k16, p2, k1 (1, 2, 2, 2), p2, k2 (2, 3, 3, 3), p6, k2 (2, 3, 3, 3); repeat from * once more, then p2, k1 (1, 2, 2, 2), p2, k16, p2, k2 (2, 3, 3, 3), p2, k16, p2, k1 (1, 2, 2, 2), p2.

Begin with Row 1, work skirt chart from D to B once, then from E to B twice.

Work through last (RS) of Skirt chart.

Under-bust Band

Decrease row (WS) With smaller needles, work in stitch pattern as established, and AT THE SAME TIME p2tog twice across all cables (4 stitches become 2), and k2tog once in center of lace panels (6 stitches become 5)—47 (47, 60, 60, 60) stitches.

Continuing on smaller needles, knit 1 (RS) row, then work

4 rows reverse stockinette (beginning with a knit row and ending with a purl row), then purl 1 row.

TOP

Next row (RS) With larger needles, *[k2, p1 (1, 2, 2, 2)] 4 times, k5, p1 (1, 2, 2, 2); repeat from * once more, then [k2, p1 (1, 2, 2, 2)] 3 times, k2.

Set up, increase row (WS) P2, * k1 (1, 2, 2, 2), [increase in p1] twice, k1 (1, 2, 2, 2), [increase in p1] twice, k1 (1, 2, 2, 2,), p2, k1 (1, 2, 2, 2), p2, increase in p1, p2, k1 (1, 2, 2, 2), p2, repeat from * once, k1 (1, 2, 2, 2), [increase in p1] twice, k1(1, 2, 2, 2), [increae in p1] twice, k1 (1, 2, 2, 2), p2—61 (61, 74, 74, 74) stitches.

Begin with Row 1, work top chart from K to L once, then from J to G once.

Continue top chart for 5 more rows.

Increase row (RS) K2, increase 1 in next stitch, work to last 3 stitches, increase 1 in next stitch, k2—63 (63, 76, 76, 76) stitches.

Continue top chart, with extra purl stitches at sides, to same length as Front above under-bust band. End after working a wrong-side row.

SHAPE ARMHOLE

(Continue Top chart as established through all following shaping.)

Work 2 rows even.

Decrease row (RS) K1, skp, work to last 3 stitches, k2tog, k1.

Work 1 (WS) row even.

Repeat the last 2 rows 3 (3, 5, 5, 5) times more.

Special decrease instructions When 2 stitches remain outside first and last cables, cross these cables on right-side rows, then p2tog twice across these cables on next wrong-side row.

Final decrease row (RS) K1, p2tog, work to last 3 stitches, p2tog, k1—49 (49, 58, 58, 58) stitches.

Work even to approximately 2" (5cm) shorter than Front armhole. End after working the wrong-side row after a cable cross.

Right Back Neck

Work to 16 (16, 18, 18, 18) stitches on the right needle. Place next 33 (33, 40, 40, 40) stitches on holder. Turn. *Bind off 4 (4, 6, 6, 6) stitches at the next neck edge, 2 stitches at the next neck edge, 1 stitch at the next 2 neck edges—8 stitches.

Work to same length as Front above armhole. End after working a cable cross row.

Next row (WS) P1, k1, [p2tog] twice, k1, p1.

Bind off final 6 stitches.

Left Back Neck

Return to remaining 33 (33, 40, 40, 40) stitches, right side facing. Place first 17 (17, 22, 22, 22) stitches on holder. Work 2 rows over 16 (16, 18, 18, 18) stitches. Work as Right Back Neck from * to end.

FINISHING

Block all pieces before seaming.
Seam side and shoulder seams.

Neck Edging

With shorter and smaller circular needle and with right side facing, begin at right shoulder seam to pick up and knit as follows:

5 stitches for every 6 rows along rows worked even, 1 stitch for every bind-off stitch and 1 stitch for every 2-row step between bind-off stitches around Front and Back neck shaping, 1 stitch for every stitch on holder, k2tog twice across all cables.

—40–50 stitches picked up around Back neck, 85–95 stitches picked up around Front neck.

(The numbers of stitches for all edgings are approximate; they depend upon size and row gauge. If you think you have too many stitches, decrease on the next row and/or bind off tightly.)

Next round With right side facing, k1. Turn (to wrong side facing), slip 1 purlwise, knit to end of round.

Knit 1 more (WS) round, then bind off.

Armhole Edgings

With shorter and smaller circular needle, and with right side facing, begin at side seam to pick up and knit as follows: 5 stitches for every 6 rows, and 1 stitch for every bind-off stitch at underarm—65–85 stitches. (Again, the number of stitches is approximate.)

Next round With right side facing, k1. Turn (to wrong-side facing), slip 1 purlwise, knit to end of round.

Knit 1 more (WS) round, then bind off.

Lower Edging

With longer and smaller circular needle and with right side facing, begin at side seam to pick up and knit 1 stitch in every cast-on stitch.

(If cast-on stitches are tight together—which happens at occasional k2—only pick up and k1.)

Next round With right side facing, k1. Turn (to wrong side facing), slip 1 purlwise, knit to end of round.

Knit 1 more (WS) round, then bind off.

LACE AND CABLE JUMPER

Top Chart

Skirt Chart

Top of Chart

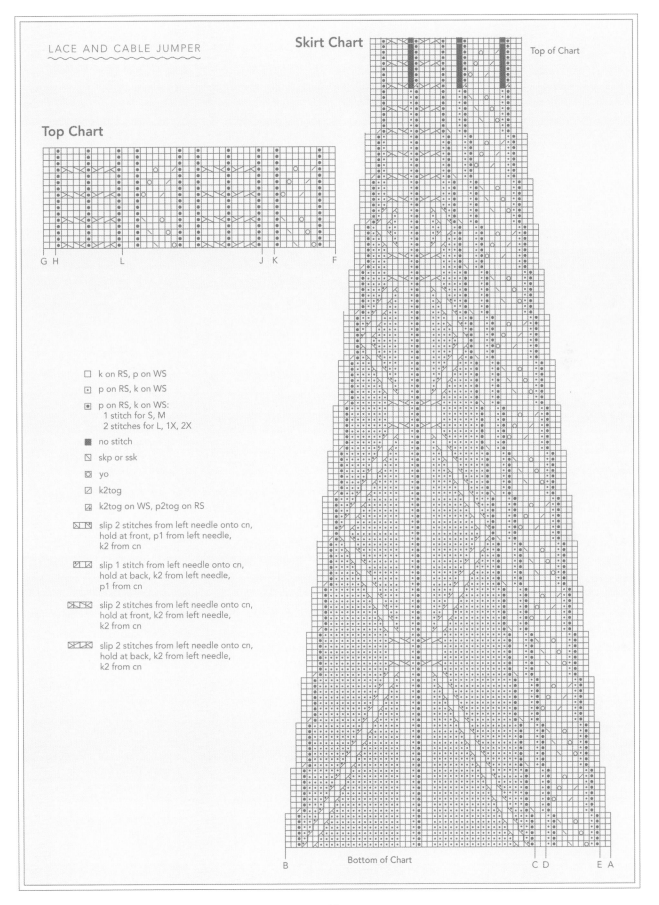

G H   L   J K   F

- □ k on RS, p on WS
- ⊡ p on RS, k on WS
- ▣ p on RS, k on WS:
  1 stitch for S, M
  2 stitches for L, 1X, 2X
- ▦ no stitch
- ◹ skp or ssk
- ⊘ yo
- ◺ k2tog
- ◪ k2tog on WS, p2tog on RS
- ◹◺ slip 2 stitches from left needle onto cn,
  hold at front, p1 from left needle,
  k2 from cn
- ◺◹ slip 1 stitch from left needle onto cn,
  hold at back, k2 from left needle,
  p1 from cn
- ◹◺ slip 2 stitches from left needle onto cn,
  hold at front, k2 from left needle,
  k2 from cn
- ◺◹ slip 2 stitches from left needle onto cn,
  hold at back, k2 from left needle,
  k2 from cn

B   Bottom of Chart   C D   E A

⚔ MINI-DRESS ⚓

Designed by Caddy

DON'T BE FOOLED BY THE NAME! JUST BECAUSE IT WALKS LIKE A DRESS AND TALKS LIKE A DRESS, DOESN'T MEAN THAT IT IS, IN FACT, A DRESS. IT LOOKS JUST AS GREAT OVER PANTS OR A SKIRT AS IT DOES OVER TIGHTS. AND YOU CAN, OF COURSE, MAKE IT LONGER OR SHORTER. THE REAL FUN, HOWEVER, IS NOT IN THE LENGTH (OR LACK THEREOF) BUT IN THE CENTER AND THE SIDES. THE WAIST APPEARS SMALLER BE-CAUSE THE CENTER STRIPE IS CUT SHORT BY THE VERTICAL STRIPES AT THE SIDES THAT ALSO HAPPEN TO TRACE YOUR GORGEOUS SILHOUETTE.

SKILL LEVEL
Intermediate

SIZES
- XS (S, M, L, 1X)
- Finished bust 30½ (34½, 38½, 42½, 46½)" (77 [87.5, 97.5, 108, 118] cm)
- Finished hem 34 (38, 42, 46, 50)" (86.5 [96.5, 106.5, 117, 127] cm)
- Finished length 28 (28½, 29, 29½, 30)" (71 [72.5, 73.5, 75, 76]cm)
- Finished waist length 15½ (16, 16½, 17, 17½)" (39 [40.5, 42, 43, 44.5]cm)
- Finished shoulder width 12 (12½, 13½, 14½, 15½)" (30.5 [32, 34.5, 37, 39.5]cm)
- Finished sleeve length 9½ (9¾, 10¾, 11¾, 12¼)" (24 [25, 27.5, 30, 31]cm)

MATERIALS
- 425 (465, 520, 565, 615) yd (385 [420, 470, 510, 555]m) / 3 (3, 4, 4, 4) skeins Louet Merlin (70% merino wool, 30% linen, each approximately 3½ oz [100g] and 156 yd [140m]), in color 43 Pewter (MC), (4) medium/worsted weight
- 150 (155, 200, 250, 260) yd (135 [140, 180, 225, 235]m) / 1 (1, 2, 2, 2) skeins Louet Merlin, in color 49 Charcoal (A)
- 80 (80, 160, 240, 240) yd (72 [72, 145, 215, 215]m) / 1 (1, 2, 2) skeins Louet Merlin, in color 01 Champagne (B)
- One pair size 8 (5mm) needles, or size needed to obtain gauge
- Stitch holder
- Tapestry needle

GAUGE
18 stitches and 24 rows = 4" in stockinette stitch

PATTERN NOTES
- This garment is long and shaped. Its finished length could be to your ideal mid-length, to your ideal long sweater length, between the two, or longer still. It is also high-waisted. You may adjust waist length between the waistband and the armhole and finished length before the waistband (page 17).
- Before you begin, divide color A and color B into 2 balls (if you don't have 2 balls of each already).
- Work in colors as established unless directed otherwise.
- Twist the yarn when changing color by taking the color-just-worked color over the next color.
- Work all increases as lifted increase.
- The sleeves are picked up around the armhole and knit down.

FRONT
With MC, long-tail cast on 79 (88, 97, 106, 115) stitches.
Knit 1 row, purl 1 row, then knit 1 (WS) row.
Next row (RS) In color A k6 (6, 8, 10, 10), in color B k2 (2, 4, 6, 6), in MC k63 (72, 73, 74, 83), in color B k2 (2, 4, 6, 6), in color A k6 (6, 8, 10, 10).
Next row (WS) Purl (in colors as established).
Repeat last 2 rows twice more. End after working a wrong-side row.
*Decrease row (RS) K9 (9, 13, 17, 17), skp, knit to last 3 stitches in MC, k2tog, knit to end.
Work 7 rows even.
(Shorten or lengthen for finished length by changing

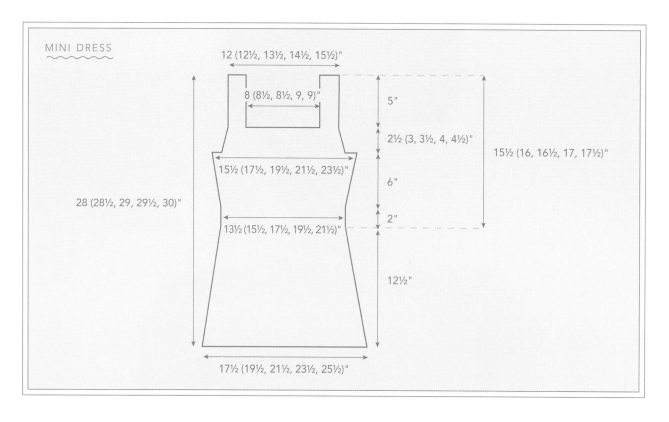

MINI DRESS

12 (12½, 13½, 14½, 15½)"

8 (8½, 8½, 9, 9)"

5"

2½ (3, 3½, 4, 4½)"

15½ (16, 16½, 17, 17½)"

15½ (17½, 19½, 21½, 23½)"

6"

28 (28½, 29, 29½, 30)"

2"

13½ (15½, 17½, 19½, 21½)"

12½"

17½ (19½, 21½, 23½, 25½)"

the number of rows worked even between decreases, page 18.)

Repeat from * 7 times more, then repeat decrease row—61 (70, 79, 88, 97) stitches.

Work 1 wrong-side row.

Piece measures approximately 12½" (32cm).

Waist Stripe

Next row (RS) K8 (8, 12, 16, 16), in color B knit center 45 (54, 55, 56, 65) stitches, k8 (8, 12, 16, 16).

Next row (WS) P8 (8, 12, 16, 16), in color B purl center 45 (54, 55, 56, 65) stitches, p8 (8, 12, 16, 16).

Repeat last 2 rows until waist stripe measures 2" (5cm). End after working a wrong-side row.

Next row (RS) K8 (8, 12, 16, 16) stitches, in MC k45 (54, 55, 56, 65), k8 (8, 12, 16, 16).

Next row (WS) Purl.

Increase row (RS) K9 (9, 13, 17, 17), increase 1 in next stitch, knit to last 2 stitches in MC, increase 1 in next stitch, knit to end.

Work 5 rows even.

Repeat the last 6 rows 4 times more—71 (80, 89, 98, 107) stitches.

(Shorten or lengthen for waist length by changing the number of rows worked even between increases, page 18.)

Work even until piece measures 6" (15 cm) from top of waist stripe. End after working a wrong-side row.

SHAPE ARMOLE

Next row (RS) Bind off 3 (4, 6, 8, 8) stitches at the beginning of the next 2 rows—65 (72, 77, 82, 91) stitches.

First decrease row (RS) K2 (2, 4, 6, 6), skp (in color B), knit to last 4 (4, 6, 8, 8) stitches, k2tog (in color B), knit to end. (There is only 1 stitch in color B at each side from here to end.)

Next and all wrong-side rows Purl.

Second decrease row (RS) K3 (3, 3, 5, 5), skp (in MC), knit to last 5 (5, 5, 7, 7) stitches, k2tog (in MC), knit to end.

Third decrease row (RS) K3 (3, 2, 4, 4), skp, knit to last 5 (5, 4, 6, 6) stitches, k2tog, knit to end.

Fourth decrease row (RS) K3 (3, 3, 3, 3), skp, knit to last 5 (5, 5, 5, 5) stitches, k2tog, knit to end.

Fifth decrease row (RS) K3 (3, 3, 4, 4), skp, knit to last 5 (5, 5, 6, 6) stitches, k2tog, knit to end.

Next row (WS) Purl.

Repeat the last 2 rows 0 (2, 2, 2, 5) times more—55 (58, 63, 68, 71) stitches. End after working a wrong-side row. (Adjust shoulder width here, page 19.)

Work even until armhole measures 2½ (3, 3½, 4, 4½)" 6.5 [7.5, 9, 10, 11.5]cm). End after working a wrong-side row.

SHAPE NECK

Next row (RS) K9 (10, 12, 14, 15), place these stitches on a holder, bind off center 37 (38, 39, 40, 41) stitches, k9 (10, 12, 14, 15).

Beginning with a purl row, work even in stockinette until neck measures 5" (12.5 cm), then bind off.

Return to stitches on holder, ready to work a wrong-side row.

Beginning with a purl row, work even in stockinette until neck measures 5" (12.5 cm), then bind off.

BACK

Work as Front to Shape Neck, but continue until armhole measures 4½ (5, 5½, 6, 6½)" (11.5 [12.5, 14, 15, 16.5]cm). End after working a wrong-side row.

Next row (RS) K9 (10, 12, 14, 15), place these stitches on a holder, bind off center 37 (38, 39, 40, 41) stitches (for Back neck), k9 (10, 12, 14, 15).

Return to stitches on holder, ready to work a wrong-side row.

Beginning with a purl row, work even in stockinette until neck measures 3" (7.5 cm), then bind off.

FINISHING

Block both pieces.
Sew right shoulder seam

Neck Edging

With MC, right side facing, and beginning at left front neck edge, pick up and knit 1 stitch for every 2 rows, and 1 stitch for every stitch around entire neck edge.

Knit 1 (WS) row, purl 1 row, then bind off.

Sew left shoulder and edging seam.

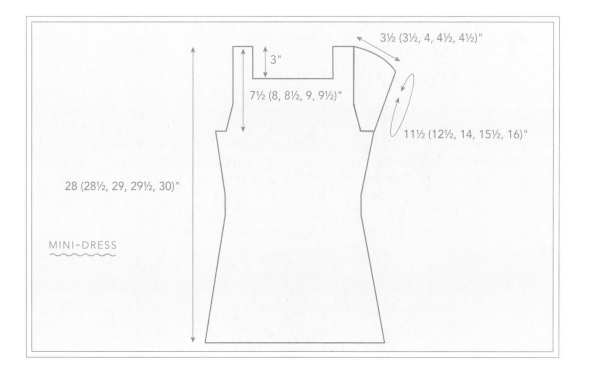

3½ (3½, 4, 4½, 4½)"

3"

7½ (8, 8½, 9, 9½)"

11½ (12½, 14, 15½, 16)"

28 (28½, 29, 29½, 30)"

MINI-DRESS

HOW ARE YOUR DESIGNS DIFFERENT FROM YOUR DAUGHTER/MOM?

SALLY: I know that Caddy's designs have an edginess that I can wear but couldn't replicate. And it's the most amazing experience to see it manifest. I've worn my Camelot Coat with her Tabbed Cuffs—a great outfit! The women my age admire the coat, but the young women are all over the cuffs!

CADDY: I like to try to blow my mom's mind with my designs. It's really funny when she freaks out; sometimes she even screams. This is not because my designs are so amazingly intricate that my mom can't figure them out (Yeah, right!) but because they are usually so shockingly simple!

SLEEVES

With A, right side facing, and beginning at underarm seam, pick up and knit 1 stitch for every bind-off stitch, and 1 stitch for every 2 rows around entire armhole edge—51 (56, 63, 70, 73) stitches. (If needed, increase or decrease in the next row to attain this number.)
Next row (WS) Purl.
Next row (RS) Bind off 3 stitches, knit to end.
Next row (WS) Bind off 3 stitches, purl to end.
Next row (RS) Bind off 2 stitches, knit to end.
Next row (WS) Bind off 2 stitches, purl to end.
Repeat the last 2 rows 5 (5, 6, 7, 7) times more—21 (26, 29, 32, 35) stitches. End after working a wrong-side row.
Bind off 6 (7, 8, 9, 10) stitches at the beginning of the next 2 rows—9 (12, 13, 14, 15) stitches.
Bind off.

Sleeve Edgings

With A, right side facing, and beginning at an underarm seam, pick up and knit 1 stitch for every bind-off stitch around entire Sleeve edge—51 (53, 60, 70, 73) stitches. Knit 1 (WS) row, purl 1 row, then bind off.

Block Sleeves.
Sew Sleeve and edging together at underarm.
Sew side seams.

CRINKLY BLOUSE SWEATER

Designed by Sally

WHEN IS A GARMENT A BLOUSE AND NOT A CARDIGAN? IS IT THE SHAPE, THE COLLAR, OR THE FABRIC THAT DEFINES IT? I'M NOT ENTIRELY SURE, BUT I DO KNOW THAT THIS PIECE WAS DESIGNED TO REPLICATE ONE OF MY FAVORITE BLOUSES—A LOOSE-FIT PIECE IN A CRINKLY FABRIC—AND SUCCEEDED PERFECTLY. THE LACE LOWER EDGE AND PROGRESSION TO SMALLER AND SMALLER NEEDLES GAVE THE GARMENT ITS DISTINCTIVE SHAPE, AND THE MISTAKE RIB DUPLICATED THE FABRIC. IN ADDITION, THE LINEN YARN EXPRESSES THE STITCH PATTERNS, THE SHAPE, AND THE STYLE OF THE ORIGINAL BEAUTIFULLY.

SKILL LEVEL
Intermediate

SIZES
- S (M, L, 1X, 2X)
- Finished bust 38 (42, 46, 50, 54)" (96.5 [106.5, 117, 127, 137]cm)
- Finished hem 61½ (68, 77½, 81, 87)" (154 [170, 194, 202.5, 217.5]cm)
- Finished length 24 (24½, 25, 25½, 26)" (61 [62, 63.5, 64.5, 66]cm)
- Finished length above lace 19½ (20, 20½, 21, 21½)" (49.5 [50.5, 52, 53, 54.5]cm)
- Finished shoulder width 14 (14, 15½, 15½, 15½)" (35.5 [35.5, 39.5, 39.5, 39.5]cm)
- Finished sleeve length 29 (29, 30½, 31½, 32)" (73.5 [73.5, 77, 80, 81]cm)

MATERIALS
- 1440 (1600, 1760, 1920, 2080) yd (1295 [1440, 1585, 1740, 1870]m) / 8 (8, 9, 10, 11) skeins Louet Euroflax Worsted Weight (100% linen, each approximately 3½ oz [100g] and 200 yd [180m]), in color Seaway Mix, (4) medium/worsted weight
- One pair size 8 (5mm) needles, or size needed to obtain gauge
- One pair size 7 (4.5mm) needles
- One pair size 6 (4mm) needles, or size needed to obtain gauge
- Stitch holder
- Tapestry needle
- One size E-4 (3.5mm) crochet hook
- 7 Buttons, ⅝–¾" wide

GAUGE
15 stitches and 26 rows = 4" (10cm) in diamond lace, over largest needles and after pressing
16 stitches and 24 rows = 4" (10cm) in mistake rib, over largest needles and after pressing
24 stitches and 26 rows = 4" (10cm) in mistake rib, over smallest needles and after pressing

PATTERN NOTES
- This garment is long and A-line (accomplished by using different-size needles). It could be made to a length between your ideal mid-length and long sweater. But it also has a demarcation (the change between lace and rib) that could fall to your ideal short sweater length (page 17).
- The shoulders will stretch at least 1" wider when worn, and the neck will stretch wider than the schematic shows.
- When one number appears, it applies to all sizes.
- To work, or to work even, or to continue means to not disrupt the stitch pattern through changes in needles or shaping.
- Slip all stitches purlwise and with yarn to wrong side.

STITCH PATTERNS
Diamond Lace (over a multiple of 6 stitches + 9)
(On Rows 7 & 15, the chart will show 5 stitches at the end, but there will be 6 on the needle.)
Row 1 (RS) K4, *yo, skp, k4; repeat from * to last 5 stitches, yo, skp, k3.
All WS rows Purl.
Row 3 K2, k2tog, yo, *k1, yo, skp, k1, k2tog, yo; repeat from * to last 5 stitches, k1, yo, skp, k2.

Row 5 K1, k2tog, yo, k1, *k2, yo, sk2p, yo, k1; repeat from * to last 5 stitches, k2, yo, skp, k1.

Row 7 K3, yo, *sk2p, yo, k3, yo; repeat from * to last 6 stitches, sk2p, yo, k3.

Row 9 As Row 1.

Row 11 K1, yo, skp, k1, *k3, yo, skp, k1; repeat from * to last 5 stitches, k3, yo, skp.

Row 13 K2, yo, skp, *k1, k2tog, yo, k1, yo, skp; repeat from * to last 5 stitches, k1, k2tog, yo, k2.

Row 15 As Row 7.

Row 17 As Row 5.

Row 19 As Row 11.

Row 20 Purl. (See chart, page 150.)

Mistake Rib (over a multiple of 4 stitches + 1)

RS Rows K2, *p1, k3; repeat from * to last 3 stitches, p1, k2.

WS rows *P1, k3; repeat from * to last stitch, p1.

BACK

With largest needle, cable cast on 113 (125, 137, 149, 161) stitches.

Next row (RS) K1, beginning with Row 1, work diamond lace to last stitch, k1.

Next row (WS) P1, work Row 2 of diamond lace to last stitch, p1.

Continue (in diamond lace and with 1 stockinette stitch at each edge) to 30 rows.

(Piece measures approximately 4½" [11.5cm]).

(Shorten or lengthen here for difference between finished length and ideal short sweater length, page 18.)

Continuing on larger needles, work mistake rib until piece measures 9" (23cm).

Continue mistake rib to end.

Change to middle-size needles, then continue until piece measures 13" (33cm).

Change to smallest needles, then continue until piece measures 16" (40.5cm). End after working a wrong-side row.

(Shorten or lengthen for ideal short sweater length here, page 18.)

SHAPE ARMHOLE

Bind off 4 (5, 7, 9, 11) stitches at the beginning of the next 2 rows—105 (115, 123, 131, 139) stitches.

Decrease row (RS) K1, skp, work to last 3 stitches, k2tog, k1.

Work 1 (WS) row.

Repeat the last 2 rows 9 (14, 14, 18, 22) times more—85 (85, 93, 93, 93) stitches.

(Adjust shoulder width here, page 19.)

Work even until armhole measures 7 (7½, 8, 8½, 9)"

(17.5 [19, 20.5, 21.5, 23]cm). End after working a wrong-side row.

SHAPE RIGHT SHOULDER AND BACK NECK

(Working 2 together during the bind off keeps the shoulders from stretching.)

Bind off 7 stitches at the beginning of the next right-side row—AT THE SAME TIME k2tog 3 times while binding off—then continue to 22 (22, 26, 26, 26) stitches on right needle. Place remaining 56 (56, 60, 60, 60) stitches on holder. Turn.

*Continue mistake rib, but work bind-offs as indicated.

Bind off 1 stitch at the next 2 neck edges.

Bind off 7 (7, 9, 9, 9) stitches at the next 2 armhole edges—AT THE SAME TIME k2tog 3 (3, 4, 4, 4) times while binding off—6 stitches remain.

At final armhole edge, [k2tog, and bind off] 3 times—0 stitches.

SHAPE LEFT SHOULDER AND BACK NECK

Return to remaining 56 (56, 60, 60, 60) stitches, right side facing.

Bind off center 27 stitches, work 1 right-side row over 29 (29, 33, 33, 33) stitches.

Bind off 7 stitches at the next armhole edge—AT THE SAME TIME p2tog 3 times while binding off.

Work as Shape Right Shoulder and Back Neck from * to end, but p2tog through bind-off.

LEFT FRONT

With largest needle, cable cast on 59 (65, 71, 77, 83) stitches.

Next row (RS) K1, beginning with Row 1, work diamond lace to last stitch, slip 1.

Next row (WS) P1, work Row 2 of diamond lace to last stitch, p1.

Continue (in diamond lace and with 1 stockinette stitch at each edge except for slip stitch at end of right-side rows) to one fewer row than Back.

Last lace row (WS) P2tog 2 (0, 2, 0, 2) times across row—57 (65, 69, 75, 81) stitches.

Continuing on larger needles, work mistake rib until piece measures 9" (23cm).

Change to middle-size needles, then continue until piece measures 13" (33cm).

Change to smallest needles, then continue to same length as Back to armhole. End after working a wrong-side row.

SHAPE ARMHOLE

Bind off 4 (5, 7, 9, 11) stitches at the beginning of the next right-side row—53 (60, 62, 68, 70) stitches.

Decrease row (RS) K1, skp, work to last stitch, slip 1. Work 1 (WS) row.

Repeat the last 2 rows 7 (14, 12, 18, 20) times more—45 (45, 49, 49, 49) stitches.

Work even until armhole measures 4 (4½, 5, 5½, 6)" (10 [11.5, 12.5, 14, 15]cm). End after working a right-side row.

SHAPE NECK

Work as established through all shaping, but discontinue slip stitch at the end of right-side rows.

*Bind off 8 stitches at the next neck edge, 3 stitches at the next neck edge, 2 stitches at the next neck edge, 1 stitch at the next 5 neck edges—27 (27, 31, 31, 31) stitches.

Work even until armhole measures same as Back. End after working a wrong-side row.

SHAPE SHOULDER

Continue as established, but work bind-offs as indicated. Bind off 7 stitches at the next armhole edge—AT THE SAME TIME k2tog 3 times while binding off—then work to end.

Work 1 row even.

Bind off 7 (7, 9, 9, 9) stitches at the next 2 armhole edges—AT THE SAME TIME k2tog 3 (3, 4, 4, 4) times while binding off.

At final armhole edge, [k2tog, and bind off] 3 times—0 stitches.

RIGHT FRONT

Mark 5 spots on Left Front for buttons: place the first 1" (2.5cm) above the end of diamond lace, place the last 1" (2.5) cm from the top, space the remaining 3 evenly between. (There should be 3½–4" [9–10cm] between buttons.)

With largest needle, cable cast on 59 (65, 71, 77, 83) stitches.

Next row (RS) K1, beginning with Row 1, work diamond lace to last stitch, k1.

Next row (WS) P1, work Row 2 of diamond Lace to last stitch, slip 1.

Continue as established (in diamond lace and with 1 stockinette stitch at each edge except for slip stitch at end of wrong-side rows) to 1 fewer row than Back.

Last lace row (WS) P2tog 2 (0, 2, 0, 2) times across row—57 (65, 69, 75, 81) stitches.

Continuing on larger needles, work as follows to make buttonholes that match placement of buttons.

Next row (RS), make buttonhole K2, p1, yo, skp, work to end.

Continue on larger needles until piece measures 9" (23cm).

Change to middle-size needles, then continue to placement of second buttonhole. End after working a wrong-side row.

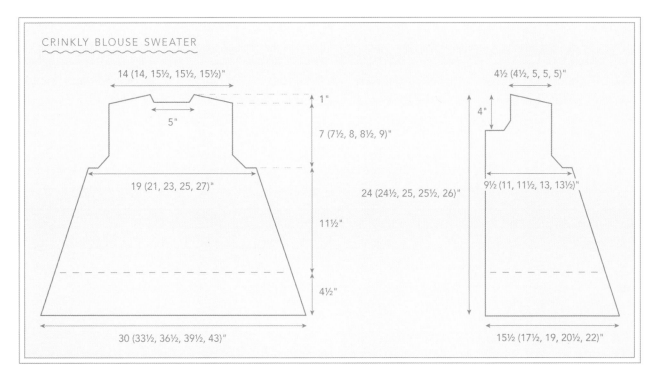

CRINKLY BLOUSE SWEATER

14 (14, 15½, 15½, 15½)"

5"

1"

7 (7½, 8, 8½, 9)"

19 (21, 23, 25, 27)"

11½"

4½"

30 (33½, 36½, 39½, 43)"

4½ (4½, 5, 5, 5)"

4"

24 (24½, 25, 25½, 26)"

9½ (11, 11½, 13, 13½)"

15½ (17½, 19, 20½, 22)"

Next row Make buttonhole as above.

Continue until piece measures 13" (33cm).

Change to smallest needles, then continue to placement of third buttonhole. End after working a wrong-side row.

Next row Make buttonhole as above.

Continue to same length as Back to armhole. End after working a right-side row.

SHAPE ARMHOLE

Bind off 4 (5, 7, 9, 11) stitches at the beginning of the next wrong-side row—53 (60, 62, 68, 70) stitches.

When appropriate, work 4th and 5th buttonholes as above.

Decrease row (RS) K1, work mistake rib to last 3 stitches, k2tog, k1.

Work 1 (WS) row.

Repeat the last 2 rows 7 (14, 12, 18, 20) times more—45 (45, 49, 49, 49) stitches.

Work even as established until armhole measures 4 (4½, 5, 5½, 6)" (10 [11.5, 12.5, 14, 15]cm). End after working a wrong-side row.

SHAPE NECK

Work as established through all shaping, but discontinue slip stitch at end of wrong-side rows.

Work as Left Front, Shape Neck from * to end, but end after working a right-side row.

SHAPE SHOULDER

Work as Left Front, Shape Shoulder, but p2tog through bind-offs.

SLEEVES

With largest needles, cable cast on 49 (53, 53, 57, 57) stitches.

Work mistake rib until piece measures 2" (5cm).

Change to middle-size needles, and work until piece measures 3" (7.5cm).

Change to smallest needles, and work until piece measures 4" (10cm). End after working a wrong side row.

Increase row (RS) K1, M1, work to last stitch, M1, k1.

Continue for 7 (7, 5, 3, 3) rows.

Repeat the last 8 (8, 6, 4, 4) rows 9 (9, 13, 15, 19) times more—69 (73, 81, 89, 97) stitches.

Continue as established until piece measures 17½" (44.5cm). End after working a wrong-side row. (Shorten or lengthen for Sleeve length here, page 20.)

SHAPE SLEEVE CAP

Bind off 4 (5, 7, 9, 11) stitches at the beginning of the next 2 rows—61 (63, 67, 71, 75) stitches.

Decrease row (RS) K1, skp, work to last 3 stitches, k2tog, k1.

Work 1 (WS) row.

Repeat the last 2 rows 13 (14, 16, 18, 20) times more—33 stitches. End after working a wrong-side row.

Next row (RS) K1, [k2tog and bind off] 16 times—0 stitches.

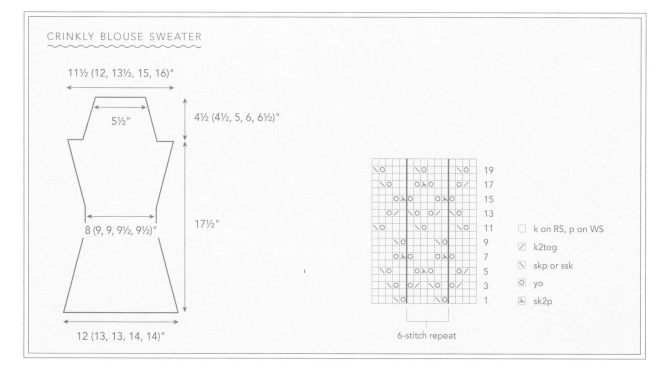

CRINKLY BLOUSE SWEATER

11½ (12, 13½, 15, 16)"

5½"

4½ (4½, 5, 6, 6½)"

8 (9, 9, 9½, 9½)"

17½"

12 (13, 13, 14, 14)"

19
17
15
13
11
9
7
5
3
1

☐ k on RS, p on WS

☑ k2tog

◨ skp or ssk

◯ yo

⧄ sk2p

6-stitch repeat

FINISHING
Sew shoulder seams.

Collar
With smallest needles and right side facing, pick up and knit as follows:
1 stitch for every bind-off stitch and 1 stitch for every 2-row step between bind-off stitches around front and back neck shaping,
3 stitches for every 4 rows along rows worked even,
1 stitch for every bind-off stitch across back neck,
1 stitch at each end of bind-off at back neck (to close holes, if needed).
—103 stitches.
(Count stitches on needle. If needed, increase or decrease in next row to attain this number.)
WS rows Slip 1, work wrong-side row of mistake rib to last stitch, slip 1.
RS rows K1, work right-side row of mistake rib to last stitch, k1.
Continue on smaller needles until Collar measures 1½" (4cm). End after working a wrong-side row.
Next row (RS), make buttonhole K2, p1, yo, skp, work to end.
Change to middle-size needles, and work until Collar measures 3" (7.5cm). End after working a wrong-side row.

Next row Make buttonhole as above.
Change to largest needles, and work until Collar measures 5–5½" (12.5–14cm). End after working a wrong-side row. Bind off, and pull yarn through, but do not cut.

Crocheted Edgings
(The Collar will fold over; what was the wrong side of the knitting now becomes the right side of the Collar.)
With crochet hook and right side of Collar facing, work as follows: beginning at top corner of Left Front Collar, *make 1 single crochet in next 3 bind-off stitches, skip 1 bind-off stitch, repeat from * to end of Collar. Cut yarn.
With crochet hook and right side facing, work as follows along each Front and Collar edge: make 1 single crochet in every slip stitch (working loosely across diamond lace rows). Cut yarn.

FINISHING
Press diamond lace and crocheted edgings.
Press mistake rib to desired degrees of flatness.
Sew Sleeves into armholes.
Sew side and Sleeve seams.
Sew buttons onto Left Front to correspond to buttonholes on Right Front.

❧ APPENDIX ❧

❧ TECHNIQUES AND ABBREVIATIONS ❧

3-needle bind-off

Hold two needles with stitches in the left hand and with right sides together: with a third needle, work 2 stitches together (1 from each left-hand needle) as you bind off as usual.

Bind off

Work 2 stitches, pass the first stitch over the second, *work 1 stitch, pass the previous stitch over the stitch just worked, repeat from *. (Always bind off in pattern unless directed otherwise.)

CC

Contrast color.

Cable cast on

Begin with 2 e-wrap stitches, *insert the right needle behind the leading stitch, draw through yarn (as if to knit a new stitch), but, without removing the old stitch from the left needle, place the new stitch onto the left needle: repeat from *; after a few stitches are cast on, remove the first e-wrap cast-on stitch.

Cast on

Add a number of stitches to the left needle. (If we think you should use a particular cast on, we will tell you so: otherwise, use your preferred method.)

cn

Cable needle.

crochet chain

Start with a slip knot on the crochet hook; with the crochet hook, draw the yarn through the slip knot—1 chain stitch formed. Continue to draw the yarn through the loop on the hook to the number of chains directed.

e-wrap cast-on

With both tail and needle in the left hand, *take the right index finger under the working yarn (from back to front), turn the finger 180 degrees to the left, then insert the needle through the loop on the finger. Repeat from *.

garter (stitch)

Knit every row.

garter ridge

The ridge formed by two knit rows

I-cord

(This is usually done on double-pointed needles, but it can be done on a circular.) Cast on stitches (usually 2 or 3). *Knit the stitches from the left needle onto the right. Without turning the right needle, slide these stitches to the beginning of the needle. This now becomes the left needle. Repeat from *.

k

Knit.

k2tog

Insert the right needle into the second and then the first stitch on the left needle, then knit both together—1 stitch decreased with a right-side, right-slanting decrease.

kf&b

Knit into the front and then the back of the next stitch—1 stitch increased.

knitted cast-on

Begin with a slip knot, insert the right needle, draw through yarn (as if to knit a new stitch), but without removing the slip knot from the left needle, place the new stitch onto the left needle. Continue to knit into the leading stitch and form new stitches by putting them back onto the left needle.

knitwise

As if to knit.

lifted increase

Work into the stitch below or into the right "leg" of the stitch below the next stitch on the left needle (knitwise or purlwise, as directed by the stitch pattern), then work the stitch on the left needle (as directed by the stitch pattern). If the pattern does not indicate, then always work both stitches knitwise—1 stitch increased.

long-tail cast-on

Have a long tail over the front of the right needle and the rest of the yarn in the back. Hold both strands of yarn in the left hand, then spread the yarn apart with the left thumb and index finger. Take the right needle under the front of the "thumb" yarn, over the "finger" yarn, then draw the "finger" yarn through the space produced by the "thumb" yarn. Pull both taut. (Pulling on the "thumb" yarn tightens the cast-on edge.)

MC

Main color.

M1

Lift the yarn that sits between the stitch just worked and the next stitch on the left needle; knit it to twist it—1 stitch increased.

p

Purl.

p2tog
Insert the right needle into the first and then the second stitch on the left needle, purl both together—1 stitch decreased with a right-side, right-slanting decrease.

pb&f
Purl into the back and then the front of the next stitch—1 stitch increased.

pick up and knit
Insert the right needle through an edge, one stitch from the edge or below the cast-on or bind-off edge. (This takes 1 selvedge stitch or the bind-off or the cast-on edge into the seam allowance.) To not get holes, insert needle so as to have 2 threads on the needle. Draw through yarn to make a stitch—1 stitch picked up and knit.

pm
Place marker.

psso
Pass the slip stitch over.

purlwise
As if to purl.

reading charts
Read all charts from right to left on right-side rows and from left to right on wrong-side rows. If repeat lines are indicated, repeat the stitches within these lines.

reverse stockinette (stitch)
Purl right-side rows; knit wrong-side rows.

RS
Right side.

seaming
Hold pieces with right sides facing. Taking 1 stitch from each edge or the bind-off edge or the cast-on edge into the seam allowances, sew pieces together.

short row
Turn before the end of the row.

single crochet
Begin with a loop on the crochet hook. Insert the hook into the work, and wrap the yarn around the hook, then draw this loop through (two loops are now on hook), take the hook over the work, wrap the yarn around the hook, and draw this yarn through both loops on the hook—1 single crochet made.

skp
Slip 1 knitwise, Knit 1, pass the slip stitch over—1 stitch decreased with a right-side, left slanting decrease.

sk2p
Slip 1 knitwise, knit the next 2 stitches together, pass the slip stitch over—2 stitches decreased with a right-side, left-slanting decrease.

slip
Slip the next stitch from the left needle onto the right. We tell you to slip knitwise or purlwise. Also, if not told to do so, do not move the yarn.

slip knot
Hold the tail in the left hand. Wrap the yarn behind the fingers of the left hand, then to the back again and under the yarn behind the left fingers; draw the yarn through to form a knot.

slip-stitch crochet
Begin with a loop on the crochet hook. Insert the crochet hook into the work and wrap the yarn around the hook; draw this loop through the work and through the loop on the crochet hook—1 slip-stitch crochet made.

ssk
Slip the next 2 stitches, one-at-a-time and knitwise from the left needle onto the right, insert the left needle into the front of the two stitches, and knit them together—1 stitch decreased with a right-side, left-slanting decrease.

ssp
Slip the next 2 stitches one-at-a-time and knitwise from the left needle onto the right, pass the slipped stitches back onto the left needle, purl these 2 stitches together through the back—1 stitch decreased with a right-side, left slanting decrease.

stockinette (stitch)
Knit right-side rows; purl wrong-side rows.

working in the round
Working on double-pointed needles or on a circular needle, continue working from the left needle onto the right without turning the work.

wyib
With the yarn in the back of the work (away from you).

wyif
With the yarn in the front of the work (toward you).

WS
Wrong side.

yo
On a knit row, bring the yarn to the front, then knit the next stitch as usual—1 new stitch made. On a purl row, wrap the yarn around the right needle—1 new stitch made. On the next row, never twist this stitch unless directed to do so.

❈ YARN INDEX ❧

All of the projects in this book call for materials that are usually available at yarn or craft stores. This yarn index, plus the following resource list, should help you find all the materials you need to complete the projects in the book.

Sometimes a yarn's weight can straddle more than one weight category (as offered in the CYCA chart). Its label may only offer one category whereas the pattern knits it to an alternative. In the patterns and in the list below, we have listed the yarn by weight according to how it is labeled. This will be most helpful as you make substitutions. But do make a gauge swatch to ensure accuracy.

Weight 2 (fine) 🄽

Louet Euroflax Sport Weight (100% linen, each approximately 3½ oz [100g] and 270 yd [246m]), in color 01 (Champagne) for Classic Shirt, page 58

Needful Mohair Royal (80% kid mohair, 20% nylon, each approximately ⅞ oz [25g] and 235 yd [215m]), in color 1650 (off-white) for Classic Shirt, page 58

Rowan Kidsilk Spray (70% kid mohair, 30% silk, each approximately ⅞ oz [25g] and 229 yd [210m]), in color 572 (Pebbles) for Mother-of-the-Bride Cardigan, page 83

Weight 3 (light) 🄽

Classic Elite Classic One Fifty (100% merino wool, each approximately 1¾ oz [50g] and 150 yd [137m]), in color 7275 (Granite) for A Gray Cardigan, page 106, and in color 7238 (Chestnut) for Box-Pleat Skirt, page 103

Estelle Young Touch Cotton DK (100% cotton, each approximately 1¾ oz [50g] and 114 yd [105m]), in color 23 (maroon) for No-Mess Headband, page 24, and Tabbed Cuffs, page 28

Filatura di Crosa Zara (100% wool, each approximately 1¾ oz [50g] and 136 yd [125m]), in color 27 (light gray) for Cable-Edged Vest, page 77

Lanaknits Hemp for Knitting All Hemp 6 (100% long fiber hemp, each approximately 3½ oz [100g] and 165 yd [150m]), in color 015 (teal) and 029 (black) for Inside-Out Panel Suit, page 113, and in color 018 (Sapphire) for Eco-Tote, page 121

Rowan Calmer (75% cotton, 25% acrylic/microfiber, each approximately 1¾ oz [50g] and 175 yd [160m]), in color 492 (Garnet) for Sophisticated Hoodie, page 69

Weight 4 (medium) 🄽

Berocco Bonsai (97% bamboo, 3% nylon, each approximately 1¾ oz [50g] and 77 yd [71m]), in color 4143 (Kin gold) for Swing Top, page 65

Berocco Suede (100% nylon, each approximately 1¾ oz [50g] and 120 yd [111m]), in color 3746 (Palomino) for Swing Top, page 65

Berroco Peruvia (100% wool, each approximately 3½ oz [100g] and 174 yd [160m]), in color 7114 (brown) for Tabbed Spats/Legwarmers, page 31

Berroco Suede Deluxe (85% nylon, 10% rayon, 5% polyester, each approximately 1¾ oz [50g] and 100 yd [92m]), in color 3904 (Hopalong Gold) for Corsage Choker/Headband, page 93

Classic Elite Princess (40% merino, 28% viscose, 10% cashmere, each approximately 1¾ oz [50g] and 150 yd [135m]), in color 3458 (Royal red) for Corsage Choker/Headband, page 93, and in color 3495 (Privileged Plum) for Garden Party Scarf, page 91

Lana Grossa Luxor (31% merino wool, 49% microfiber, each approximately 1¾ oz [50g] and 165 yd [150m]), in color 009 (brown) for Tabbed Spats/Legwarmers, page 31, and in colors 005 (charcoal) and 006 (silver) for Two-Way Shrug, page 37

Louet Euroflax Worsted Weight (100% linen, each approximately 3½ oz [100g] and 200 yd [180m]), in color (Seaway Mix) for Crinkly Blouse sweater, page 146

Louet Merlin (70% merino wool, 30% linen, each approximately 3½ oz [100g] and 156 yd [140m]), in colors 43 (Pewter), 49 (Charcoal), and 01 (Champagne) for Minidress, page 140

Nashua Julia (50% mohair, 25% kid mohair, 25% alpaca, each approximately 1¾ oz [50g] and 93 yd [85m]) in color 6086 (Velvet moss) for Scarf-Closing Cardigan, page 53

Needful Yarns Kelly (55% cotton, 45% acrylic, each approximately 1¾ oz [50g] and 107 yd [98m]) in color 64 (taupe + green) for Femme Tie, page 126

Needful Yarns Kim (55% cotton, 45% acrylic, each approximately 1¾ oz [50g] and 107 yd [96m]), in color 340 (ivory) for Reversible Tank Top, page 123

Needful Yarn London Tweed (95% wool, 5% viscose, each approximately 1¾ oz [50g] and 92 yd [85m]), in color 10 (green) for Lace-and-Cable Jumper, page 135, and Altered Austen Jacket, page 129

Prism Tulle (100% nylon, each approximately 1oz [30g] and 96 yd [87m]), in color Fog for Corset Belt, page 95, and in color Smoke for Flirty Top, page 99

Prism Pebbles (MC) (100% nylon, each approximately 2 oz [60g] and 123 yd [111m]), in color Smoke for Flirty Top, page 99

Skacel Zitron loft (100% merino wool, each approximately 1¾ oz [50g] and 110 yd [100m]), in color 1211 (taupe) for Mother-of-the-Bride Cardigan, page 83

Tahki Yarns New Tweed (60% merino wool, 26% viscose, 14% silk, each approximately 1¾ oz [50g] and 92 yd [85m]), in color 051 (yellow-green) for Knit-Across Sweater, page 46

Weight 5 (bulky) 🄽

Cascade Eco+ (100% wool, each approximately 8¾ oz [250g] and 478yd [437m]), in color 6922 (coral) or 6902 (periwinkle) for Camelot Coat, page 39

Classic Elite Duchess (40% merino, 28% viscose, 10% cashmere, 7% angora, 15% nylon, each approximately 1¾ oz [50g] and 75 yd [68m]), in color 1016 (Natural) for The Slouch, page 34

Autunno Dive (100% merino wool, each approximately 1¾ oz [50g] and 98 yd [90m]), in color yellow/green-brown-turquoise 32965 (turquoise/brown/green) for The Long-and-Short-of-It Pullover, page 49

Weight 6 (super-bulky) 🄽

Malabrigo Aquarella (100% wool, each approximately 3½ oz [100g] and 65 yd [58m]), in color 02 (Soriano) for Buttoned Muffler, page 27

❧ RESOURCE LIST ❧

It does happen, in the process of writing a book, that a yarn is discontinued. You may contact the yarn company for substitution help. And you may contact us at www.sallymelvilleknits.com.

Berroco Inc.
PO Box 367, 14 Elmdale Rd.
Uxbridge, MA USA 01569
508–278–2527
www.berroco.com

Cascade Yarns Inc.
(for Dive yarns)
1224 Andover Park E.
Tukwilia, WA USA 98188
206–574–0440
www.cascadeyarns.com

Classic Elite Yarns
122 Western Ave.
Lowell, MA USA 01851–1434
800–548–1048
www.classiceliteyarns.com

Estelle Yarns
(for Estelle and Lana Grossa)
2220 Midland Avenue, Unit 65
Scarborough, ON Canada M1P 3E6
1–800–387–5167
www.estelleyarns.com

Lanaknits Hemp for Knitting
3B, 320 Vernon St.
Nelson, BC Canada V1L 4E4
888.301.0011
www.hempforknitting.com

Louet Sales
3425 Hands Rd.
Prescott, ON Canada K0E 1T0
613–925–4502
www.louet.com

Malabrigo Yarn
8424 NW 56th St.
Suite #mvd 80496, Miami, FL USA
786–866–6187[S3]
www.malabrigoyarn.com

Needful Yarns
155 Champagne Dr., Unit 8
Toronto, ON Canada M3J 2C6
or
60 Industrial Parkway PMB #233
Cheektowaga NY USA 14227
866–800–4700
www.needfulyarnsinc.com

Prism Arts Inc.
3140 30th Ave N.
St. Petersburg, FL USA 33714–4530
727–528–3800
www.prismyarn.com

Skacel
PO Box 88110
Seattle, WA USA 98138–2110
800–255–1278
www.skacelknitting.com

Tahki • Stacy Charles Inc.
(for Tahki and Filatura di Crosa),
70–30 80th St. Bldg #36
Glendale, NY, USA 11385
800–338–9276
www.tahkistacycharles.com

Westminster Fibers
(for Rowan and Nashua)
165 Ledge St.
Nashua, NH USA
800–445–9276
www.knitrowan.com

⚜ CYCA YARN WEIGHTS ⚜

1 🔒	2 🔒	3 🔒	4 🔒	5 🔒	6 🔒
SUPER FINE	FINE	LIGHT	MEDIUM	BULKY	SUPER BULKY

These weights are also known as the following.

sock	sport	DK	worsted	chunky	bulky
fingering	baby	light worsted	afghan	craft	roving

This is the range of stitches they would achieve, worked in stockinette and over 4" (10cm)

27–32	23–26	21–24	16–20	12–15	6–11

This is their (CYCA) recommended needle size, U.S. sizes.

1–3	3–5	5–7	7–9	9–11	11 and larger

This is their (CYCA) recommended needle size, metric sizes.

2.25–3.25mm	3.25–3.75mm	3.75–4.5mm	4.5–5.5mm	5.5–8mm	9–16mm

⚜ SIZING CHART / STANDARD BODY MEASUREMENTS ⚜

SIZE	BUST	WAIST	HIPS
XS	28–30	20–22	30–32
S	32–34	24–26	34–36
M	36–38	28–30	38–40
L	40–42	32–34	42–44
1X	44–46	36–38	46–48
2X	48–50	40–42	50–52

These are the standard measurements we have used to determine the sizes for this book. When determining which size you should knit, use these body measurements. We have then added the appropriate ease to the actual garment based on its style or yarn or stitch pattern.

All finished lengths are made to fit someone 5'4"-5'6". If your height is different, shorten or lengthen as needed where directed in the pattern.

NEEDLE AND HOOK SIZES

US	MM	HOOK
0	2	A
1	2.25	B
2	2.75	C
3	3.25	D
4	3.5	E
5	3.75	F
6	4	G
7	4.5	7

US	MM	HOOK
8	5	H
9	5.5	I
10	6	J
10½	6.5	K
10¾	7	
11	8	L
13	9	M
15	10	N

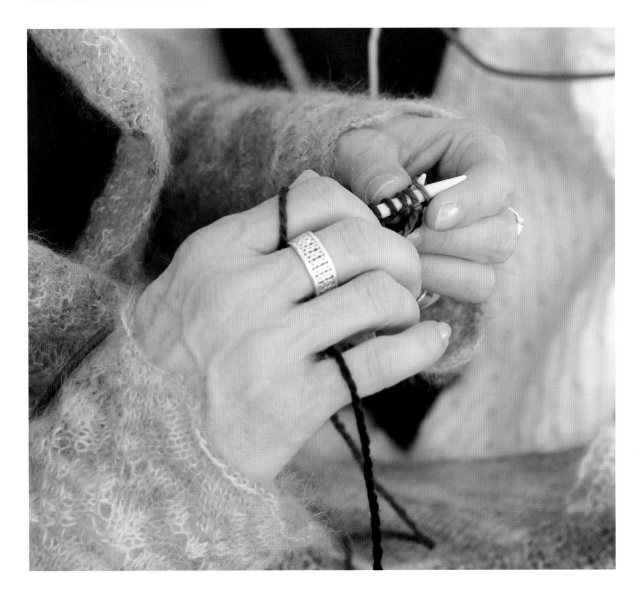

❧ INDEX ❧